SAVING OUR SERVICE ACADEMIES

SAVING OUR SERVICE ACADEMIES

My Battle with, and for, the US Naval Academy to Make Thinking Officers

BRUCE FLEMING

Post Hill
PRESS

A POST HILL PRESS BOOK

ISBN: 979-8-88845-046-8
ISBN (eBook): 979-8-88845-047-5

Saving Our Service Academies:
My Battle with, and for, the US Naval Academy to Make Thinking Officers
© 2024 by Bruce Fleming
All Rights Reserved

Cover design by Conroy Accord

Post Hill Press, LLC
New York • Nashville
posthillpress.com

Published in the United States of America

To my students over more than 30 years at the US Naval Academy. It's been fun; heartfelt thanks. And to my wife, who suffered the ups and downs alongside me.

CONTENTS

WHO AM I TO TAKE ON THE US NAVY?

When I arrived at the US Naval Academy (USNA) in 1987 to teach English to future officers in the Navy and Marine Corps, I was excited, pumped, and totally *oohrah*—as the Marine Corps has it. "GET SOME!" they yell before charging at an obstacle. And by golly, I was going to "GET SOME." I'd gotten my PhD at Vanderbilt in 1982 and spent five years abroad, as a Fulbright Scholar in West Berlin, two years as a lecturer at the University of Freiburg, Germany, and two years as the Fulbright Professor of English at the National University of Rwanda—luckily before their civil war. When I got the job offer at Annapolis, which is largely staffed by civilian PhDs like me—unlike the other service academies of West Point, Air Force, Coast Guard, and arguably Merchant Marine—I couldn't believe my good luck. A Maryland native, I was coming home. Moreover, my vision of the Academy as filled with the best and the brightest, the ideal combination of Athens and Sparta, spoke to my deepest yearnings. *Mens sana in corpore sano*! To push yourself mentally and physically and never ever give up—that was my idea of the right kind of life, rare (I had discovered) in contemporary academia, or indeed perhaps in our society at large. And to be able to mentor young men and women who shared my goals—what an opportunity! Was I the luckiest guy on the planet or what?

It took almost the first two decades of classes, EI (Extra Instruction: one-on-one tutoring in my office), and workouts in our gyms, weight rooms, and pools along with the midshipmen for me to realize that behind the well-groomed façade of the Academy so energetically tended and boasted by the military brass lay something quite different. (These high-ranking officers live for three or four years in their beautiful Victorian houses on our campus, called The Yard, and insulated from the reality of what actually goes on by their command bubble where all they hear is "Yes, sir.") The students, I saw, were the unhappiest and least motivated group of human beings I had ever encountered. And I learned that the service academies now produce a fraction of the total officers (currently about 18 percent) they once did, at astronomical costs to tax-payers (about half a million dollars per student) with little to no better quality of output compared to other commissioning sources. So why do we still have them? Tradition? Perhaps because the alumni, recipients of the most golden of tickets—free and actually paid education, guaranteed employment after, and prestige in getting civilian jobs after leaving the Navy or Marine Corps (about 25 percent of the current USNA graduates become Marine Corps 2LTs [Second Lieutenants])—would raise a ruckus if we tried to change them in any material way. Certainly the military brass like how they looked running them: we heard that the post of Superintendent of the Naval Academy, a two-star admiral when I arrived and now a three-star (this sweetening was in response to our massive cheating scandal in the early 1990s—that'll show them who's boss!), was a consolation prize to the man who didn't get the job of Chief of Naval Operations, CNO. So, the Academy mirrors and to some degree determines what we call Big Navy. That's the scariest part of this story.

You're probably surprised. That's not what the USNA administration says, is it? According to their hype, the academies are the font of duty, honor, country, and all midshipmen (and cadets, at West Point) are the "best and brightest," as they are told multiple times a week. However, none of that is true. I wish to heaven it were. I've discovered this over three decades and counting, so I know that the brass's version of things is self-serving smoke and mirrors. Some of the younger officers know this is all PR on steroids, but neither they nor the midshipmen are allowed to talk about it to outsiders. So, I guess that leaves me, as a professor, whose professional code of honor is to tell the truth as I see it. Besides, I have a personal interest in this question: I'm a civilian tax-payer the military exists to defend. And so, probably, are you.

So as the golden haze of hype began to clear and the scales fell from my eyes about this institution I had so respected and been so proud to be a part of, I began to write about what I saw for outlets like the *Washington Post*, the *New York Times*, *The Atlantic*, the US Naval Institute's *Proceedings*, the *Chronicle of Higher Education*, and the *Christian Science Monitor* (all linked at the end). That's what professors do: we don't pick up a pitchfork; we write articles.

These articles diverged from the rah-rah hype put out by the administration, because I felt a sense of responsibility for civilians to know what they were paying for in the academies and what, to some degree—I came to see from talking with my former students who were officers—was true of the military as a whole. It didn't seem particularly daring, because I knew the Constitution protected my free speech, and all military officers raise their right hand to protect and defend the Constitution. Besides, I thought I was protected by my USNA-awarded tenure as a professor (explanation of "I thought" below).

Most fundamentally, I knew what I was talking about, was in a privileged position, and had taken my time—it was more than a decade and a half before I began writing these articles. (Officers at USNA spent, at most, a few years and had to toe the party line because they're in the military. Now we have a small handful of officer teachers who stay for the rest of their time in the military, as so-called Permanent Military Professors.) I had spent countless hours listening to students, both in the classrooms as they blew off steam before we started the day's work about some ridiculous new action on the part of the higher-ups, and sitting individually in the big red leather chair in my office. After talking about their paper for class, the reason for their coming to see me in the first place, they tended to relax and open up about what was really on their minds. After a while, I knew what they were going to say before they said it. Dozens, then as the years passed, hundreds of students told me that the spit and polish they spent countless hours maintaining was nothing more than senseless busywork to give the place the appearance of bustle and efficiency, and that it made them less eager for military life, not more. Over the years and then decades, I came to realize that what taxpayers are told repeatedly is a temple of virtue was a Potemkin village façade, a military Disneyland for tourists with students as the cast members—who hated being the goldfish in the bowl whose job was to swim around in circles. This was more heartbreaking for me to hear because most of them, like me, had come as true believers, and their disillusionment mirrored my own.

So, my loss of faith in an institution I had revered, and still admire in theory if not in practice, came gradually. It also came to some degree suddenly, during a year serving on our Admissions Board in the mid-2000s. As part of the team of professors and officers reviewing applications, I was only responsible for saying an applicant was "qualified" or "unqualified"—actual admission was the prerogative of the brass behind closed doors. But I discovered that, with the hundreds of millions of dollars taxpayers pump into this institution yearly to produce only a fraction of new officers at multiples of the cost of other commissioning sources, the brass were running a nepotistic slush fund school to benefit their children and the children of friends. And it was one that at the same time discriminated against white applicants in order to have cast members of specific skin colors in the military Disneyland, and then the Navy—and to field a football team, among other teams, that could look respectable against civilian schools. None of these schools are taxpayer-supported job training institutions for a specific line of work, nor do they, or their parent institution, here the US Navy, hire all their graduates—as a former superintendent liked to say about Annapolis.

Probably our admissions process's selection of future officers by skin color hit me hardest. A somewhat later Chief of Naval Operations Gary Roughead, who had been a USNA Commandant in charge of military activities (I should say "military" in scare quotes rather than merely military, as the job of midshipmen is not to fight but to put on parades and go to class), was quoted as explaining that the official Navy position that "Diversity and diversity leadership remain top priorities" meant actively giving more of the slots at Annapolis and in our remedial prep school in Newport, Rhode Island, NAPS (Naval Academy Preparatory School) to nonwhites because of their skin color—and (he didn't say this) fewer based on merit if the applicants are white. That put into words what I had already seen.

So, having a Navy that "looks like America," as we frequently heard, was more important than having the best? And besides, there are all those children of the brass to give slots to, which I saw happen repeatedly—to repeat: the most golden of tickets in the government-handout sweepstakes—an expensive, but taxpayer-funded, college degree, and at least five years of guaranteed post-college employment at some of the highest salaries of any US college graduates, and prestige in the civilian world after that. The physical danger of military service is never zero, of course, but the Navy isn't typically at high risk, secure in its ships. We lost about seven thousand military members in the war zones of Iraq and Afghanistan in the two decades since our invasions of these countries post-9/11. Two hundred twenty-five of these were Navy, about 1,400 were Marines, and about 4,400 Army. Traffic fatalities in America, for context, were about forty-three thousand in 2021 alone.

And yes, the academies want to play football—something that doesn't happen in the real Navy, Army, or Air Force, for which the academies are supposed to be the preparation. To get a team of large football players and tall basketball players (who tend to sweeten the numbers of nonwhite students we brag about), we reject countless better qualified applicants—though not nearly as many as we claim (more on this subsequently).

I had, of course, noted that the students in my classes were, on average, not particularly able and didn't know much, though I was immensely fond of them, but I hadn't known why until I was on the Admissions Board. As a result of that year, seeing the preferences given for race and athletic recruits regardless of other potential, I could say why. And then I discovered that there is little evidence that USNA graduates were, on the whole, better officers than the 82 percent that came from Reserve Officers' Training Corps (ROTC) at civilian colleges and Officer Candidate School (OCS)—a several month training course for college graduates, which cost taxpayers one-quarter to one-eighth (respectively) what the Academy costs. (Documentation in the Appendix). I came to see finally that, contrary to the hype the Academy puts out and what most taxpayers believe, USNA was devoted most of all to its own self-preservation, as well as to burnishing the résumés of the brass, not to the defense of civilians.

And late in my second decade at Annapolis, the culture wars, which until then had been behind-the-scenes skirmishes, really began to hit, imposed by Congress and imported from society at large: racial and gender preferences for leadership positions; sexual assault training that assumed the man was always guilty, alienating the men and turning students against each other; and then the DEI industry—diversity, equity, and inclusion, which means racial profiling—that pushes hires of non-white, nonstraight faculty and pressured faculty members to teach works other than those by dead and usually straight white males. These were the new Topics A, B, and C at Annapolis, not the old-time goals of producing warriors or even competent officers.

So, this is the story of my discovery of what lies behind the well-tended grounds and the nicely turned-out uniforms at Annapolis. The bottom line: the service academies are nothing at all like what you think, or what I arrived thinking. But so strong was my determination to believe the hype that it took me decades to fully understand that. And the other academies are generically like Annapolis, especially the US Military Academy (USMA) at West Point, as West Point professor Tim Bakken points out in his exhaustive exposé of malfeasance there and in the larger military, *The Cost of Loyalty: Dishonesty, Hubris, and Failure in the U.S. Military.*

Can Annapolis, and the other service academies that mirror USNA, be fixed? Do they have a purpose anymore? The answer is yes, but changes—big changes—will be necessary to save them from their sad, downward spiral, produced in part by changes in society (more colleges have ROTC, which produces a big slice of new officers) and partly because of Congress's desire to use the academies, which they control, for social engineering rather than for military purposes. I want the academies to be more like what they say they are, and I want them to live up to their reputations—which they currently do not.

I've had time to do my research and to think about how they could be reconceived, which I outline here, echoing in the process a number of other professors and officers outside the academies. I don't think they will be fixed from within, because the brass are, by and large, not creative thinkers, and remember, they got where they are by saying "*Yes, sir!*" and now "*Yes, ma'am!*" I am optimistic that the service academies can be fixed so that they actually fulfill their mission statements—at Annapolis, to "develop midshipmen morally, mentally, and physically, and to imbue them with the highest ideals of duty, honor, and loyalty." But it will take creative thinking and setting aside the self-interest of the military brass whose vanity projects the academies, funded by tax dollars and protected by a smoke screen of all-is-perfect hype, have become. Though they can be fixed, the first step is seeing that they're broken and understanding how they got that way.

But let's start with where they are now, having been turned into battlegrounds of the culture wars, that rivet everyone's attention. And let's do it the military way: with a drumroll.

DRUMROLL: WELCOME TO THE CULTURE WARS

I f you've been reading the news in the last decade or more, you will have followed stories such as these:

- the rise of the aggrieved left demanding that people say things they want to hear
- the rise of the aggrieved right demanding that people say things they want to hear
- the insistence of some women that all men are potential rapists who have to be relentlessly pursued and punished
- the insistence of some men that women should be wives, mothers, and babymakers, and nothing else
- the insistence by some women that the military and college campuses, the entertainment industry, and virtually all businesses are the happy hunting grounds of predatory males out to have sex with females in their power, and that guilt of the man, if accused, should be assumed
- the insistence by many men and women that this violates the American assumption of innocence until proven guilty
- the attack on once-respected authority figures because they are the "elites" whose conclusions are merely opinions that have the same value as yours or mine
- the transformation of academia, from a neutral playing field for the marketplace of ideas that have to be justified to the weapons of advocates for particular positions

- the rise of the position that parents have the right to control what their sons and daughters hear in classrooms to bring this in line with what the parents themselves believe
- the death of the notion that education broadens minds, so that people can respect and get along with those they disagree with and be citizens in a multiviewpoint democracy
- the rise of the notion that educators who challenge ideas students bring from home need to be attacked and removed
- the insistence that free speech allows the predominance of the loudest voices, whether from the right or left
- the rise of the "heckler's veto," where one member of a large audience, or a handful, can shut down, disinvite, or disrupt an individual trying to express his or her views, even if these have been solicited by an institution of which the hecklers are members
- the attempt by people who insist they were "marginalized" (which means pushed off the printed page where they were once part of the text—it asserts action on others' part) demanding that those who marginalized them should (a) feel guilty for having done so and (b) make immediate amends, usually financial
- the insistence that definition should not be as groups defined by race (skin color), national origin, religion, sexuality, or gender, but as individuals
- the response by members of these minority groups that this fails to establish a level playing field because of historical disadvantages, such as "systemic racism"
- the insistence of traditionally powerful groups that they are doing just fine at running things
- the attempt by individuals who fail to fit into standard categories to destroy the categories for all, rather than saying merely that they are exceptions, usually expressed in gender terms
- the attempt by defenders of the standard categories (such as male/female) to allow no exceptions and brand individuals who don't fit these categories as weirdos

- the insistence that each individual gets to say that he/she/they is male or female, or both, or neither, despite the way he/she/they appears to others or his/her/their physical makeup, down to chromosomes
- the reverence for the military expressed by Americans who, when polled, identify the military as the institution they trust the most
- the inefficiency of a system where high-ranking military officers are surrounded by subordinates eager to tell them what they want to hear, rather than what may be the unpleasant truth
- the inefficiency of a civilian political system with similar misjudgments and misadventures
- the fact that the military in America is an all-volunteer force that has to advertise for members by painting a rosy picture of military life (leaving out the possibility of death and dismemberment, as well as its boring or frustrating side) and draw in recruits by lavish financial incentives and benefits supplied by taxpayers
- the military's projected image of muscular, sweaty masculinity, expressed in SEAL movies and in military recruiting commercials
- the fact that the military is engaged in a relentless campaign to make itself attractive to female volunteers to bring it in line with what Congress demands and to fill its ranks
- the fact that this campaign destroys the very aspect of the military as a "band of brothers" that is so attractive to many men
- the insistence that the military is gender-neutral and just like an office job
- the fact that it isn't, and thus the inherent problems of having men and women together under close quarters, sometimes far from home, each with his or her (or "their") libido to contend with
- the fact that the military denies that these problems are inherent to the situation they have created, but are instead only matters

of personal comportment that can be addressed with individual punishments

- the subjectivity of the Uniform Code of Military Justice (UCMJ) that allows a commanding officer (CO) to punish subordinates based merely on the CO's individual moral or political views, on the grounds that the subordinate's actions have (in the view of the CO) been "unbecoming" or "prejudicial" to good "military discipline" or that, in the view of the CO, they bring "discredit on the armed forces"
- the ability of a CO following the UCMJ to protect subordinates from punishment based merely on the CO's own personal trust of those subordinates, on the grounds that no discredit has been brought on the armed forces—or that public knowledge of the subordinate's actions would itself bring discredit on them
- the fact that the American military has not won a war since World War II aside from the 100-hour land coalition defense of Kuwait in Operation Desert Storm, as shown most recently in the chaotic withdrawal from Kabul after decades of ineffective and destructive actions in Afghanistan and thousands of American service members dead, along with countless Afghans
- the abuse of power by those in positions of authority, whether civilian or military, to punish opponents by subjecting them to aggressive, endless, and repeated "investigations"
- the American reverence for athletes who are assumed to be morally pure and worthy of their large salaries and, subsequently, of election to public office
- the reality that many athletes are not in fact scholars and ladies/ gentlemen, or indeed, use their celebrity status to achieve illicit personal gains, whether sexual or financial
- all of the above at once

These constitute our culture wars. I lived the last option at the Naval Academy: all of these at once—or at least all of these in a small period of time. Because of my involvement in these culture wars both as participant and onlooker, I was subjected to repeated attacks by the brass and their civilian administrators on my attempts to do my job, and also on my professional reputation, my honor, and my financial security. I spent my days not merely teaching midshipmen, but also defending myself against an increasing scale of punishments—star-chamber-style "investigations," official Letters of Reprimand, loss of pay raises—by those in power that were designed to bring me to heel. And I spent my nights in restless sleep, usually awakening at two a.m. with clenched fists, my heart beating wildly, my jaw tight with frustration and anger. In my view, I was defending the interests of the US citizens and doing precisely what I was hired to do; in the view of those in power, I was engaged in "conduct unbecoming."

And then they pulled the trigger and fired me, taking away my livelihood and my health care in the same week I had a major heart attack, and a stent was put in the most major artery feeding my heart. (Three others came later, along with permanent damage to the heart.) And then poof! After almost a year of no pay and an expensive though effective lawyer, it all went away when a judge reversed their actions, and I was reinstated as of the day I was fired. It was like awakening from a nightmare. Because of all this, I am the SparkNotes, the condensed and shortened version, of our common culture wars, and the Naval Academy the place where the pebble drops into the water. The water is the Severn River, where (as our school song, "Navy Blue and Gold," has it) "Severn joins the tide" of the Chesapeake Bay. But the ripples expand far outward, to the military at large and then to our whole civilian society, in this third decade of the second millennium. Looking at the central ripple at the Naval Academy, a place foreign to most people, helps us understand all the other manifestations of the same forces that many of us confront in our daily lives.

THE PROBLEM:
FALL OF KABUL, 2021

In renowned military analyst Thomas Ricks's book *The Generals*, about the contrast between World War II top-level military figures—he focuses on Army generals—and the much-diminished ones of today, Ricks argues that our rudderless military interventions and increasing reliance on military show over substance are reflected in the sometimes hapless "leadership" of generals in the post-World War II world. The thread he pulls on to unravel many others is the question of why generals in World War II were routinely relieved of command and replaced, whereas today they almost never are—except, I would add, largely for social rather than military problems, like alleged sexual misbehavior. Some Navy ship commanders, who are senior officers but not admirals (generally Commanders, O-5 rank), including dozens of Naval Academy graduates, are relieved of command nowadays for things like ship collisions, but mostly for social and image problems. We're not fighting that many battles anymore, so the focus on public image of senior officers replaces war accountability.

Contrasting the World War II general George Marshall with later generals, Ricks asks:

> [H]ow did we go from a tough-minded thinker like
> George Marshall, who made his reputation in part by
> speaking truth to power, to eminently pliable chairmen
> of the Joint Chiefs of Staff such as Air Force General
> Richard Meyers, chairman from 2001 to 2005, and his
> successor, Marine General Peter Pace [USNA 1967],
> who was chairman for two years after him? (Ricks, p. 12)

As someone who believes in a strong military and its necessity in a threatening world, I too revere the earlier era of military effectiveness. Fascism and murder in the mid-twentieth century were only defeated by the sacrifice of countless boys in uniform who never returned from World War II, and their officers—and countless civilians as well. Visiting the Normandy cemeteries of American soldiers, I couldn't hold back tears. What they did for all of us—it's too great to fathom. However, it is as difficult for me as it is for Ricks to revere the current brass—especially the admirals I saw come and go at Annapolis, the most show-over-substance poster institution of the Navy, as West Point is of the Army. The academies are both a symptom and a sign of our larger malaise. The problems of the academies, serious though they are in their own right, are even more troubling in that their problems are problems of our military as a whole in the decades since World War II.

I think this is probably causal to some degree in the direction of academies to larger military, as academy graduates dominated the upper ranks of the military through the 1980s, though steadily diminishing in importance. But to some degree, the academies' increasingly entrenched mindset of discouraging and even punishing productive disagreement, what I call loyal opposition, has certainly been determined to some degree from the opposite direction: Big Navy (as we call it) runs Annapolis, not the reverse. And the culture wars that have hollowed out academies since my arrival in 1987 (racial score settling; ham-fisted sexual assault training; DEI forcing of ethnic, racial, and gender minority prominence) came from the larger military that is controlled by Congress.

The fall of Kabul in 2021, after twenty years of US misadventures in Afghanistan, was the result of a withdrawal agreed upon by a Republican president (to a war started by a Republican president, continuing through several Democratic ones, and carried out so chaotically under another Democratic one—this isn't about political affiliation). It was also, for a new generation, what the sight of helicopters taking off from the roof of the US embassy in Saigon at the end of the equally unsuccessful Vietnam War was for my generation. What was the US doing there to begin with? Why did about two thousand US service members die in Afghanistan as a result of enemy action, not to mention the vastly greater numbers of local people, and at what financial and moral cost to their country? What did the US have to show for its expenditure of blood and treasure?

These questions haunted me perhaps more agonizingly because of my commitment for over three decades to develop thinking officers for the US Navy and Marine Corps. Many of my students have become commanders or captains, lieutenant colonels or colonels in the Marine Corps, some have been SEALs or EOD officers (explosive ordinance disposal guys), and at least one an admiral. Individual heroism and honor aside, what was the point of their service—or for that matter, of mine? (As a civilian Department of Defense employee, I get a pin and a citation every five years. My thirty-year pin with the citation praising me for that service, as the citation had it, came just before I was fired.)

Thinking officers are vital to winning wars. In the US and other democracies, civilian control of the military is a given, and is one of the aspects of our society we can be most proud of. Here, the military does not rule. But neither is it a passive machine. The military consists of living, breathing people who can reason and use their wits, as indeed they must do even under battle circumstances where decisions must come quickly and can cost lives, whether those of our soldiers and sailors or of civilians on the other side. They can present facts to the senior officers and civilians whose decisions ultimately determine the course of battle; they can influence, reason, outline possible outcomes, and speak up for their people.

I am a professor of English, though my degrees are in philosophy and comparative literature (I add modestly that I speak five languages and have read, and written, lots of books, as well as living all over the world). At its most trivial, teaching English to young adults means showing where to put commas and how to construct an essay. More importantly, it means showing them how to pay attention to data, how to think logically, and to use evidence to support their conclusions, as well as how to relate through literature to other human beings with vastly different life experiences. But I saw my job as even more than that. I saw my job, because it was at a military academy, as teaching not just students but future officers, and a specific kind of officer: thinking officers. The skills of the classroom can be transferred to real life. People who know how to look for evidence (which can be done when reading a poem or a novel), analyze it, and reach defensible conclusions that can be explained to others in exercises where no bullets are flying are far more likely to be able to do so when they graduate to the Navy or Marine Corps. These are bedrock skills for military officers—as indeed they are for all citizens, but perhaps even more vital when the decisions have to be made under chaotic conditions, as is frequently the case in armed conflict, and can cost human lives.

Thinking officers need to be able to question their superiors. Tenured civilian professors, such as we were told we had at Annapolis (alone among the service academies), need to show them how to use facts to withstand pressure from above, below, or any direction. This is what I committed myself to. And this is what the brass who run Annapolis tried to prevent by harassing and punishing me. That fact is the most worrisome: if the brass are stifling dissent at Annapolis, punishing reasoned disagreement from people who say things they'd rather not hear, what are they doing in the larger military? The disastrous fall of Kabul seems to give at least a partial answer. Yes, that war was ordered in stages and set up by civilian politicians. But the military is not without influence, which does not seem to have been exercised to good effect.

I had a draft number in the 1972 Vietnam-era draft lottery, but my number was never called, as the war was winding down. So instead of toting a rifle, I have done over three decades of what the Navy would call a shore tour as a civilian employee of the Department of Defense, teaching over three thousand young officers-in-training, as best I could, how to reason and justify their conclusions, rather than flying off the handle under pressure or according to their personal prejudices. (USNA likes to claim that half its faculty are officers, almost all on three-year assignments from the fleet. They tend to lack advanced degrees and have typically no training in the subject matter of the department to which they are assigned. This number is a generous estimate and includes ensigns on temporary active duty in the Physical Education Department. But it's true that I do exactly what the military officers are doing in the offices next to mine in the English Department.) Perhaps more importantly, I have tried to show the midshipmen by word and deed that they must resist the enormous pressure of the Academy and of the military in general to tell their commanding officer what he or she wants to hear. That mid-August weekend of 2021, with the sight of helicopters airlifting Americans from the US embassy in Kabul and the chaos of Afghans trying to board planes going out of the country to anywhere but there, the echoes of Vietnam were too strong to ignore. Why did both go so wrong?

Civilians control the military, but the military gives them data and interpretations, a process that I have tried to teach. Did the military give the wrong interpretations? Was it, as in Vietnam, too optimistic in Afghanistan about the effects of sheer American firepower? Could the battle have been won with other tactics? Should it have been started at all, or pursued this long? These are questions that must be posed and discussed, and the classroom is the place where people learn to do this. But the brass running Annapolis, that preen in front of the massed students at our parades and are waited on by white-coated servants at taxpayer-supported official functions in their high-ceilinged Victorian houses, made it their business to stop me from questioning their diktats, or from encouraging productive disagreement and promoting critical thinking. For them, this meant that their few years at the helm of a beautiful institution revered by many Americans went smoothly, and that they got promoted, as the Commandant, a Captain in charge of the military aspect of student life, invariably is, or went successfully into retirement, such as the now three-star Admiral Superintendent, who acts like a college president. But the negative cost to the students, and hence ultimately to the whole US military, was and is immense.

The commitment of the brass that run Annapolis and the other service academies wasn't to foster effective education and the production of thinking officers. It was to look good without the annoyance of a professor writing op-eds in major newspapers saying that what they were doing was outdated, a waste of money, ineffective, and/or illegal. Calling the US federal government out for waste, fraud, and abuse is legally protected, indeed encouraged. As the Government Accountability Office (GAO) Web site has it, "We want YOU! (to report fraud, waste, and abuse)" and it gives a link to do so—anonymously. I thought I didn't need this anonymity. I was wrong. What they therefore teach the young military under their command is to please their immediate superior: that's how they can get ahead. And when the students graduate, many of them take these lessons into the fleet. Pleasing your immediate superior is not the way to implement effective strategy, especially if these superiors feel that they have to please their superiors in turn, and they theirs. It all becomes an echo chamber into which reality can't enter.

Admittedly, it's hard being a thinking individual in a system that prizes conformity. What plebes (first-year students) are taught to do is make "sir (and now ma'am) sandwiches." "*Sir, yes, sir!*" "*Ma'am, yes, ma'am!*" And that means never questioning. Keeping your sense of proportion in a job where you're rewarded for kissing the ass of the person above you is very, very difficult. It's hard in industry, and it's harder in the military, which can punish you for "conduct unbecoming an officer" as your commanding officer (CO) defines this. The UCMJ that lists this offense isn't precise about what this is—that's up to your superior to say, whether he/she is good or bad as an officer—see below. Each level has to please the level above it. See the problem?

The point of education is supposed to be the opposite: using reason, not obedience—which means some people aren't going to like what they hear. Tough. Many Annapolis graduates retain their clarity of vision, but a certain number do not. And there is some evidence that it's precisely those who know how to tell their superiors what they want to hear who survive in the system long enough to become the next generation of admirals and generals. The others, disgusted, get out. The military sees a vast exodus of young officers after the rank of O-3, Navy lieutenant or Army captain, when many young men and women find the sycophancy required of them intolerable. Indeed, about half of Naval Academy graduates leave after their initial commitment of five years despite the mission statement speaking of their preparation for a "career" in the military. Even so, a "career" is defined as twenty years, so those who stay are let loose in their forties with no clear idea of how to get through the rest of their lives. (By that standard I've had almost two back-to-back careers at USNA.) Many miss the comforting embrace of being told what to do by the Navy or Marine Corps and feel rootless; typically, they are hired by military-related companies as midlevel managers.

I have seen many superintendent admirals come and go at Annapolis over more than thirty years. Almost every one was more clueless about where he was than the last, at an educational institution that was strange to them and not on board a ship under deployment (always a "he," by the way, until 2023). So what would they do if inserted into a world as strange as, say, Afghanistan? I think we saw. Having military officers with no background in education, other than having been a student decades before, run what is supposed to be a college is like having the real estate developers who built the buildings of Johns Hopkins Hospital in Baltimore, up the road from us, in control of the medical side of things. But almost to a man they have puffed out their chest, spoken loudly, and exhibited what they call "leadership," which largely seems to consist of doing what makes them look good.

The larger issue is therefore that the hounding and personalized harassment by administrative superiors I experienced is not limited to civilians who work for the Department of Defense like me. According to the reports of former students, it's also the way of the broader military, where your commanding officer can decide that s/he doesn't like you for whatever reason, or that his or her job is in jeopardy if s/he doesn't show him/herself pitiless on anything that is in the public gaze. The saying goes that military justice is to justice as military music is to music. That's not a flattering comparison. I've talked to countless young officers, my former students, who were accused of something (today's hot-button topic is actions with alleged sexual connotations) and even if found not guilty, were hounded and harassed until they left, their superiors unwilling to be seen as soft. No wonder people quickly realize that what makes life in the military tolerable is a happy superior officer, something to be bought at all costs. If s/he isn't happy, ain't nobody happy, and you're the one who suffers. By contrast, if the entire mission fails, say because you didn't tell them what they didn't want to hear, the blame is diluted, and you personally are spared.

The push was on until 2023 by a number of US senators to take the adjudication of any cases with an element of alleged sexual misconduct out of the hands of officers. The military understandably resisted this, as it destroys the almost completely personal nature of military "justice," which is its most fundamental principle. The fear on the part of politicians is apparently that the "good old boy" network is letting scofflaws off that a civilian tribunal would find guilty. In fact, the opposite is more often the rule. Commanding officers (and keep in mind that people change places continually in the military, so many of these "rotate in" after the fact and have no knowledge of the specific cases they are asked to deal with) are unwilling, especially as new arrivals, to seem at all approving of those who have even been accused (even if found innocent) of any of the marquee offenses of our day. These newly arrived commanding officers, rather like the eternally new superintendents at the US Naval Academy, will almost always protect their own careers by throwing these young—and frequently innocent—officers to the sharks. The mere accusation was enough for someone in charge to refuse to forward the junior officers' promotion papers. The young officer is not merely guilty until proven innocent, he (as it most likely is) is guilty *although* found innocent.

8

In 2023 this became a done deal. I think it highly likely that because politicians have succeeded in prying adjudication of alleged sexual-related misconduct from the military, it will be to the benefit of officers, not the contrary. Yet the personalized "I don't like this person because s/he makes me look bad" way of dispensing "justice" in the military—which was the prototype of the way USNA dealt with an annoying civilian professor—is deeply engrained in the system. USNA was acting as it usually does. Its only mistake was in thinking they could treat civilians the same way as the military. I had recourse to civilian justice. The young officers sacrificed to the careers of older officers eager to protect their own careers do not.

So this book is a warning. The military is intrinsically prone to say, "Yes, *sir*/Yes, *ma'am*" and acquiesce to what the superior officer wants. But officers and enlisted alike can be taught and encouraged to question, to reason, to keep their eyes open, and not to ignore evidence they'd rather not see. And from the other direction, down the chain of command, they can be taught not to punish subordinates who say things they don't want to hear, or that suggest that their own efforts are not producing the results they want them to. In Afghanistan, as in Vietnam, the military wanted to hear and to believe that things were getting better, and that we were winning. News that suggested otherwise from below—say from seasoned enlisted who had lived the battle—wouldn't have had much chance at making it past the multiple layers of buffer officers, all of whom wanted to tell their immediate superiors what these wanted to hear, leading back to the top.

Could I alone have prevented fiascos like Vietnam or Afghanistan, not to mention everything we've been involved in (and lost) past World War II? Of course not, but greater tolerance for fostering critical thinking and dissent in the military, indeed its encouragement from the highest levels on down, might have. This is a dark tale about what happens when looking good takes over from being good. For this leads to situations where we as a nation look anything but good—and where people die needlessly, coming back to the US Air Force base at Dover, Delaware in a box, as fallen military members do, having died in the fields of Vietnam—or Iraq and Afghanistan.

What I've realized after my three decades and counting at Annapolis is that while intrinsically small, the military actually shows in enhanced form the problems of our society as a whole, being the place where (to use another metaphor other than ripples widening out from a pebble drop) a magnifying glass focuses the sun's rays available to all—our societal obsessions—in a spot so hot it burns. And the service academies are the places at the center of the burn. The Naval Academy is where the conflicts and stresses of our society strengthen, under pressure both from without and within, and the pressures become unbearable. If we can understand the Naval Academy, we can understand our divided society—black vs. white, female vs. male, liberal vs. conservative. How do societal obsessions with the relations between men and women play out in these pressure pots where even hand-holding, much less sex, is prohibited? (Destructively.) How does the debate about race in America work when certain numerical results are guaranteed by top-down force? (Simmers under the surface.) How do the conservatives who still claim a stranglehold on these institutions relate to the liberals forcing change upon them from without? (They embrace their causes to get ahead.) The problems of the Naval Academy allow us to see the problems of our society as a whole—and perhaps, begin to address them.

SPIT AND POLISH

When I first came to the Naval Academy, I was taken, as almost everybody is, by the surface allure of the place—what they spend so much time keeping up, and which wows the tourists. What impresses visitors is, first of all, the clean-cut, short-haired students wearing these so-adult clothes, all alike, that reduces the visual chaos of a civilian college campus. Remember, what they wear are called uniforms for a reason. Plus, the fact that they are hurrying down the walkways and not ambling across the lawns (they're not to step on what is called "the Admiral's grass"), or worse, lying half-clothed on it, at least not where you can see them. For that, they have the burgundy-colored roof of Bancroft Hall, the single multiarmed dormitory, away from tourists, that midshipmen call "the red beach." The grounds are kept up by taxpayer-funded gardeners ripping out the beds of (say) tulips as soon as the plants even begin to think of passing their peak, and making piles of seemingly still-vibrant flowers on the brick walkways. These walkways link the gracious white Beaux-Arts architecture of Ernest Flagg, who made the Corcoran Gallery of Art in Washington (now part of George Washington University and its collection dispersed) and the Scribner Building in Manhattan, that are complete with flourishes like dolphins, stone cannonballs, and versions of the Michelangelo Medici tomb statues.

In addition, there is the quasireligious hush enjoined by the administration in places like Memorial Hall, one floor up in Bancroft Hall, their common dormitory that midshipmen call "Mother B," with the names of Naval Academy graduates who have given the last full measure of devotion for their country—for so the visitor is encouraged to see death in the line of duty, whether the cause was just or unjust (this question is never posed).

Or try going to the solemn crypt of John Paul Jones under the altar of the chapel (in which, sigh, my first wedding took place so long ago). When I first came to Annapolis, there were real Marines standing guard—I know now that they were hating their lives. Then these Marines, as well as our Marine gate guards, were deployed to war zones, and for a while there were midshipmen standing watch in the crypt. (Our gate guards are now Navy enlisted.) Now no one is there but tourists and old JPJ in his tomb. But it still feels like a solemn place, with the sarcophagus the French gave, after the body was found under a Paris city street when the Naval Academy bosses needed a body to anchor the church. Jones himself was actually a dicey character, a Scottish soldier of fortune who fled to Virginia after killing one of his own men, and who failed in his single attack on Britain, and then, after fighting for the Americans, sold his services to the Russians. He wasn't anyone's idea of a shining example of morality; yet the US Naval Academy needed a patron saint under the altar, so they invented one. It's all marble and columns and dolphins holding up a sarcophagus like a miniature version of Napoleon's in the Paris Invalides: scoff at your own peril. And when I first visited it at ten or twelve, coming from Maryland's Eastern Shore where I grew up, I didn't scoff. How could I?

Now go out and survey our perfectly kept lawns. You'll thrill both to the sea of muscular youth poured into flattering uniforms, the "yes, sir"/"yes, ma'am" with which the tourist is greeted, and to the very lack of your ability to have a casual conversation with the midshipmen that might produce negative publicity, beyond questions about where they are from or what year they are in. All this gives the Naval Academy its air of being more efficient, more orderly, more important, and more beautiful than the messy world outside its gates. The students have no scraggly hair, no sloppy T-shirts, and when I arrived, no backpacks—the backpacks they have now are all the same uniform black whose minuscule personalizing touches are too small to be noted by the outsider. Nothing can be added to the uniforms except earned and sanctioned pins, and the students are constantly inspected to make sure they are snappy looking. Their senior enlisted can order them to get their hair cut, and of course the women's hair is tucked back into a relentless bun or kept short. The men shave daily.

Maybe you think what impresses you is just chance? Not at all. It's the main show. The effect on the tourist of the thousands of healthy young people, who all have to pass a twice-yearly Physical Readiness Test (PRT), on a campus with gracious buildings and impeccable grass, is to make them think they have entered something close to paradise, one that it would be blasphemous to question. But more than three decades of more direct contact than visitors have with thousands of midshipmen in the classroom, my office, the weight rooms, pools, and social situations have shown me that question it we must.

Academically, USNA consists of largely required courses that the students sleep through, if at all possible, and in any case, try to get out of the way so they can check other boxes to reach the one day they all live for: graduation, when they leave this deadening place behind them. It's the happiest day of their lives. Militarily, the Academy—the students complain in class when I let them—is a lot of haphazard playacting to no purpose. Students are all dressed up with nowhere to go except class, or inspection, or parade—for four years. Most are completely wiped out emotionally by the pretending and the make-believe, and by the necessity to do things with no military purpose, aside from putting on a show. They know it's all fake, but what are they supposed to do about it? If they complain or try to fix it, they're punished. I've had many bitter students sit in my office red chair and tell me how they were slapped down by the officers for making proposals for change. After such experiences, few continue to try.

It's true that over all the years since its foundation, including a century when the Naval Academy was virtually the only commissioning source (as opposed to the current fewer than one in five), more admirals have come from Annapolis than from other commissioning pipelines. (ROTC used to provide officers only for the reserves.) And defenders of the Naval Academy brandish this fact. But this is only of historical importance and does not reflect the current day. Things changed when the percentage of Academy graduates in the fleet began to diminish as ROTC programs expanded post–World War II, and their graduates entered the active military and not just the reserves. The Naval Academy lost its status as the majority commissioning source for promotion to flag officer (admiral) rank in 1985, and studies have concluded that the commissioning source (which is to say, USNA vs. ROTC or OCS) is not a major factor nowadays in promotion to admiral. Anyway, the percentage of admirals in the fleet is very small indeed, with 229 flag officers in 2022 for an active-duty navy of just under 350,000. So, the chances of an entering plebe making admiral is almost zero, about as small as a high school basketball player becoming Kobe Bryant. So why are we still bragging about this? Smoke and mirrors.

The Academy also touts the fact that many astronauts have come from USNA. This is the case because Navy pilots were overwhelmingly selected for the early years of the astronaut program. Nobody notes that astronaut is no longer a growth job designation, and that Navy pilots compete with many other sorts of candidates these days. (Tom Wolfe's *The Right Stuff*, and the movie of the same name, celebrate this inspiring generation of badass daredevils.) This is history, which we can all be proud of. But it doesn't mean you should come to Annapolis if you want to be an astronaut. How long can you run the car on the fumes of a now-all-but-empty tank?

Previous studies, helpfully summarized in a study by William D. Lehner, himself a USNA graduate, linked below in "An analysis of Naval Officer accession programs," have attempted to calculate whether Naval Academy graduates are better than the current 82 percent of new officers who come from other pipelines. This means whether the aura of "best and brightest" (as the administration repeatedly tells the midshipmen they are) has any value outside the academies' bubble, where the officers have military command over the cadets and midshipmen. (This 2008 study is now, however, outdated and even when published, relied on data from some decades before.) Of course, no one dares say "better than" out loud outside the bubble because it would offend the 82 percent, so criteria like retention and promotion have been analyzed (in a study by William Bowman referenced by Lehner) that show in most cases differences (if any) of less than 10 percent between commissioning sources, with USNA apparently holding a slight advantage based on these decades-old statistics.

But the studies cited here, aside from more recent developments, are based on assuming that even if there are differences (and other studies fail to show these), they were due to USNA, rather than to the individuals drawn to it, who presumably would have been the same in an ROTC program. And no studies, especially not older ones, can factor in the recent toxic environment produced by the increased use of the academies for social-engineering purposes. On the positive side, it's true that USNA graduates do better at the rigorous postgraduation BUD/S training for SEALs than other pipelines. But it stands to reason that hard-charging individuals would have been drawn to an institution they thought would challenge them; most find it dispiriting instead and sit in my office red chair to voice their bitterness. It's not the place; it's the man—or as the Marine Corps puts it, the size of the fight in the dog (not the size of the dog in the fight). In any case, this extreme edge is the tiny minority of USNA graduates, and the SEALs are completely atypical, though perhaps among the most endearing. So, there's not much justification for the academies here.

Check out the recruiting material for Annapolis, or the other service academies. It'll tell you that if you are among the chosen few who are picked, you are not only stellar but virtuous: you alone are giving back, serving your country while the flag whips in the wind. Or read the *oohrah* propaganda from the USNA superintendent on our USNA web page. As I write this in spring 2023, the message is from Vice Admiral

Sean Buck (who incidentally told a group of officers that Bruce Fleming would never again be teaching at the Naval Academy so long as he was Superintendent, echoing the brag to a full faculty meeting of his predecessor Vice Admiral William Carter that he had managed to fire Bruce Fleming) and contains such inspirational claims as these:

> [The Naval Academy] is where we mold young people who will protect the freedom cherished by past and current generations and all those yet to come. This is where we develop the leaders of tomorrow and cultivate and nurture our core values of courage, honor and commitment. This is where many of our nation's finest young people make the commitment to serve their country, as so many have before them. This is where we accept responsibility for shaping a vision of America's future.

Cultivate and nurture honor, courage, and commitment? If only it were true. The music swells. What this means is, "Keep shoveling money our way!" The leaders of tomorrow! I guess only from USNA? All our graduates? And then it heads straight into "we are better than you" territory, frighteningly so, as I know what these claims mean for the daily reality of the Academy.

> The Naval Academy offers a unique opportunity where young men and women—from a diversity of races, regions, socio-economic groups and religions—gather in a special environment to learn and practice ideals that may often seem to be lacking in modern society. The result of this comprehensive process is a collective group of young leaders potentially more morally, mentally and physically sensitive than any that could be produced in another environment. That is what distinguishes the Naval Academy and its graduates.

I think he needs a new speechwriter. Physically sensitive? At least it admits "potentially." But note—these ideals "may seem lacking in modern society." Well, are they lacking or not? The sly suggestion is that they are. We're the font of all that's good! And besides, I know exactly what this sensitivity training consists of—forced indoctrination that most students resent and that ends up being counterproductive. And note that now the Naval Academy should be admired for the sensitivity of its products. That's certainly a switch from the old days when we touted their military strength. Now we're all about social engineering to achieve political goals.

Then there's this: "Among these outstanding young people will emerge the future leaders of our Navy, Marine Corps and the country." Among these will emerge? We don't say that in English. And note that it's only "future leaders." If they are only future leaders, how do you know they become these? Of course USNA makes Navy and Marine Corps officers. Is that the same as leaders? But of course, if we don't incessantly beat the drum for "leadership," we have no point. Plus they are all "outstanding" and "finest young people." Finer than the civilians they are to defend? All outstanding? In what way? Because they checked a box on the application about their race, or were recruited to play football against Temple and Southern Methodist University?

Even with all these choice claims, my favorite line in this inspirational message from VADM Buck is this one: "We stand prepared to show the American people the value of the Naval Academy—the value added by the Naval Academy—to the security, strength, vision and leadership of our nation." Yes, please, show us the value! You're on, Admiral: you say you "stand ready," so do it! Put your money where your mouth is, for the sake of the taxpayers who fund you and the people who believe propaganda. We're waiting.

Of course, by the time this book appears, VADM Buck will be safely in retirement, enjoying his pension of about $200,000 year, 100 percent of his salary plus health benefits past 30 years service (my retirement pension as a civilian federal employee, just for the record, at thirty years would be 33 percent of an average of my three highest salary years).

I don't think we should hold our breath for proof of the value of the Naval Academy, certainly not from VADM Buck.

Indeed, military retirements are lucrative even for the enlisted and lower-level officers. One article from a website called *The Military Wallet* points out that "a military retirement is worth millions of dollars" (see Appendix)—that's because we have an all-volunteer force that has to be bought. And military retirements have increased sharply in recent years, as have retention bonuses to entice people to stay in. I tell students, trying to get them to think, that this amounts to having a mercenary force. They gulp. The alternative, a draft, won't happen, so this is what we have. But it tarnishes the halo of "service" that the military brass and recruiters like to polish. And no, you probably won't die. You may be sleep-deprived and bored, but you sure can't beat the benefits. My conclusion is that it's a job—a good-paying one. Still, most people dislike it enough to leave.

If you are admitted to a service academy, you are not entering Camelot, the shrine of all that is good. But at least you are the recipient of the biggest government handout ever devised. You just won the lottery! A college degree at taxpayer expense with food, clothing, and lodging (that you get to complain about, and yes, I'll agree this is justified to some degree, as the food in King Hall at Annapolis is largely fried fat and empty carbs, the rooms are Spartan, you get put on restriction for kissing your girlfriend, and most of the clothes are synthetic and uncomfortable). But you get that "free" college (the students joke that it's an expensive education shoved a nickel at a time up their ass) and well-paid employment after that. Academy graduates get among the highest salaries of any college graduates, and this is presented as "service." Again, that's because we have an all-volunteer force, so we have to entice them in by money. Currently as I write this, unemployment is so low all the services are having trouble meeting their recruiting goals. Or is it because they are too "woke," as some commentators have suggested (see Appendix)?

I say all this to my students: Don't give yourself airs. Be grateful for what you are being given. Some students are resentful that I am raining on their parade where they believed they are the most self-sacrificing (certainly among the most miserable), the most deserving, and the most virtuous of college students. That's what the brass tells them, after all, simultaneously kissing their ass while it beats them over the head with a million senseless regulations arbitrarily enforced. Of course, most of them figured out by about October of their plebe year (so I call it the October surprise) that the people around them are neither the best nor the brightest, as they were repeatedly told, that academics are not taken seriously, and that the military side of things is a sham. My job is to reassure them they are not crazy: no, it's nothing at all like what they were told. Most midshipmen are grateful they finally have somebody who isn't lying to them, and I hear from some of them for years afterward. But some hate being disabused of their fantasies. It takes a lot to acknowledge that you were lied to and are caught in a system that isn't worth your respect.

It's the lies about the outside world they are ostensibly being trained to serve that get me; that and the self-serving purpose of the lies. That's just one way that Annapolis reminds me of East Berlin, which I visited often for theater and museums when I lived in West Berlin as a Fulbright Scholar. The Academy has, and East Berlin had, a wall, which midshipmen used to consider a joke and scale at night when they went out after curfew. No longer. Now it has lights and sensors—no guard towers yet, though the gate guards carry guns.

But it's not just the wall. East Berlin lied consistently about how awful the world outside the wall was, and so does USNA—and how rosy the world inside is. For East Berlin, inside was the socialist paradise of workers and farmers and outside was drug-addicted unemployment. East Germany, with barely ten million people, was touted by its dictators as among the top ten industrial countries in the world. Yet when the wall fell, it became clear how shoddy their goods were—they could sell only to their own people and the rest of the Eastern Bloc under Soviet domination—and that they had polluted their fields and streams. Overnight, their production collapsed as no one wanted their low-quality gadgets. The service academies have a monopoly similar to

East Germany in selling their products: the US government is obliged to take them all. If the socialism of this system disappeared, I wonder how many graduates would get jobs? And as for happy lives behind the wall—ha.

In neither case do most of the inmates have any illusions about what's what. East Germans could get West TV, and the government had to put them in prison, branding it as unpatriotic as well as a crime, to discourage it. Leaving the country legally was all but impossible except for the very old, whom East Germany was glad to let the West pay pensions for. Leaving illegally (if you didn't get shot trying) was called fleeing the fatherland—*Landflucht*. How is that fundamentally different from the moral opprobrium heaped on letting down the team at USNA by leaving in the first two years, which midshipmen can do without penalty, financial or legal (after that not), and the dire warnings about certain unemployment in the world outside? And yes, if you just up and leave, they can put you in prison. Military prison.

Technology makes walls useless. In East Germany, it was West TV, despite possibly having neighbors and family members turn you in for watching. Keeping the world at bay in a walled place like Annapolis or the other service academies is even more difficult now with the internet. So, the administration has taken the basic East Berlin step of forbidding plebes to access the internet. This is policed by roommates and fellow students, and by the upper class that function like the Stasi, the East German *Staatssicherheitsdienst*. But they don't forbid it all four years. And the result is that the midshipmen know too much about the world beyond the wall to believe the hype about the world it encloses.

For over three decades, I listened in my office to students seeking guidance on their journey of disillusion. It broke my heart, especially because by that point decades into my career, I knew what they would say. They came in with such high hopes for duty, honor, country, intense physical challenges, and hopes of running alongside people as motivated as they. What they found was people admitted because of their skin color or to play a sport that required a specific body type and skills unrelated to being an officer, and midshipmen "remediated" rather than thrown out for cheating or lying. No higher moral standard here, just an emphasis on passing on warm bodies to be junior officers and keep graduation statistics brag worthy.

Some of the African American kids are the most disappointed of all. One brilliant young woman from New York City announced in my office some years ago, "I should have gone to Howard."

"Why?" I said.

"Because I am so tired of being stereotyped as black," she said. "In New York nobody is anything. But here they want me to join the gospel choir. I can't sing. And I hate this channeling of the black kids so the administration looks good."

"Yeah," I said. "It's a problem. But don't give up. Just be you."

"Hmmm," she said. "Hard at this place."

"Tell me about it," I said.

The plebes are almost universally disillusioned with what they see. They are taught to revere the seniors (rank: MIDN—Midshipman, 1/C—First Class) as sterling examples of character and fitness. They address the seniors as "sir" and "ma'am"—as indeed they must address all three classes above plebe, an exercise ostensibly to teach obedience but productive only of resentment and disillusion. These people are, in many cases, not even a year older than the person addressing them with these terms of respect, and not always so, as some plebes have been enlisted and are older, or have been sent to the prep school. And it has no relation to the real Navy: you don't address somebody in the fleet as "sir" or "ma'am" because that person has been in uniform a year longer than you.

I tried to motivate them. I tell them that fine, the seniors are admittedly rarely role models, being careless about their uniforms, sloppy about personal interactions, and frequently so drunk when they come back late at night on the weekends that they vomit all over the floor— but they are so because they themselves have been disillusioned in their turn. The system does this to them all. That's your future, I tell the plebes—if you give in to cynicism and despair. I tell plebes the bottom line is that they have to stay positive and become good officers despite the institution, given that they will not become so as a result of it. I know what it means to stay positive despite the institution.

Some defend all these disappointing role models by saying, "If you can put up with the bullshit here, you can put up with the bullshit anywhere." Or this: "You can learn as much from bad leadership as from good leadership." Or this: "It shows you what not to do." What I say in response to them is this: The world is full of bad examples and immorality. Taxpayers don't need to pay half a million dollars per student to put on a horror show for you of what not to do. You'll find enough examples of that anyway.

What plebes learn is that USNA is nothing at all like what its hype presents it as. And why the need for the intensive hype anyway? That alone is suspect. Other schools, of course, put their best foot forward in their recruiting literature, but they are not so shameless as to portray themselves as the mother lode of virtue at taxpayer expense, defenders of the country who are better than those they defend because they have held out their hand to accept the taxpayer largesse that is being thrust upon them. Remember: if midshipmen are the "best," they have to be better than the people outside they are supposed to be working for.

I say: Be grateful! Thank a taxpayer! Instead, people come up to them in the airport when they are on the way home to say, "Thank you for your service." They are supposed to say, "Thank you for your support." The more self-aware of them say to me, "I feel bad because I'm just a student, but I can't say that to them." They also say: "Whether you become a good officer or not depends on the individual. Not the institution." So I say, "Right. So, tell me why you shouldn't have done ROTC at Ohio State. Or just gone to college and OCS after."

Over the decades, this realization that the graduates of the Naval Academy are not better "leaders" than any other group of young people (or old) has pushed me to define, and discuss with students, what I, and they, think a leader should be. What is a leader? Can leaders be produced by a process, such as the Academy insists they can? Is this, in fact, what the Academy does? Perhaps it is possible to mass produce leaders. I don't think it is. At any rate, no discussion of either the pretense of being able to make "leaders" or the particular process by which this is done is allowed. There's simply no discussion, probably because the conclusion might be that it's all hooey: what the brass does is the best of all possible actions. Now just say, "*SIR, YES, SIR!*" Oh, and by the way: "*SIR, BEAT ARMY, SIR!*"

Amusingly to me, the effort is unrelenting to suggest to the midshipmen that their institution on terra firma is, in fact, a ship. Hallways are p-ways (passageways), bathrooms are "the head"—and you don't go up or down a floor in buildings, but a deck. But USNA is not a ship. It's a boarding school. They live together in one huge coed dormitory. For four years. Where's the war? The deployment? It's not really a military base except to the extent it's proclaimed such; we could simply reclassify it as something else as a first step.

Too, the total ban on sex comes from calling the academies military bases, and the students being in the real military. This ban was unremarkable until 1976 when women arrived, as the students were all male, and there was no out homosexuality: straightness was assumed. So how, with women and so many other options, can this rule be maintained? It pushes their sexuality into off-campus screwings that are, they have told me over the years, positively Hobbesian: nasty, brutish, and short. The Academy can't offer guidance on healthy relationships (it offers guidance on almost everything else) because it sees all sexual contact of any degree as a transgression. Why can't we reclassify the Naval Academy as something other than a ship and four years by the Bay as something other than active duty? Why do they have to be in the Navy at all? Things have changed since women were admitted in 1976 and since homosexuality ceased to be punished by expulsion.

We need some creative thinking. We almost certainly won't get it from the military brass. They got where they are by agreeing with their superiors. And the Academy is better than Mary Poppins, who was only *practically* perfect in every way. The Academy removes the qualifier. Or at least they don't want interference from anybody with different views, even if that anybody has (like, um, me) interacted with far more midshipmen than they ever will, for far longer, and on a far more informative level—not (like them) in situations where the midshipman stands at attention to be reamed out or knows s/he cannot say anything to displease the senior. But military strength requires the ability to deal with people who disagree or who have access to other sources of data (as I do: no military administrator at USNA can talk to students as frankly as I do or has stayed for decades). Those at the top live in a command bubble—everyone around them says "Yes, sir"/"Yes, ma'am" and can be ordered around—and unwelcome information from lower down the chain of command is filtered out; it never reaches the brass. Keeping your next-layer-up commander happy gets you good fitreps (fitness reports). Even the rare disagreement is preceded by "with all due respect, sir/ma'am"—as if functional human beings couldn't hear another opinion without the assurance that they are the ultimate deciders. The military as a result has a natural tendency to do wrong-headed things and for far longer than they should. They are profoundly self-protective and don't welcome disagreement. This leads to mistakes, inefficiencies, and yes, deaths—of your children, if they are enlisted.

I hope you aren't surprised. You shouldn't be. Rich people are usually the same—they feel they deserve their money. And politicians. For that matter, exceptionally attractive people usually have a sense of their greater innate worth. As Lord Acton, the nineteenth-century British politician, said, "Power tends to corrupt and absolute power corrupts absolutely." Nor is this true only of people at the top of the heap. The world is full of mini-Caesars at all levels—someone with just a little more power than you who makes your life miserable: office dictators, the newly promoted, people looking to get a sense of self-worth by bossing others around. But I'd say, based on decades of experience with the military, that the military is more prone than other organizations to this sort of weakness because the uniform defines the person. To some degree, the office boss is always the office boss, of course, but in the military, you salute the uniform, not the person. You might lose your job if you talk back in an office, but in the military, you can be thrown in jail. Military jail. And remember: military justice is to justice what military music is to music. You signed away your rights when you enlisted.

Some individuals are able to resist this all-too-human tendency to lord it over others if they get a chance, and the military has many people serving honorably and humanely. But everybody in the military looks both up and down—that's the nature of a chain of command. The American military is the greatest in the world to the extent that more of its members find this balance. I believe the service academies and the attitudes they create are making this increasingly difficult to achieve.

HOW DID WE FIND OURSELVES IN THIS STRANGE PLACE?

The paradox of the service academies nowadays is that they are a hard-left veneer forced onto a hard-right base in a world that has changed out from under them. The military, a conservative institution, finds itself aggressively pursuing the left-wing preoccupations of racial profiling to the benefit of nonwhites and the punishment of men to the benefit of women in an institution that until recently was, let's admit it, all (or almost all) white and all male. Meanwhile, it recruits students with the image of bygone days, so that the students who arrive discover the truth and become unmotivated and cynical. Progressives outside may like this force-feeding of their favorite (civilian, peacetime) societal causes. But in institutions set up for radically different purposes than to be the avant-garde for a certain view of peacetime civilian society, this is merely contradictory. It doesn't make the military progressive. It just makes it confused. And the students bear the brunt of this war of cross-purposes. And then so does the military. And then so do you.

And please don't use as a counterexample Harry S. Truman's forceful integration of the military after World War II to claim that the military has always been more progressive than society at large, or at least has been forced to be by politicians. That step was taken because the needs of the military demanded it, an acknowledgment that the military had a specific and different function than society at large. The current emphasis on recruitment and promotion focused on skin color rather than individual quality, and blaming individual men for structural problems involved with throwing men and women together for long periods of time away from home, do not achieve military goals. They may please outsiders but are disastrous to the military. They turn races and genders against each other, re-racializing rather than uniting, and creating rather than defusing tension between men and women. And the silencing of discussion and dissent within the ranks and by civilian employees of the Department of Defense about the problems forcing this set of unwise changes creates an atmosphere of repressive authoritarianism rather than collaboration, making a less efficient military, as well as an unhappy one—not a more effective one. By jumping on the bandwagon of these programs in the military, the brass are acting to weaken our defense, not enhance it. But it certainly generates promotions. If you endorse this year's marquee program, no matter how destructive it is, this shows you're a "team player" and worthy of advancement.

The question members of Congress need to ask the Pentagon is this: Do we need the service academies at all? If so, why? Should they be funded as the racist football schools they have become? (The June 2023 Supreme Court ruling prohibiting educational institutions from admitting based on preferences for nonwhite applicants specifically excepts the service academies—see below. So alone among colleges, or "colleges," they can continue to use your tax dollars to discriminate. Perhaps Congress should intervene?) The answer to the first question may be yes! One caller on an NPR broadcast I was on insisted that the service academies were a "national treasure"—but he had graduated from one. I'd say that the people who have been handed the golden ticket of paid education followed with guaranteed employment that sets them up for life don't get a vote in whether they approve of this government program, any more than welfare recipients should get to say whether they want to continue to get handouts. And there may be answers to why. But as of now, we hear none of these answers, and the question is regarded by the military brass, and perhaps by many Americans in general, as a sort of lèse-majesté, an affront to the men and women who come back to Dover in a box, most of whom had nothing to do with the service academies. For many people, even asking for a justification of the service academies is a clear sign that the asker is almost certainly a Communist or an Islamic terrorist rather than a taxpaying American wondering why a specific government program is still going after all these years. VADM Buck also uses the phrase "national treasure" in his inspirational message on the USNA Web site. But then he would, wouldn't he?

Congress, however, has asked these questions in the past, in repeated attempts to close, alter, or downsize the academies—again usefully summarized by William D. Lehner in the study mentioned above. Some suggestions have been remarkably close to my own proposal, below—one in particular that all officers in the Navy do a training course at Annapolis after college education elsewhere, rather than having it be a stand-alone undergraduate college for a small minority of officers.

A combination of inertia, the weight of tradition, and the loud protests of Academy alumni (the recipients of this huge government handout) and of the brass that like them as bright shiny objects—and the source of the famed Army–Navy football game—have defeated these proposals in the past. Every time we have another major cheating scandal (such as in the early 1990s—and we had another one in 2021, with several in between), the proposal seems pertinent to Congress, which punted on major change by simply reducing the size of the student body in the 1990s, since reversed. (The superintendent's extra star remained.) But legislators forget quickly, and besides, undoubtedly don't want to be seen as antimilitary or unpatriotic.

Now, however, things have reached a tipping point—and the issues I raise based on more than thirty years' experience are far from the bloodless comparison of retention and promotion studies that are usually the criteria for asking whether we need the military academies. The bottom line has repeatedly been some form of "Well, they've been there a long time, we need varieties of commissioning sources, and besides, maybe it's too drastic to do much about them." (I ask: why do we need varieties of commissioning sources? When the service academies were in their prime, prior to World War II, we had essentially only one source, the academies. Was that bad?) So, they lumber on as institutions with no clear purpose except their own existence.

These discussions need to be reopened, because the situation is dire. The question to ask now is not just whether they should exist at all, but also the more nuanced one of whether we should have them in their current form as undergraduate institutions primarily about social engineering to enact larger societal preoccupations. The academies in recent decades have become toxic to their students (and yes, faculty—and by extension to the civilians the military exists to protect) because they have jettisoned the productive questioning that is necessary to make thinking officers, demanding instead unquestioning obedience to whatever racial- and gender-based program is imported from society at large, all forced down the throats of soldiers and sailors with the iron arm of the UCMJ by officers eager for promotion. The academies are no longer about defense—though of course they continue to graduate people they commission as officers. They're all hat and no cattle, to put it in Texas terms, and demotivate the students who cannot wait to leave. They have a storied past, but they have been perverted by a combination of outside forces and internal mismanagement. We need to say, "Enough!" Houston, we have a problem. A big problem. Let's fix it.

Shocking as this discussion may be to defensive alumni or the parents of current midshipmen, the questions I raise have been in circulation in academia for some time. What I have to offer here that's new are the personal experiences to back up my analysis of problems and possible responses. To repeat, the three most basic facts about the academies, which are well known to writers on this subject but among the most surprising to outsiders, are these. First, that nowadays (as opposed to the time up to and including World War II) the service academies produce not almost all officers, as many civilians assume they still do, but fewer than one in five, and at other times since World War II have produced far fewer, single digits of percentage. Second, that they do so at exorbitant cost to taxpayers that are many multiples of the cost of other commissioning sources. And third, that no metric convincingly shows that academy graduates are better as officers, whose job it is to protect and defend civilians. For me, however, it's a fourth fact—their toxic daily reality that I experienced for over thirty years—that is my reason for saying they are broken and must change, perhaps radically.

Other writers have pointed out the first three facts cited above, and some have proposed alterations similar to those I offer at the end of this insider narrative. For example, a 2018 article from George Mason University underlines what it calls the "systemic issue" with the service academies, namely "that these institutions are not fulfilling any function that ROTC and OCS are failing to perform." It considers three possibilities: abolishing them entirely and sending all applicants to ROTC and OCS, cutting funding so students pay something, and (my preferred solution, below, and also that of the author, identified as "Spring 2018 M-VETS Student-Advisor") getting out of the undergraduate education business and transforming the academies into campuses for training courses of shorter duration.

Others have suggested even more radical solutions to fix the fact that the academies produce too few officers at too great a cost for no better outcomes than other programs—and moreover, propagate an unjustified culture of nepotism and insider snobbery that plays badly in the fleet. I add that they are used to force-feed military members, who cannot object, social engineering programs dear to Congress to the detriment of any emphasis on defense.

An article in 2009 by Tom Ricks was entitled "Why We Should Get Rid of West Point." (He printed my response to the pushback by the West Point Public Affairs Officer in *Foreign Policy*.) Ricks advocates expanding ROTC and getting academy students out of their bubble. As he says:

> Not only do ROTC graduates make fine officers—
> three of the last six chairmen of the Joint Chiefs of
> Staff reached the military that way—they also would

be educated alongside future doctors, judges, teachers, executives, mayors and members of Congress. That would be good for both the military and the society it protects.

Another op-ed in the *Washington Post* in 2015, this one by military veteran Scott Beauchamp, was entitled "Abolish West Point—and the other service academies, too." Beauchamp agrees with me that "they are not the hallowed arbiters of quality promised by their myths." And he continues: "Their traditions mask bloated government money-sucks that consistently underperform. They are centers of nepotism that turn below-average students into average officers. They are indulgences that taxpayers, who fund them, can no longer afford." Actually, he's wrong about that last bit: Sure, given the cost of other things in the military, of course we can afford them. But should we? His bottom line is also more explosive than mine (op-ed writers have to make their points boldly to get readers): "They've outlived their use, and it's time to shut them down."

The realization within the last decade or so that the service academies are problematic is found on both ends of the political spectrum. An article in *The American Conservative* by West Point professor Tim Bakken (who cites me extensively in his book *The Cost of Loyalty*) is entitled "Corruption in US Military Academies Is Harming Our National Security." It largely considers West Point's lies in claiming highly selective admissions percentages, which are the same sort as the lies from Annapolis—a topic considered in Chapter 5. The liberal twin to this from *The Nation* is called "How America's Broken Service Academies Create a Broken Military" (links to articles in the Appendix).

Perhaps voices from within the service academies should be heeded? Bakken's biography notes this:

Tim Bakken is the first civilian promoted to professor of law in West Point's history. He became a federal whistleblower after reporting corruption at West Point and, after the Army retaliated against him, became one of the few federal employees to win a retaliation case against the US military.

I should add that I'm another. Bakken writes, in *The Price of Loyalty*:

> The military's loyalty to itself and determined separa-
> tion from society have produced an authoritarian insti-
> tution that is contributing to the erosion of American
> democracy. The hubris, arrogance, and self-righteous-
> ness of officers have isolated the military from modern
> thinking and mores. As a result, the military operates
> in an intellectual fog, relying on a philosophy and prac-
> tices that quite literally originated at West Point 200
> years ago. By dint of their rank, officers implicitly trust
> their own judgment, even when it runs counter to
> basic facts.
>
> Besides creating a culture based purely on loyalty and
> fear, the officers' stubbornness affects their performance
> on the battlefield as well. (Bakken, p. 258)

Most of these commentators (except Bakken) were writing from the outside—so the institutions couldn't fire them, as mine did me. But I knew things they didn't. Who better to describe the way things are on a daily basis than someone who has talked to almost four thousand midshipmen both singly and in groups, away from the officers they have to please? I thought (and still think) I had a responsibility to report the truth as a taxpayer and a professor; the administration took measures to stop that. Remember once again that all members of the military (including the superintendent) take an oath to uphold the Constitution, which protects my freedom of speech, and that the faculty tenure that USNA ostensibly awarded me when I was promoted from my entry rank of Assistant to Associate Professor (the rank beyond that, which I have held for decades, is simply Professor) was supposed to protect my academic freedom. And federal laws make it my protected legal (and moral) duty to report what I see as waste, fraud, and abuse in government programs. The administration apparently saw only their so carefully tended reputation being tarnished, which is pure self-interest. Apparently, Bakken is right.

When I arrived, only Annapolis among the service academies had what it claimed were tenured civilian professors; the *USNA Faculty Handbook* states that it abides by AAUP (American Association of University Professors) definitions of tenure. Not that having tenure (as I thought I had) or more than thirty years' experience as a professor helped me in the end, as USNA simply brushed aside the question of violating my tenure, saying that it chose when to deviate from AAUP guidelines—younger and still green USNA faculty take note. It turns out that was more smoke and mirrors; my only protection was as a federal employee. (As Bakken documents, West Point civilian professors are now told they have "academic tenure," but in fact, similarly do not.)

On a not irrelevant side note, civilian employees of the Department of Defense (such as I am) hold up (almost) half the sky—to echo (of all people) Mao—and so cannot be characterized as clueless outsiders. We are more than the number in the military reserves: in 2022, there were about 950,000 civilians compared to 600,000 reserves (sometimes we read in the 800,000s, which includes the National Guard). And civilians represent a contribution that numbers about 70 percent of the 1.4 million active duty. So, the clubbiness of the "he's not one of us" reaction by then-Superintendent Rodney Rempt at my first publication (Chapter 5) is insulting and wrong. He was walking proof that the USNA bubble created skewed perceptions. And by the way, the Secretaries of Defense, Army, Air Force, and Navy are all part of this civilian contribution to the Department of Defense.

The service academies exhibit all the preoccupations of opening these institutions to be more inclusive, while retaining the absolute control of the military during the days when they were completely exclusive. The service academies are the nightmare vision of conservatives finding their own weapons of everyone marching in step being used against them by liberals who insist on using this power to force their own agenda. Now with the Supreme Court decision on affirmative action of 2023, only the service academies among US educational institutions can continue to admit students based almost exclusively on race, and will certainly continue to do so. National defense has long ago gone by the wayside. The dream of these places being training grounds to produce tough "warriors" is dead.

We got to this odd place one step at a time through the military trying to run colleges that mirror civilian society's preoccupations. These preoccupations include advancing pro-female, pro-nonwhite, and pro-college athletics agendas, but at the same time implausibly keeping outdated strictures against sex and student partying that civilian schools have long ago abandoned, along with keeping the micro-control of every aspect of their lives once common in colleges that thought of themselves as continuing the role of strict parents. We can focus either on getting the most effective officers for defense after graduation, or on creating a student body before graduation that is the set of skin colors, genders, and big-time sports teams we want. We have chosen the latter, but rather than just making the concessions necessary to allow this to happen like civilian colleges, we have tightened the controls while pretending that these do not place stresses and strains on our mission. They do.

Remember, we're a job-training institution for one job guaranteed upon graduation—being military officers. It's as if the government had a stand-alone college that paid students to become accountants, all of whom were hired by the government (which had a monopoly on accountants) upon graduation. Civilian colleges and universities do not have the single mission and narrow purpose of the service academies—and students pay them, not the reverse. Their graduates compete for jobs and do many things upon graduation, or nothing. And civilian colleges and universities simply allow the better students to pursue academics in what, in state universities, are usually called honors colleges, while everybody else goes to the games and parties and has sex as they choose. I don't necessarily approve of this hedonistic solution either, but at least they're not doing it with 100 percent taxpayer funding, and the government doesn't hire all graduates for something important.

In civilian colleges, there is some effort to create groupings by class year, and self-identification as students at university or college X or Y, but at the service academies this bonding is intense. You chant your class number as you march and have different legal relations with members of other classes. And the whole student body at Annapolis, the Brigade, is composed of divisions such as battalions, regiments, and companies. You're a member of a series of Russian nesting dolls that determine your life, all bristling with military valor.

Because civilian colleges send students in so many different directions after graduation and simply gave up trying to control a good deal of student behavior as they altered and changed, it was easier for them to cope with coeducation and the nonacademic takeover by big-time sports that characterizes the post-World War II academic landscape. To be sure, the result is dilution of the educational mission in most civilian colleges, or the acceptance that there may be no common mission. But at least they don't seem ready to explode. The service academies do.

This is so because they have adopted some of the same changes as the civilian schools, but they've done this more abruptly—and far more forcefully. These changes are centrifugal in nature, in that they have nothing to do with the goal of effective national defense, but are instead societal concerns of what is seen as inclusion of specific groups. And so, in order to keep some vestige of the idea of common mission, the centripetal forces have been intensified. The best example is control of sex. Civilian schools went coed and stopped patrolling sex in the 1960s and 1970s. They also ceased punishing students for having sex, until the attempts to patrol what is called sexual assault (Chapter 7). Women came to the academies in 1976. But the administration have not ceased patrolling sex. In fact, the control has gotten tighter.

Women, national sports recruits, and racial profiling and score-settling are all centrifugal forces in institutions that formerly were defined by their unity and homogeneity (yes, at the cost of exclusion). If we loosened the control, the service academies would be virtually identical to civilian schools. And then there would be no reason for taxpayers to fund them, and the brass would lose their bright shiny military Disneylands. So, the administration simply increases the pressure: more punishments, courts-martial, constant hectoring, mandatory training, lying about problems, and blaming individuals rather than the system. Only increased centripetal force keeps the whole thing from falling apart. But it also increases stresses within.

The service academies took so many turns off their original path that they have ended up in the middle of nowhere. Once upon a time, however, they made sense. The Naval Academy started as a technical school in 1845 to teach "midshipmen" who formerly learned about ships at a young age by shimmying up the rigging "amidships"—hence the rank—the things that spending two years before the mast no longer could, in an era that was more complex than that of simpler sailing ships. West Point was founded in 1802 in the Napoleonic age of strategy that required moving large masses of soldiers around on a battlefield, something almost all scholars agree is a thing of the past. No more Normandy beach landings either, most agree. The conflicts of the future are technical, mechanical (drones, for instance), and distanced (the Navy sits on its ships and fires torpedoes, and all services drop bombs from planes). Of course, this is not true for the Marine Corps infantry or Army Rangers and Navy SEALs. But only a small number of these come from West Point or Annapolis.

Clearly the world in the nineteenth century was getting more technical, and the educational institutions of the time did not fit military needs. American and British colleges in the first half of the nineteenth century were for gentlemen, and devoted to the study of classics and religion. The legislation that was the origin of the agricultural and technical land-grant college was passed during the Civil War, but they only began to receive dedicated funding in the 1890s. Most of these have become X State University, or A and M University. Other colleges were for teachers, or arts schools. The military needed something else. The service academies they founded were not colleges. They did not give bachelor's degrees. Almost all classes at Annapolis were in engineering or nautical skills and were required. They were for men only. Chapel was mandatory, and students marched in ranks to class. Then they became the new officers of the Navy. None of that is true now.

Other things have changed too. The military was basically male and was seen as the institution that "made men out of boys." So, at the service academies, the marginally older men were given free rein to haze the newbies. (Read James Webb's novel about the Naval Academy, *A Sense of Honor*.) At least that's how we see it now; then it was seen as a necessary rite of passage that the younger men secretly (or not so secretly) welcomed, even if they dreaded it. It was like Parris Island for the Marine Corps. Physicality was the language of men, with men punishing and hurting men. It was a form of sadomasochism, of course, but conversations with my students over decades have convinced me that many of them long for these good old days when they could be made to do pushups until they puked, and when they could be shoved and slapped around by bigger men: now the upper class cannot touch the plebes without their permission. That's not because we are kinder and gentler, or at least not totally. It's because of women. Women who cannot be muscled around have irrevocably changed things. For the better, perhaps. But the change is undeniable.

From the all-male, all-white days of mandatory chapel and marching to class, no academic degree, and almost all mandatory classes, move first to 1933, when Annapolis began giving a bachelor of science degree, and then to the 1960s, when majors were introduced, including a limited number of nontechnical majors including English and history (while still requiring a heavy load of mandatory science and technical courses). Then: no more chapel; no more marching to class. Electives! The service academies were suddenly unpopular because of Vietnam: time to get nice. (Webb hates this set of changes; see his article "Women Can't Fight" referenced below—and hold your fire on the misleading title: that's not what it says at all.) Then jump again to 1976, when women were first introduced to the academies over the protests of the military, because that was what was happening to almost all the other formerly all-male schools. (Webb hates this even more, because they could not be URL, unrestricted line officers.) As the decades went by, women expanded as a percentage of the student body well above the number of female officers in the fleet, because the brass had a mandate to forward women, and because they control the admissions to the service academies. Now they brag that the proportion of the entering class is more than a third female. Soon I am sure it will be 51 percent or even more. They can make that happen, no problem, even without many females applying.

While the service academies were becoming more like colleges, colleges were adopting some of the aspects of the service academies. Universities were no longer, as they had been prior to the twentieth century, largely philosophy, religion, and classics for gentlemen. The state universities, which always had an agricultural and technical or mechanical aspect (some schools are called A and T, in addition to some being A and M), were more practical than the East Coast intellectual schools. Technical institutes (e.g., Caltech, MIT) were founded initially as largely engineering schools before they were pure science schools. That meant that the engineering and technology courses of the service academies were no longer different from what was offered elsewhere. Nowadays, if most colleges have engineering courses and all have the same other ones we teach, if ROTC can teach a course in (say) Naval history, and if only a small percentage of officers comes from Annapolis or West Point, we can't continue to claim that our academics are in any way special. So, the brass had to focus on the uniforms, punishments, and regimentation; what was once secondary now had become primary. We're all about the show.

Another alteration was in the cost of civilian colleges, and hence the gap in costs between the service academies and any other option, that has skewed their allure to students. At the service academies, it remains as true as it always was that students pay nothing and are fed, housed, and given a salary—and of course are guaranteed high-paying jobs after. However, what has changed is schools outside. In the 1960s, the University of California provided free tuition to in-state residents. In 2022, Berkeley cost about $15,000 for in-state students—just tuition.

But now it costs to out-of-state students for tuition almost what private universities cost—about $45,000. Stanford and other private universities cost about $56,000 for tuition alone and $78,000 including room and board. Again: tuition at the service academies: $0; in fact, the students are paid for being in the Navy and get free room, board, and medical care. (They also get GI Bill benefits for later education.) Fees at all universities have risen much faster than inflation for decades. When I was a student at Haverford College in the early 1970s, it cost $4,000—tuition, room, and board. Adjusted for inflation, that would be about $24,000 in 2022. In fact, the sticker price of Haverford in 2022 is approximately $81,000. And no guaranteed jobs after. I had to pay for graduate education and scramble.

With financial aid for less well-off students, the average price of Stanford is said to be about $14,000. Richer ones pay the full price. But at the service academies, even wealthier families pay nothing. The students are paid. And many (they tell me) come for the "free education," something that is only a dream in the world outside. This means that they are not intrinsically committed to the military, only putting up with it as a way to finance their education. It doesn't necessarily mean they will be less-effective officers, if they decide later to be committed to the military, but the financial incentive of free college means a lot more nowadays than it used to. I've often wondered how many applicants we'd get if our universities, like those in (say) Germany (I've attended two, Munich and Berlin, and taught at a third, Freiburg), had no tuition, like Berkeley in the 1960s. That would take the huge financial pull off the table. How popular would the service academies be if colleges outside hadn't altered so drastically?

There were other changes too that all happened in civilian schools more naturally, and in the military institutions by force. Until 1994, gay students were kicked out of the service academies, just as gay servicepeople were kicked out of the military at large (remember, students at Annapolis or West Point are actually in the Navy or Army). This was attenuated a bit under what we called "Don't Ask, Don't Tell" (DADT), coming into effect in that year, which meant that your CO could no longer proactively seek to find out if you were gay, nor could s/he ask you directly. But with time, even this was felt to be restrictive, and with the lifting of DADT in 2011, gay servicemembers and hence service academy students were no longer thrown out at all. Even transgender people were accepted for a time, then not, and now are back again. (The military, remember, is having trouble reaching its recruiting goals.)

In the last half-century or so, many hitherto excluded groups—racial, sexual, ethnic, and gender—have gained rights that they did not have before. These have been victories. Women have asserted their rights, people of color can no longer be legally discriminated against, and ethnic or linguistic backgrounds are no longer grounds for exclusion or denigratory treatment. The story of the achievement of what is, at last, legal parity for many minority groups is perhaps the greatest victory of American democracy of the last half-century, as I am told that the now all-but-universal use of car seatbelts is the biggest victory for public health of the same period. That, and arguably the change in public attitudes toward smoking and the consequent diminution of that practice.

But now we've gone way beyond parity, into discrimination against whites. And in 2023 the Supreme Court said it was legal for the service academies, though not for any other institutions of higher education. Our first black graduate was one Wesley Brown, in 1949, after whom a huge sports facility on our campus is now named, and stories abound of his mistreatment by his classmates. Not good. In short order, however, we went from the extreme of excluding, then later allowing harassment of, black students, to our policy (mirroring many civilian schools) of actively recruiting them, because they are black, and, as I discuss below, admitting them to lower standards than white students. The current policy to police perceived racial bias is even more drastic, what is called DEI (Diversity, Equity, and Inclusion), that creates a system for clandestine reporting of alleged incidents of racial bias. It's comparable to the way women a few years before were encouraged to report alleged incidents of gender bias under the programs regarding sexual harassment

(Chapter 7). No semblance of due process is to be found in any of this, as I learned, and innocence of the accused is not presupposed.

With the focus on what is called harassment of women and more recently, of nonwhites, the viewpoint of these previously excluded groups has become primary at both the military institutions and civilian ones. If a woman says, even months after, that she only gave in because she felt coerced to have what the man may have thought was consensual sex, the man can be ridden out of his university on a rail. In the service academies, it's similar but even worse: he can be court-martialed and put in the brig. If a professor at a civilian institution isn't teaching works that speak to minority concerns, or says something, even inadvertently, that a nonwhite or nonstraight student takes offense at, s/he can be "counseled" by superiors. It's even worse at military institutions, where civilians are treated—even if illegally—as if they were in the military, as I came to learn.

This seems a victory for individual viewpoints that had been excluded before, and much of civilian society—certainly the education sector—has embraced these whole-heartedly. But it's a paradox that these policies have been pursued so relentlessly in the military, have been imposed more forcibly and enforced with more draconian consequences. It's a paradox because very little in the military is geared to the development of the individual, which is the goal of social justice warriors demanding equal (and sometimes more than equal) rights for African Americans, Hispanics, immigrant groups of various points of origin, women, gays, and now most recently transgender individuals. So, while civilian society is suffering indigestion at demands for inclusion of individual points of view, the military, faced with the same demands for individual valorization, has become mortally ill. Civilian society has a healthy, perhaps too healthy, tradition of the defense of individual rights. It's in our Constitution, after all. Not to mention the "Life, Liberty and the pursuit of Happiness" of the Declaration of Independence. Of course, this can go too far too fast for some people, and leads to what some people see as a trampling on the rights of the collective: does a Christian baker who thinks that now-legal gay marriage is immoral have to make a cake for a gay couple? But at least it's firmly in the mainstream of American political thought.

Not so for the military. The military has never known this push for individual rights to self-expression. The military, by its very nature, is about a very un-Enlightenment, un-Kantian use of individuals, not as ends in themselves but as means to an end. Midshipmen are taught the scale of values from most to least: ship, shipmate, self. Self comes last, not first. Indeed, nothing in the military is geared to individual self-expression, not in clothes, not in taste for food (uniforms and the mess hall, respectively), not in suddenly wanting to hop in your car and go into town if you feel like it, not in freedom to quit your job when you've had enough, not in your decision of how to style your hair, to exercise or not; not in anything. What personal expression there is, is severely limited. Midshipmen have a single corkboard of less than four square feet in their otherwise identical rooms: all personal photos must fit within its borders. Decoration is communal, in the form of bulletin boards in the halls that plebes fill with colorful scenes from construction paper like in third grade, only theirs are of death-dealing airplanes spitting fire and warriors wielding swords to lop off heads and limbs.

So, even if you're not nostalgic for the "good old days" of white boys beating each other up between bench presses, it's hard to defend the current day. The old days may have been like *Game of Thrones*, but a lot of people liked *Game of Thrones* (the CGI dragons were cool). And at least they made sense in a world that equated masculinity with violence, as many young men still do, and please don't just say "Tut tut, we'll change all that!" Because you won't. Now why bother? The machines do the fighting, and we're all about gender and racial representation and playing football.

Sure, the service academies have changed, perhaps even for the better, but not in ways that argue for their necessity. Instead, they are increasingly without specialized purpose to justify their cost to taxpayers and their restrictions on students. With uniforms. And parades. And control. Lots of control.

The control is necessary to keep the lid on a pot boiling ever more violently. Annapolis has loosened up but also gotten more controlled. We have courses in psychology and philosophy (if no majors in these) and courses in LGBT literature and Gender Studies and graphic novels, as well as in African American literature. Christian chapel is optional; we have a synagogue and a mosque, and the only marching is at noon meal formation and for parades, not to class. We brag about the increasing number of nonwhites and women and inclusivity of all sexual persuasions. It's mordantly funny to someone like me who saw how ferociously they resisted all these things in the past. From being Peck's Bad Boy, they are now teacher's pet.

Teacher is civilian society, and the whip hand is usually Congress—or the military preemptively, as it tries to please politicians. All changes in the military come via orders and are enforced with great intensity. Thus, the military whipsaws in ways that the real world, that has to develop more gradually, does not. So, the two factors that coincide to make the military and the military academies the pressure cooker of social stresses they have become are that outsiders tell it what to do, and the insiders force the changes demanded from without immediately and with no possible resistance or discussion. The love of the military for force and the unwillingness of most of its people to have their orders questioned make an extremely effective instrument for politicians eager to affect at least one visible aspect of society immediately and to their liking. In real society, changes take longer and have to be discussed. Not in the military.

Usually, the military doesn't want too much interference from civilians once it's been given the go-ahead order. But civilian direction of the military has gotten stronger in recent decades as its actual fighting function has receded, and the military has become, to a large degree, about show. Politicians tell the military what it is going to do, and the military figures out how to do it. (This isn't intrinsically bad: none of us wants the military running the show, as in Egypt, Pakistan, or Thailand. At least, I don't think we do.) As, for example, politicians told the military that women were going to be admitted to the service academies in 1976.

Nobody denied that this would open opportunities to women, which seemed the only issue. Would it also destroy something? Of course, but making this point was held to be male chauvinism at its worst. So, things are bad at the service academies. We have, you might say, trouble. Right here in River City, as the musical *The Music Man* has it. Only our river is the Severn, and the city is Annapolis.

But I hear people objecting, what about the rankings? Bruce Fleming has to be full of shit as USNA and USMA and also Air Force are called among the handful of best "national liberal arts colleges" in the USA! Who's right here? To find the answer, you have to look at the definitions of "best," "liberal arts," and "colleges."

Some years ago, USNA climbed into the top group of colleges according to the *U.S. News & World Report* list, and in 2022 was listed as the sixth best "national liberal arts college" in the whole US. (USMA, West Point, is listed as number nine, and Air Force as number eighteen.) *U.S. News* is the most cited of these many ranking services, and everybody at Annapolis, from plebes through professors and all officers, received a US Navy ribbon for "Meritorious Unit Commendation" when we climbed into the top cluster. The flag signifying this flies in front of the administration building—and I still have the pin somewhere. It came in a little plastic bag in all the faculty mailboxes—thousands of them handed out to students, faculty, and administrators. (Of course, this is also the institution whose superintendent canceled classes after Navy's unexpected win in a football game over Notre Dame, which, of course, we are otherwise guaranteed to lose.)

Another influential ranking is by *Forbes*, which notes that it ranks "colleges and universities in the US based on the return on investment and outcomes they delivered for their students. Schools placed well if their students graduated on time, secured high salaries and low debt, and went on to have successful careers." *Forbes* is a financial publication and loves the service academies, to which it devotes a shout-out article, because the students incur no debt (in fact, are paid for being in the military, at Annapolis 35 percent of an officer's salary in addition to room, board, and education) and get some of the highest salaries after graduation of any college graduates. Of course, that's because they are guaranteed employment—in fact are required to take it—at salaries that are so high because we have an all-volunteer military force. It's pure socialism: as one superintendent liked to say, repeatedly (so I'll repeat it here), "We hire all our graduates." If the State of Maryland paid over-market rates to all University of Maryland graduates with guaranteed employment, UMD would be ranked even higher than it is.

Forbes just doesn't seem to understand the service academies very well, which may be understandable, as nobody knows what to do with government financing, military control, and a government monopoly on hiring. In 2009, the second year of the *Forbes* rankings, they even ranked West Point the best college in the country—and a reporter called me up for my reaction. I tried to explain what I am describing here: that this was like having a government monopoly compete against free-market businesses, or a natural bodybuilder to one on steroids, or a healthy person to one kept alive by constant blood transfusions and kidney dialysis. To no avail. However, in 2021, they seemed to admit this overreach somewhat shamefacedly, citing their 2009 enthusiasm for West Point, but noting that "the military academies are slightly different animals." Um, radically different animals, I'd say. They're like a baseball team that wins by greasing the ball against one playing by the rules.

When I arrived at Annapolis, I was interested enough in the idea of cardinal rankings of very different schools to read the annual *U.S. News* rankings. At that point, the service academies were listed not as "liberal arts colleges" but in a separate box. Then, some years later, they were reclassified and included in the same list as institutions such as Amherst, Williams, Wellesley, Swarthmore, Haverford (my college), and Bryn Mawr colleges—much, I heard, to the horror of the USNA administration, who liked neither "liberal" nor "arts," nor for that matter, "college." (They quickly decided they liked the honor.) The justification for this was the definition of "liberal arts college" following the Carnegie Basic Classifications: an institution that focuses on undergraduate education and that gives more than half its bachelor's degrees in the arts and sciences. The purpose of this is to bracket out "specialty schools" (a separate classification) like those that are focused on performing arts or business. The service academies are undergraduate institutions that give 100 percent of their graduates a bachelor's degree—at USNA, a Bachelor of Science (BS) even if your major was English or History. QED. Liberal arts colleges!

The same man, Robert Morse, has run these rankings for decades. As Morse and his co-author Eric Brooks noted in 2022, "we do not factor nonacademic elements like social life and athletics." So, the controlled nature of the academies plays no role in being proclaimed "best national liberal arts colleges"—nor do more murky things like student eagerness to learn (low at Annapolis), morale (very low), or whether the students actually retain anything at the end. Midshipmen universally tell me that classes are largely run on a memorize-for-the-test-and-mind-dump-after system.

To me, it seems ridiculous to include federally funded institutions with guaranteed, highly paid jobs after graduation with the free-market schools students pay for and where graduates have to compete on the open market for jobs upon graduation. But that's what the inclusion of the service academies as "liberal arts colleges" does. So, let's look at the breakdown of where the so-influential *U.S. News* ranking comes from in terms of percentages for various factors. In almost all cases, ranking the service academies with free-market, nongovernment-monopoly institutions is like comparing apples to orangutans: because they are paying for cadets and midshipmen to be in the military, as they are at the academies, and to be officers afterward, these institutions are close to the top of the heap.

To begin with, 10 percent of the ranking is based on an institution's level of "graduate indebtedness" (zero, by definition, at the service academies), "graduate indebtedness total" (ditto) and "graduate indebtedness proportion with debt" (still ditto, zero). The students are in the military—they are paid. And are hired after at high salaries. Et voilà! No debt. There are all-scholarship specialty schools like the Curtis Institute of Music in Philadelphia, but these are not ranked as national liberal arts colleges. And employment after leaving is not guaranteed. Then there is "financial resources per student": 10 percent of the *U.S. News* ranking. We do extremely well here too but for the wrong reasons. You're paying for it all, and the sky's the limit. For Congress, it's not considered education; it's military funding, which grows and grows. Congress doesn't fund any "colleges" but these, and they're not funded as colleges but as branches of the military.

And then there's our putative selectivity: 7 percent of the *U.S. News* ranking. USNA claims less than 10 percent acceptance rates, among the lowest in the country. But this is simply a lie, or at least, a made-up definition. It includes groups USNA thinks should be included but that no other school does, such as the applicants to an eleventh-grade summer seminar at USNA—the justification being that these are counted as "preliminary" applications to USNA, even if the student doesn't actually later apply (see below). And it counts, or at least counted, all 7,500 students who apply to this program with 2,500 spaces. USNA claimed for years a total of close to 20,000 applications (the class of 2026 is down to about 13,000), but the Admissions Board (on which I served) considered fewer than one quarter of that number. We offered about 1,800 admits for about 4,500 applications actually considered—and not all of these were complete either. Daniel de Vise, a reporter for the *Washington Post*, noted the following in a 2011 article: "The Naval Academy reported an admission rate of 7.5 percent last year, one of the lowest in all of higher education. But academy officials now acknowledge that roughly two-thirds of the 19,146 applications were incomplete and never seriously considered for admission."

If you Google "USNA acceptance rate" you get the figure of 8.4 percent for 2021. USMA, West Point, is listed as 10.7 percent for the same year; see Tim Bakken's article, mentioned above, for the same admissions policies at West Point/USMA as at USNA. Acceptance rate, impressively (and suspiciously) low for the service academies, is calculated by starting with the number of applications and tallying this with the acceptances. So the more applications you count, the lower your acceptance rate. In a USNA response to a Freedom of Information Act request I made early on when I became interested in these issues, USNA admitted that it counts these incomplete applications as part of its number of applications. (When they realized what I was doing with these requests, they started refusing to answer questions or sending pages of blacked-out data.) I heard from reliable sources that what they count as an application is frequently nothing but a name and a computer-generated applicant identification number, even if the student does not subsequently fill out the application—that according to reports are handed out at recruiting events, frequently staged in heavily-minority areas.

However, a name and address and a computer identification number is not what the US Department of Education, to which all schools must report their admissions selectivity, says counts as an "applicant." Here's what the federal guidelines say as the definition of "acceptance rate": "The proportion of first-time students submitting an application to this school that were accepted for admission. An application is considered submitted only after all required portions of the application are complete. Applicants that do not submit a complete application are not included in the calculation of this rate." Perhaps USNA simply defines only a name and address as "required"? I ran USNA criteria by the admissions director at an Ivy League university. I asked her, "Does your school use incomplete applications?" "Absolutely not," she said.

After I began writing about these things (articles at end), Sam Fellman, a reporter for *Military Times*, which publishes *Navy Times* and *Army Times*, followed up this topic with the then-dean of USNA admissions Bruce Latta. After noting that in 2012 USNA said it turns down 16 out of 17 applicants, Fellman continues:

> But the academy's nearly peerless selectivity relies on counting methods that appear to diverge from the higher education standard, experts say. The school counts as "applicants" those who haven't completed an undergraduate application but have shown interest in another way—a catch-all category that includes everyone who begins an online application or applies for a Navy ROTC scholarship or the school's weeklong

Summer Seminar for high school seniors, the academy's admissions head confirmed.

So, to be clear, if you apply for an ROTC scholarship to study at a civilian school, USNA counts (counted?) you as an Annapolis applicant. The justification, we heard when these topics were discussed and making the rounds, was that they assumed if you wanted to go to ROTC at, say, Penn or Vanderbilt, you really wanted to go to Annapolis. Say what?

The Academy thinks it can do what it wants, as is clear from Latta's response to Fellman asking why the Academy diverges from accepted practices (even though, to repeat, their bottom line has to be reported to the Department of Education and is used by ratings agencies) as it repeatedly does (for example, in applying AAUP guidelines as it wishes, or for that matter conducting its "investigations" with no regard for due process). Asked if it was fair for the Academy to use a different standard, Latta replied: "Their application processes are completely different from the Naval Academy's or a service academy's. So I don't know that I would compare myself to other schools." Right. But that's just what the rankings do, and what people who Google acceptance rates are doing. If you don't want to be compared to other schools, don't put out these misleading (lying?) statistics. But of course they do want to be compared (favorably) to other schools. The military craves the adulation of the people it exists to protect.

For the Class of 2026, again, the number of reported applications is down to a few shy of 13,000; perhaps they have finally stopped counting the eleventh-grade applicants to the USNA summer seminar? The number of offers of admission for this class was 1,390; all but about 200 accepted the offer. (If you're interested enough in a service academy to apply, you're probably going to go if they say yes—they're that odd.) I assume they are still counting the incomplete applications; are they still counting ROTC? If not, it's only because of the bad publicity I generated for them, which is the only thing USNA ever responds to. They're all about looking good, and they respond only to external pressure. So far as I can see, they have no internal moral compass. But it seems clear that these numbers of applicants are still self-defined and wildly inflated, because the academies don't think they have to use the standards other schools do.

A colleague of mine broached this topic of falsified (or if you prefer, made-up) selectivity with the Middle States evaluation committee that came to assess us for accreditation; their reaction was that this was not a topic they would consider. So, who will? I've pieced together a picture of systematic deception based on what I saw and what I have been able to research, but this is spotty at best because the administration doesn't want a nosy professor looking into what they do. So the data are sparce, anecdotal, and not handed out willingly. Congress needs to send people to see what's really going on, with the power to examine every step of the admissions process and not be fobbed off by assurances that everything is A-OK, nothing to see here. What I have learned most fundamentally is that just because the USNA administration says something, that doesn't mean it's true. In fact, it's usually the opposite. I don't think it means they set out to lie, it's just that they think the world revolves around them and they can do what they want. They live in their bubble, and they see no reason to allow reality to intrude. And that is a problem with the brass that makes it do stupid things, both at the service academies and outside, like losing wars.

What I learned is that the service academies are rogue actors, making up policies as they go along and applying them as they wish. Even the government seems to know the academies are rogue actors. A GAO—then General Accounting Office (now Government Accountability Office)—report from 1991, more than thirty years ago, on this subject of overall performance of the academies, recommends increased external oversight: "To strengthen the oversight of the service academies, the Secretary of Defense should evaluate alternative means of providing external oversight and advice to the academies." This would have been a step forward. However, the Department of Defense (DOD), under whose aegis the academies operate, rejected this, with the results we see today: "DOD did not agree that the system needs reevaluation and it does not intend to act on this recommendation." A report from 1992 on all commissioning sources (the academies, ROTC, OCS, and direct commissions, which usually makes finished doctors and lawyers officers at the lieutenant or lieutenant commander level) also recommended more coordinated oversight, a recommendation that was marked as "not implemented." Another report from the GAO, from 2003, summarized its findings as follows:

> GAO recommends that the Secretary of Defense direct the Office of the Under Secretary of Defense for Personnel and Readiness (OUSD/P&R), in concert with the services, to further enhance performance goals and measures to improve oversight of the operations and performance of the service academies. In comments on a draft of this report, DOD concurred with GAO's recommendation.

However, in a 2012 letter from the GAO to the Armed Services Committee of both houses of Congress, the GAO noted that "more than 7 years later, DOD has not fully implemented any of the recommendations." Later GAO reports, such as from 2022, have focused on specific issues of interest, such as minority recruiting, retention, and sexual harassment, but the issue of comprehensive oversight from outside seems to have disappeared, or at least been ineffectively applied. And the 2022 report seemed to conclude that there was no way to know what was going on inside the academies even on these issues, given the methodological flaws of their internal surveys.

> The United States Military Academy, United States Naval Academy, and United States Air Force Academy collect information about their organizational climate using a variety of tools. However, the DOD climate survey—the academies' primary tool for collecting information—does not provide complete and reliable information. Specifically, the survey has methodological issues concerning security, response rates, and

> post-survey weighting that limit its usability…. This will limit the academies' ability to identify problems, implement actions, and measure outcomes.

So even the GAO can't get inside the service academies, or apparently, control them. But let's get back to those *U.S. News* rankings, the big gorilla in the college rankings industry (at least for now: several major law schools have pulled out of the rankings in 2022 by refusing to submit data, and discontent is growing with the whole pretense of being able to make cardinal rankings of different schools with particular qualities that go unacknowledged by the criteria used to rank them [see articles listed at the end]). Twenty percent of the *U.S. News* ranking is derived from "undergraduate academic reputation" and "peer assessment survey." Talk about smoke and mirrors! I call this the beauty quotient, which of course is highly subjective. No denying these schools rank high in beauty. The students are young and fit, all have their hair cut or, the women, pulled back; the boys are shaved, and the grounds are kept immaculate at taxpayer expense—and no walking on the Admiral's grass! Your tax dollars pay to have USNA- and USMA-funded Madison Avenue ad(wo)men who tout these institutions as educating "future leaders" and "the best and the brightest." And that's what the high school guidance counselors and deans at other colleges reflect by apparently thinking, "Well, surely they wouldn't say it if it weren't true. And look at their selectivity!" Nobody likes to accuse the military of lying.

Then there are the points for graduating a lot of the class in six years. Namely: 8 percent of the score is devoted to "graduate rate performance," 22 percent to "graduation and retention rates," of which 17.6 percent comes from "average six-year graduation rate." Of course, we do well on these metrics because we own the students—they're in the military. At Annapolis, we can order them to go to tutoring at the so-called Academic Center, have them retake a failed class (at your expense), send them to mandatory faculty office hours to reteach the material one-on-one (boy oh boy, do I know about these sessions!), yank them from teams until they get back on track, send them to summer school (again, at your expense), and lecture them about how they are letting down the team or their company (one of the thirty divisions into which the student body, the Brigade, is divided) by doing badly in classes, most of which are required. I've been a team faculty representative for various sports, tasked with keeping track of GPAs and intervening if a student is in academic trouble; each company has an upperclass student with the same function, the so-called academic (Ac) officer. What does *U.S. News* not get about the power of military command? If students at civilian schools were subject to the UCMJ, more of them would graduate on time than currently do, I'm sure. The difference is that at civilian schools, you have to want to. Why are these institutions being ranked with institutions of education rather than with other military training?

And, oh yes, these rankings are based on what the institutions themselves report. Clearly Annapolis believes its inflated hype, and think of the plunge in rank if suddenly they told the truth! (See the USNA admissions dean's defiant brush-off, above, of any attempt to have USNA do things the way others do.) Years ago, I sent Robert Morse documentation that USNA was lying about its selectivity, and got no response. Other schools that have later been demoted in the rankings have fessed up—USNA never will. As the now-finally-gone toxic dean who pursued me repeatedly asserted at my legal challenge to their firing in the hearing they lost so completely: "USNA is military. It's different." Right. So, they shouldn't be ranked with actual liberal arts colleges that are devoted to learning and that aren't sucking away at the government teat, or have the power of the UCMJ over their students.

U.S. News and Carnegie Basic were right the first time. The service academies are not colleges, much less colleges of the liberal arts. They don't do education; they do training, and not very effective training at that. I tried to educate in my classroom, because it's clear that citizens need thinking officers to defend them who can respond creatively to fast-changing circumstances. The administration begged to differ.

DOUBLE WHAMMY

So, in the same week in August 2018, I was fired as a tenured professor of thirty-one years and had a major heart attack, though a few days apart and in reverse order. A double whammy. On Monday, I was taken to the emergency room in an ambulance and subsequently given a stent that opened a completely blocked artery, the one from the so-important left heart ventricle responsible for most of the blood the heart delivers. Another major artery was also completely blocked, but my clever body had utilized other smaller blood vessels as work-arounds (so they explained), and surgery on that was put off for another month. Anyway, that blockage wasn't going to kill me; the left ventricle one could.

As it was, the attack damaged my heart. A lot. The doctors said I had undoubtedly had the heart attack because of stress and perhaps also some heredity. Hmmm, I thought: my father lived to ninety and my mother, still doing well at ninety-nine as of mid-2023, didn't have a stent or two until her mid-eighties. I was sixty-four. The stress came from the Naval Academy and the years-long conflict between my view of what tenured civilian professors at a military school should be doing, namely teaching students to question their world (including the world of the military and the Naval Academy), and what the administration demanded from me, which was that I toe whatever administrative line was currently being toed. No questions, no disagreement. Just do what we say.

There have been civilian professors at Annapolis since it was founded in 1845. Teddy Roosevelt thought education for officers was important, and so he imported a gaggle of Yale PhDs in the early years of the twentieth century. But now that we've morphed into what is sold as a college, there are more of us, and people like me arrive who were assured in the *Faculty Handbook* the academic freedom of a college and AAUP-defined tenure—though it turned out we don't have that, despite the administration saying we do. And all this opening up to the world has made the military panicked and afraid of what it might mean to actually have tenured professors exercising academic freedom. They can't have it both ways: both a military and a real college. They say it's college—that's to entice unsuspecting students, but the reality is they want military control of what is taught.

I arrived in 1987, to repeat the timeline, after a BA at Haverford College, an MA from the University of Chicago, a PhD at Vanderbilt, a Fulbright Scholarship in Berlin, and two years each of teaching at the University of Freiburg, Germany, and the National University of Rwanda, as the Fulbright Professor, in central Africa. And after the usual period of probation as an assistant professor, I was (they said) awarded tenure and promoted to associate professor, and then in due time and many books and articles later (I won the Academywide research award), to professor.

I'm arguably a different kind of English professor: not fussy, not tweedy, aware of the youth of my students, but without a sense that I was put on Earth to open their eyes to the evils of racism, sexism, imperialism, and colonialism. I knew that literature could help them figure out who they are as individuals, so I had to connect it to the real world as much as possible. And that was easy. Connect literature to their lives with the military and at this institution? Check—it's as full of power and corruption and ideals as anything Shakespeare ever wrote and full of examples that resonate with them. Connect literature to newspaper headlines? Check—soldiers were dying in Iraq and Afghanistan, as they themselves might, and Annapolis floods every time it rains: the Pentagon says climate change will be behind our future wars. Connect literature to their lives as young people? I remembered being where they were in their life trajectory, basically clueless but full of confidence. So, check. And to their lives as men and women? I'm a man and see the world (at least sometimes) through gendered lenses. Male-female relations are the subject of a good deal of literature. So, check, check there too.

That's not the way literature is usually taught these days, but as it happens, I think that's wrong for any student, not just future officers. Frequently, literature these days is used as a crowbar to force change that a usually youthful professor wants to see, taught as resentment literature of outsider groups. I'm trying to change individuals with literature, not the world, or to use it to right perceived injustice (which usually means, advance a striver group that wants a bigger slice of the pie—and a lot of groups want a bigger slice). So, I swim against the current academic stream as well as infuriating the military brass by questioning their assertions. (What else are civilian professors there for?) Being different isn't better than not different—not intrinsically. But when everybody around you is doing what seems to be the wrong thing or going along to get along, different is the only way to go. It gets people angry, but that seems a small price to pay. And it can have benefits for everybody but the people who are pissed off. Maybe even for them too, in the long run.

John Stuart Mill agreed, arguing in his seminal essay "On Liberty" that people who "think different" (as the bumper sticker has it) are a benefit to society, because they may see things others don't—or at least are willing to say what they see and let others think about it. They may be right—not necessarily, but maybe. That's the function of professors. Especially professors teaching students who become military officers, as is the case at the Naval Academy. All of us need to be able to use our judgment to look at situations and arrive at a set of best possible actions or responses. But military officers need it most of all, because they have the lives of the enlisted—and to some degree their fellow officers—in their charge. These enlisted, some 90 percent of the military, may be your children. And professors are the ones society has designated to organize the discussion their officers are supposed to have during their classroom education period. But that's not how the brass see things. Considering going to a service academy? Maybe that's not such a good idea after all if you actually want an education.

The benefits of teaching officers-to-be to think independently can be huge. And the price of not doing it can be even higher. You want thinking officers who can question what they are told—especially since those doing the telling are typically not on the field and hence unable to see what the situation is. I am the one on the field, having been in the classrooms, offices, and gyms with midshipmen for more than three decades, while the brass cycle in and out of the front office and hear only what they want to hear. The joke about admirals is that when people attain that rank, they will never eat a bad meal again, or hear the truth: they are pampered and told what they want to hear. And then they give the orders that subordinates must carry out and follow, and which may lead to death. At the Naval Academy, they determine the policies that have made it such a contradictory place. I'd say the only ones the taxpayer-funded sea of student misery makes happy are the parents of the midshipmen, whose children have gotten the most golden of golden tickets in today's US of A: a prestigious degree at somebody else's expense, but free to them, and guaranteed well-paid employment after graduation for a minimum of five years, usually more if they want it. Well, politicians like it too, because they get to give out the nominations that are necessary components of an application, and thereby reward constituents. And of course, tourists, for whom we regularly put on snappy shows.

Have you ever been to one of our spring or fall parades with all those Ken dolls lined up on the field slapping their rifles in unison with their white-gloved hands and raising their heads en masse at the same command so you see the flat, round, white covers glint in the sun? Yes, Ken dolls. Some are female, but you wouldn't know it from the bleachers, as all wear the same clothes, and the women always have their hair short or in severe buns—no facial hair for the men, of course. No trick is unplayed to maximize the effect for you, the visitor. The music swells, cars moving along the edge of the parade field are stopped, the brass gleam with their chests full of ribbons (which, by the way, are just for longevity showing each particular assignment or job, and not for heroism), and the sailing team even takes the boats up and back on the Severn beyond the parade field with their colorful spinnakers out to give some color and a nautical feel to things. Nowadays, the student parachute team sends guys to land in a circle on the field, and our bagpipe band plays.

Makes you happy to be alive, all these gorgeous young people! What they can't tell you is that they hate drill (parades), and they hate being the goldfish you are looking at in their bowl. I know because they tell me. They won't tell you. They are directed to refer all questions to the Public Affairs Office and to say, like robots, "Thank you for your support." They aren't robots, as I know from decades with them. But they have to act as if they are. Mickey and Minnie don't talk at Disneyland either, and this is military Disneyland.

I went to the hospital Monday. On Friday, I was fired through a letter to my lawyer from the dean who had been after me for years. I'd retained the lawyer years ago, when the Academy started weaponizing investigations of their own invention (i.e., not following any known protocol that assumes good faith, or even innocence, on the part of the tenured professor, and sending out mass emails to the Brigade to solicit complaints against Fleming) and using them to harass and punish me. This was the same civilian dean who had arrived some years before and promptly denied me a merit pay raise because, as he said in front of a witness, I should not have allowed to be published a newspaper op-ed critical of Naval Academy policies (remember the government fraud, waste, and abuse thing?). That prompted the intervention by the Office of Special Counsel, the federal office that defends whistleblowers in government. That was only the shot across the bow. Gotta give this guy credit. He kept after me.

My salary comes from you, the taxpayer. That means I work for you; I don't work for the brass. For those who want to "starve the beast" (of government) and dismantle or downsize it, that means what I do is useless or bad. Want to cut government? Sure. Why not start with the service academies? I've suggested this in print, and explained why the military should probably get out of the business of running colleges. I guess it's logical that the brass, faced with my criticism of their comfy lifestyles in the high-ceilinged Victorian houses with groundskeepers, would want to take me out.

There are four, arguably five, federal service academies: Annapolis/ Navy, West Point/Army, Colorado Springs/Air Force are those run by the Department of Defense. Coast Guard/New London is run by the Coast Guard. The students of all four are actually in the military, thus can be controlled by the UCMJ, and ordered to do X, Y, or Z on threat of court-martial and the brig. The Merchant Marine Academy, sometimes listed as the fifth, is run by the Department of Transportation, and its students have the status of Navy Reserve midshipmen but are not subject to the UCMJ. What I am writing here applies most strongly to the first three academies: Coast Guard is different in that all Coast Guard officers, whether commissioned through four years at New London, through Coast Guard OCS, or direct commissioning, spend at least some weeks at the school, something not true of the others. So, there is a commonality of experience for all officers that does not exist at the first three, and (I have heard) less of a "ring knocker" and "we're better" mentality associated with Coast Guard. (A "ring-knocker" is the derogatory term for a military officer who ostentatiously flaunts or bangs on the table the huge college ring attesting to his or her status as a service academy graduate; the enlisted military members reportedly find this offensive, as do many other officers from other commissioning sources.) Anyway, the Coast Guard is purely defensive, and thus fails to speak to the bellicose aspirations of many students at the first three schools.

In fact, people aren't wrong to think primarily of West Point and Annapolis (again, founded in 1802 and 1845, respectively) when they think of US service academies. The Air Force was separated from the Army only after World War II; before that it was the Army Air Corps, so the new (and architecturally remarkable) Air Force Academy in Colorado Springs dates only to its founding a few months before I was born, in April 1954, and took some years to complete. Besides, the "Big

Game" is Army-Navy, which means Annapolis's recruited team plays against West Point's recruited team.

I bet you thought Naval Academy midshipmen and graduates were squeaky clean like Scouts, didn't you? Many of the officers removed from command in the 2010s for malfeasance have been Naval Academy graduates. More recently, numerous Naval Academy graduates have been implicated in the so-called Fat Leonard bribery scandal where officers accepted wild parties with hookers from a Malaysian businessman to steer US ships to his docking facilities. Several of the last superintendent admirals of the Naval Academy have been retired early or punished after the fact: one, who lectured midshipmen on morality, for being involved in the Fat Leonard scandal, another one for presiding over an illegal system to bribe athletic recruits from a so-called slush fund, and another for grabbing a Marine gate guard when he came back late and apparently drunk on New Year's Eve and failed to comply with the 100 percent ID policy of his own Naval Academy—and then got the Marine transferred the next day in an apparent attempt to cover it up (see Appendix). That's just the superintendents.

We have, as noted, a midshipman cheating scandal every few years, the most recent in 2021—though the early 1990s saw several in a row. In fact, the 1990s were a wild ride. Among other newsworthy scandals, there was a murder triangle involving a female midshipman who killed her boyfriend's former girlfriend—the boyfriend was a cadet at the Air Force Academy. The conviction of a midshipman on child pornography charges happened in 2021, and that of a retired Navy commander USNA graduate for the same offense. In 2018, a midshipman was convicted of dealing drugs to other midshipmen. And did you read about the Marine major in the USNA History Department who was having an affair a couple of years ago with not one but two female midshipmen and got his buddy to lie to cover it up?

The amount of underage drinking among midshipmen that goes on doesn't seem to be less than at a civilian school, with upperclassmen coming back late at night shit-faced and vomiting on the floors of Bancroft Hall—the plebes have countless stories about this. The indefatigable

Annapolis *Capital Gazette* reporter Earl Kelly (coauthored with Tina Reed) turned in a blockbuster story in 2009 about the Academy's drug culture, called "Capital Investigation: Drug Use, Party Culture at Naval Academy," following an official investigation into the use of synthetic marijuana that resulted in the expulsion of twenty-seven midshipmen. Kelly wrote:

> The investigation ended the military careers of at least 27 midshipmen, including those allowed to resign while being investigated for drug use and an undetermined number suspected of drug use who were dismissed for collateral reasons....[It] also uncovered a drug culture replete with users and dealers. Agents not only found use of synthetic marijuana, called "spice," but that some mids had used cocaine, mephedrone, mescaline and psychedelic mushrooms. Some mids possessed soda bottles with secret compartments to hide their drugs, and fake bladders called "Whizzinators" to avoid detection of their drug use in urine tests.

So, drugs, alcohol, and cheating. That's not worse than civilian schools, probably, but it's more noteworthy because the administration keeps up such a relentless drumbeat of higher morality and squeaky cleanness among the students whom taxpayers are funding. They're just people. But finding this out is like catching the preacher doing the very things he denounces from the pulpit on Sunday. So, it's galling that Academy graduates tend to say things like this: We went through hell so we're better! (I've had midshipmen say exactly this to me.) That doesn't play well with the ROTC or OCS officers, and it certainly doesn't play well with the enlisted. Yet, the brass tell the midshipmen many times a week that they are the "best and the brightest." That only makes the situation worse. To be sure, many of the more self-aware graduates cease to believe this when they get into the fleet—then they come back to me and say, "Well, it depends on the individual." What a surprise. Getting out of USNA bubble teaches people things.

As I am pleased to repeat, we do have some true superstars, a small handful of winners of national scholarships (in a student body of about 4500), the intellectual cream of the cream, and believe me, the Academy puts them front and center. But also on the physical side, which I firmly support, there are the absolute animals, a compliment at Annapolis, the relentless machinelike physical and mental overachievers who run ultramarathons and become SEALs, EOD, or Marine infantry, and who never, ever give up. They are attracted to Annapolis because they believed the hype that they would be surrounded by their kind. They are the most disillusioned because they had the highest expectations, and almost no one else is even near their level. I love these guys and a few gals. And I don't think I'm bragging by saying, yeah, they love me too.

If there is a type of midshipman who gravitates to me—and of course there is—it's these ultraalphas, usually but not always male, who smoke (as they say—absolutely crush) the PRT, the Physical Readiness Test that all midshipmen, in theory, must pass, which is to say these "animals" pass the PRT with perfect scores and without even breaking a sweat. (I say "in theory" because, if you're an athlete, you can be overweight for four years, and typically they won't throw out the racial recruits who fail the PRT repeatedly.) The "animals" hear about Professor Fleming from their buddies, even if they aren't in my classes, and knock on my door, or make sure to take my classes when they can. These are the ones who seem to need me most—the ultrasmart ones adrift in a sea of mediocrity but also the ultrastuds (as we call the physical beasts at Annapolis) who sit in my office's red chair and pour out their frustration at being turned into walking suits, cast members at our military Disneyland for tourists. It's a Disneyland that instead of being the happiest place on Earth is the unhappiest.

How typical are they? Not at all.

That's not what you hear in the hype the ad agencies put out—with your money. The brass aren't paying for anything themselves. So, the sky's the limit. In addition, the service academies are big sources of taxpayer-supported perks for the brass, because the superintendent (an admiral) gets to let in the children of his buddies as well as the football team he and the older alumni are dying to have. Then there are those parents. Remember, if you are lucky enough to have a kid accepted at a service academy, you save a heck ton load of money and get your kids degrees from what are still (largely as the result of this hype) prestigious institutions, with guaranteed employment at taxpayer expense!

They tried denying me pay raises for what I write, then (because the OSC, the federal watchdog office, intervened) for what I said in class, and then for one kid's version of what I am supposed to have said in a tutoring session in my office. (In fact, it turned out he himself hadn't complained; they had complained on his behalf. They gave me a copy of the entire "investigation" in two spiral-bound covers.) They didn't even ask me about this last one before sending out emails to my students encouraging them to bring negative comments about me to the faculty committee, and I didn't even find out what the allegation was until they had done their dirty work.

I'd been reading Arthur Koestler's *Darkness at Noon*, about Stalinist trials, but their use of "investigations" to punish and with foreordained results wasn't even that organized: I called it "Kafka meets the Keystone Cops." I was kept in ignorance about the whole thing until the end; that was the Kafkaesque part—I didn't even know what I was accused of or who had accused me—in the end it turned out, only the adminis-tration. They had to abandon this particular assault because they didn't even have the instruction (rule) saying they could do this, rather than just having a student who felt offended (though he apparently didn't!) talk to me, though this power grab by the administration was in the works. (The toothless Faculty Senate had objected, but was ignored. Welcome to Annapolis!) When the dean realized his error, he rammed through the instruction giving him permission to forgo the usual chain of command, and awarding disciplinary power directly to him, and put it online. Then someone must have realized it was dated too late to be useful in this case, so they reissued it dated earlier. That's the Keystone Cops aspect. Thank goodness I had screenshots of both. A public shout-out and thank you to my lawyer. So after all this—the emails to the entire student body soliciting complaints, the hellish interview with a faculty committee run by a vitriolic female history professor who clearly relished the power she had been given, the two spiral notebooks with hundreds of pages—it all went away. No apology, no explanation, just silence. Better luck next time, I thought, not understanding that of course there would be a next time, with the dean's new instruction in the system.

This instruction said: if you want to complain about a professor, bring the complaints to us; we'll take it from there. Even if you don't want to complain but we hear about something the professor is alleged to have done or said, we'll still take it from there. Taking it from there means sending out mass emails to the whole student body asking for complaints about that person, compiling a roster of second-hand quotes by other people taken out of context that the administration gets to interpret any way they choose, drawing any conclusions the administration chooses to draw, and meting out any punishment the administration chooses for however they define the infraction they decide upon (there are no rules for this; it's all up to them). It's illegal, of course, but inside the Naval Academy, who is to stop them? I had to wait to be fired to get redress outside of USNA. Any wonder I had a heart attack apparently largely from stress, or awoke at 2 a.m. with my fists clenched and my heart beating wildly?

It went in a sort of crescendo, as they figured out how to dispose of me. What they'd learned from the OSC defense of my article was that they couldn't punish me for what I write that is critical of the current state of the Academy, and then later, probably not for what I said in class that was critical of their programs like the botched sexual harassment training, considered below. So, all their investigations and punishments for these things failing to shut me up, they decided to trash my reputation, concocting a case from one student who was furious he hadn't gotten a higher grade, and who claimed that my class explanations of things like gender change/affirmation surgery were "pornographic" and had made him "uncomfortable."

Their allegation was that I was guilty of "conduct unbecoming a federal employee." What is that precisely? It's not defined anywhere, so they never said—they knew it when they saw it, apparently. (It's been used in the past in other agencies against federal employees who refuse mandated vaccines or, in one case, against a man who brought a stripper to work, took photographs of her naked, and then published the photographs.) Clearly, it was their attempt to apply to civilian professors the equivalent of Article 133 of the UCMJ (to which I am not subject), the "conduct unbecoming an officer" clause that gives the military complete control over its members. Because this allegation itself has little meaning, the agency (here, USNA) must prove all the allegations that lead to this label, and the Naval Academy proved none of them. Zero. It was a nothingburger case that cost me a bundle—and not just in money.

Coming at the end of a string of increasing punishments over a decade and a half for everything they didn't like about Professor Fleming and the bad publicity he was creating about this government program they benefitted from, it was clear that this case wasn't about the specific kid or their over-a-dozen disparate allegations of "conduct unbecoming." But that's all they had, so I guess the military brass, and their minions, the deans they had hired, figured they'd give it a try. Clearly, they hated me that much. And seeing it their way, I can see why they did. I say that the Naval Academy is run not for the benefit of the taxpayers but for the benefit of the military brass. That's harsh. But if I'm right, shouldn't we want to do something about it? I'm sure it all made sense to them. They can control all the military, so why not civilian professors who work for the military? What are you going to do next, put a horse head in my bed?

Only there's one problem: the function of tenured civilian professors, even at a military institution, is to be able to question things, not to follow orders. That's how the system of academic promotions and tenure is set up and why. Professors aren't vagrants who come in off the street: we're vetted to get into graduate school, to write our PhD thesis, to get a job, to keep a job, and to be promoted and given tenure, and to be promoted again. We're hardly crazy loose cannons. Granted, people who would never think of challenging the system and who themselves just like the comfort of an assured position fill many tenured slots; as a result, some perfectly rational people have suggested that tenure should be abolished. But this only means that some professors don't actually use their tenure. So sure, it's wasted on them. It's invented for people like me who do use it.

The American Association of University Professors (AAUP) protested when I was ripped from the classroom from one day to the next in February 2018 before they began "investigating" me, and again when I was fired. The Naval Academy brushed this aside. They're the biggest, baddest gorilla around, after all. We're the Naval Academy: we do what we want. The then-superintendent who signed this letter blowing off the AAUP—named Carter—became, on retirement from the Navy and on leaving Annapolis, the president of a major midwestern state university. Say what?

But what this means is that USNA is lying when it tells professors they have academic tenure, and the whole circus of a Yardwide "Promotion and Tenure" committee is a sham—because our legal status as professors is not different after being awarded "tenure" than it was before. Academic tenure as defined by the AAUP spells out the few justifiable causes for firing a tenured professor, including elimination of the program in which this person teaches or failure to do the job, and is a legally binding contract that can be litigated in court. It goes without saying that none of these causes applied—and I did not have recourse to a civilian court for their breaking a contract. My only protection was as a federal employee, and to its internal court system, which was a protection I had had for years before being awarded this sham "tenure."

I'd say I was fired for doing my job as a professor, which is to determine what I have found to be true, and say why. In order to be reinstated, I had to take on the Department of the Navy and the Naval Academy, with the AAUP supporting me, because they too thought I had been awarded AAUP-defined tenure (that's what the *USNA Faculty Handbook* says, after all). I also had the support of my invaluable lawyer, who, as he likes to say, has won every one of his numerous cases against

USNA. I won, because it seems there still is rule of law in this country, and was reinstated with retroactive effect one day before my sixty-fifth birthday, July 24, 2019. The judgment was in the case *Fleming v. Department of the Navy.*

The judge noted that Professor Fleming ("the appellant") "appears to be a rather unique professor at the academy. He is irreverent, theatrical, fashion-conscious, outspoken in his criticism of the academy (both in the classroom and his writings), and liberally sprinkles his classes with profanity and discussions of sexually-related topics (from condom use to transgender surgery). The appellant is also a 'work-out fiend,' and in good enough shape to regularly exercise with the well-conditioned midshipmen at the gyms and swimming pools on campus (where typical attire is swim trunks and other workout gear). Moreover, the overwhelming majority of his students enjoyed the appellant and his teaching style." The judge then proceeded to take apart piece by piece and reject each of the multiple charges the Academy had brought against me and reinstated me forthwith.

Here's how it works. Because I am a federal employee, actions like this—firing a tenured professor for an invented infraction—can be challenged before an internal federal judge system called the Merit Systems Protection Board, MSPB. The MSPB for our region is a suite of offices with a courtroom in a glass, high-rise office building a block from City Hall on Market Street in Philadelphia.

The hearing before the administrative judge was scheduled for two long days but took less than one, because the lineup of witnesses the "agency" (USNA) had arranged, largely midshipmen, fizzled one after another. They failed to provide testimony that would substantiate the ugly translations the administration had provided of their complaints and that were repeated to the press so long as the matter was solely within USNA hands. (It became clear from the hearing that the plebe they had chosen as their star witness had rustled up some friends to write letters to give him some cover.) The Naval Academy, for example, told the press that I had been accused of "unwanted touching." This is an echo of a #MeToo-type allegation, of course. Wow, that Fleming! Rip him from the classroom and fire him! But the midshipman who was behind this ugly version of things, encouraged by his buddy (the star witness) and apparently by the administration, testified before the judge that what this meant was that I had patted him on the back two separate times when I took the only empty seat in the overfilled circle of desks to let a student present to the class and that it didn't bother him. Of course I patted him on the back. I liked him, as I like all (well, almost all) the students, and I was afraid he would be discombobulated by the professor taking the seat next to him. I wanted to reassure him that I wasn't scary, and apparently, I did. And in case you're a Martian, I'll explain that's how men interact positively with other men, especially subordinates: they pat on the back. So, no "unwanted touching." Strike one out of over a dozen strikes for one huge, colossal strikeout (documentation in the Appendix, along with a transcript of the hearing).

Similarly, the core of the Academy's repeated assertion that I failed to provide "respect" to midshipmen was a recent Chinese immigrant student whom I had completely forgotten, and still didn't remember when I saw him, who testified in a barely audible voice that I had (in his view) "purposely" mispronounced his name and that his family honor resided in his name here as in China. And the centerpiece of the Academy's insistence to the press that I had sent a "shirtless picture" to students was an email responding to a fellow weight-lifter student who asked what I had looked like twenty years ago as compared to now. The only way to answer this was with a visual. So I sent him a professional model photo of me, wearing a Speedo and goggles, that was part of my model card at my two agencies in Washington twenty years before, and that was on the website background of one of them for several years.

The Commandant, a Navy Captain who has no authority over civilian professors, was called to mouth platitudes about "dignity and respect" at USNA (meaning that Fleming didn't provide them). He responded to my lawyer's showing him numerous official Academy pictures of shirtless male midshipmen wrestling in lard, both with each other and with women in bathing suits, to climb the greased obelisk known as Herndon, and being hugged by clothed first-class midshipmen, their

69

legal superiors, by saying that it was OK as this was an "official Academy function." Roger that. The intended star witness of the Academy's argument was the plebe who had written a sixteen-page rant months after his first semester English class with me was over, covering every tiny scrap over an entire semester that had any sexual connotation whatsoever, including that Herndon was a phallic symbol (duh), and (most shocking!) that transgender surgery was this and such and had these steps. Why did I explain this last one in an English class? The then–US president had argued against transsexuals in the military because of the cost of the surgery, and the students asked what this was. Professors are there to answer student questions, so I did.

This kid got everything I'd said right, with an astonishing level of recall for anything related to reproduction. He was also offended that I had said (and once again he got it right) it was ridiculous that college students were punished even for holding hands, or for having sex in the dormitory—prohibited because this place is classified as a military base, something I argue should be changed. Things like this are what this self-righteous kid characterized as "X-rated" and "pornographic" in his official complaint. When my lawyer asked what the kid meant by "pornographic," the kid, whose last name is DeSantis (and who came from Florida), as was reported in the press, disgustedly cited my information about transgender surgery. The judge leaned over and asked, "Do you come from a religious family?"

"Yes," he said.

"Do you consider yourself religious?" the judge asked.

"Yes," he said. It made him "uncomfortable," plus he disapproved. Bam. End of story.

Plus he was egged on by his parents. Over semester break, he said he talked to his parents about this Professor Fleming and what he had said in class. His father insisted that this was "not right," and his mother cried. And then they acted. They were going to control what their adult son in the military heard. Go 'rents!

Note that he objected to my saying that the campuswide ban on sex should be lifted. That too was pornographic—the mere expression of that point of view, that is. And the administration liked that well enough to include it in their accusations. Can't have anybody opposing the official line. And if they could get a student to be upset by that point of view, that's how they were going to take down Fleming.

Roger that also. Can't hear anything in college you didn't hear at home. That's clearly "conduct unbecoming," up to every freshman to define. These happen to be right-wing objections, but it's comparable to left-wing objections that lead to undergraduates screaming at Ivy League professors, or students rioting to prevent an author they disapprove of from speaking.

But, you might object, didn't the Academy have the responsibility to tell this kid, a mere freshman and clearly very sheltered, that biology or Freudian theories weren't "pornographic," that my views about prohibiting sex on campus were protected by the First Amendment, and that I was doing my job as a professor by sparking debate and providing information? Didn't they have the responsibility to ask the kid I patted on the back whether the pat was "unwanted"? Didn't they realize they had to prove that my alleged mispronunciation of the Chinese kid's name was "intentional"? Sure. Well, probably. I can't even say anymore what they thought. But that wasn't where they wanted things to go, and they couldn't be sure I'd fight back—and in the meantime, I was fired, so they thought that was that. It was like being trapped in a speeding train driven by maniacs.

In fact, the DeSantis kid's creepily laser-sharp memory for being able to list months after he sat in my class all the disparate crumbs of anything that had to do with gender or sexuality (scattered, of course, through discussions of short stories and current events relevant to the Naval Academy) suggested to me that he was actually thrilled to hear about things that apparently (to judge from his parents' reactions) were forbidden at home and during his upbringing. I think it likely he was hanging on every word. And his jokey emails to me complete with pictures of men in Speedos running down Main Street in Annapolis in the annual "Santa Speedo run"? I'll leave that one uncommented on. It's in the transcript of the hearing.

As it happens, I grew up with someone who underwent transgender surgery many decades ago, and I know that for this person, it was completely the right decision. That said, the irony is that even those opposed to transgender surgery or procedures, or to transgender people in the military, should know how serious a series of interventions and operations the process is. Giving information is not adopting a position one way or another—though, of course, professors regularly adopt positions they don't personally believe, in an effort to get students to discuss issues. At least English professors do. Transgender medical procedures aren't a walk in the park, and that's true whether you're for it or against it. For this young man—or rather, his parents, who he said were horrified when he told them about it—this was pornographic. We don't talk about genitals in the military, or in college. Maybe we don't have any? Remember, these are members of the US military, not third graders.

The main witness on my behalf, a former English Department chair and Faculty Senate president, testified that three past superintendents, whom she named (including the then-most-recent one, Carter) talked publicly about finding a way to fire Fleming, so it's possible that this power-hungry Academic Dean and Provost was himself under pressure. And I'd heard rumors that the anti-Fleming impetus originated in the Pentagon. Just because you're paranoid doesn't mean they aren't out to get you. So, the students were themselves being used.

The dramatic high point of the hearing (otherwise a dull recitation of motivational nonsense from representatives of the administration, and from midshipmen presented by the administration as Fleming killers, who actually had nothing to say) was this young man announcing loudly (his voice began to fade the longer he talked) that he wanted to be nothing like Fleming. How devastating—no chance of that I'd say, so no worries. He then (probably unwisely) admitted that the emails he'd sent me saying he was disappointed not to get me the following semester and that he wanted to stay in touch were because he wanted a good grade—which he didn't think he got. So over semester break he rethought things, with the help of mom and dad. Under the judge's questioning, he said he was indignant that, while he got an A in "college level" English (a high school AP class) back in Florida, he got a C—his lowest grade!—from Fleming. Had he ever heard of dropping a course? My lawyer asked. He didn't know freshmen could do that, he said. Anyway, he was apparently hoping I'd like him more and sweeten his overall grade for that reason. (The final grade was in large part based on a series of graded papers, and they get two sets of interim grades during the semester, so he knew where the grade was going well before the course was over.) So, he waited until he got the grade he deserved, rather than the higher one he'd hoped to flatter me into giving him, to take his revenge with his sixteen-page complaint to the administration, clearly far too organized to have been written by him alone. Who helped? Mom and dad? The deans? All of these? And the Academy licked its chops and pounced. Finally, we've got Fleming!

I knew while it was happening to me how Soviet and un-American all this was (i.e., illegal), but apparently the Academy assumed it was kosher. And that includes the civilian professors they deputized to do their dirty work. In this case, the equivalent of the sneering female history professor who ran the previous "investigation" (the one they had to abandon after all their work, where the Asian athlete wasn't complaining, so they complained on his behalf) was a broken-down engineering professor who seemed genuinely puzzled that such things as life, death, and sex could ever be discussed in an English class. He also observed at the hearing—as if it mattered—that he would never say anything like that in his engineering classes. He did approve of my telling the students before Thanksgiving break to use the condoms they get for free at your expense in the student health center—other things he wasn't so sure about. Tell me why I should care what an old fart engineering professor personally approves of or not? Except that it was precisely personal disapproval by other individuals—this kid's parents, say, or the lanky Marine colonel who was the division director and who officially recommended my firing in a letter dated mere days before his retirement—that this whole thing turned on. That's the way the military works—and it's why you, the taxpayers the military exists to protect, should be worried. As an organization, the military raises personal reactions to the level of law.

A subsequent Faculty Senate report on the way other institutions handle complaints against faculty members—which found that USNA's way bore no resemblance to those of other institutions in offering no protections to the faculty member against whom the complaint was lodged and no due process—was met with indifference. When asked if USNA had consulted what it holds to be peer schools for guidance before making its own system, the vice dean (the one whose letter ripped me from the classroom) was reportedly nonplussed and responded by saying something to the effect of "Of course not. Why should we?" It must be nice to be a Navy of one.

Maybe it isn't chance that the administration's authoritarianism embraced USNA snowflake students who believed their personal reactions must be valorized? This is how all our current culture wars play out at the service academies, and in exaggerated form. All of a sudden, being "uncomfortable" or "offended" is a powerful position, even for the lowest-ranking military members, or civilian college freshmen. Of course, the administration had been lying in wait to get a student to complain about something, anything, so they could rip Fleming from the classroom (based on, asserted the vice dean who signed the letter doing so, "credible" accusations—of what, he never said—explaining a medical procedure, apparently). They were using months of damaging emails from a committee winging it with leading questions (Did Professor Fleming ever talk about X or Y?) to pry from my students any complaints they could use and finally fired me, with loss of my reputation and pay, along with my health insurance, in the middle of a crisis.

The students were merely pawns of an enraged administration. But in an earlier age, no students at any academic institution, and certainly not at the service academies that peddle respect for authority and the chain of command, would have felt that they had the moral obligation to attack and tar the reputation of a professor who made them "uncomfortable" (a much-used word at this hearing). This is how the new age has reached those vestiges of the old, the Victorian holdovers known as the military academies. (I had written an article called "The Service Academies: Eminent Victorians" for the sociology journal *Society* about precisely what a time warp many of their aspects are caught in, more at home in the nineteenth century than the twenty-first.) It's actually not about the students; it's about total authoritarian control of the civilians who work for them. The administration already can control military subordinates, many of whom (the students tell me) feel free to subject the midshipmen to obscenity-laced diatribes whose whole purpose is to make the students feel "uncomfortable." But that's clearly fine, the way half-naked students wrestling with each other covered with lard on the giant phallic symbol is okay, because it's sanctioned by the administration. It's those dratted civilian professors who have to be made to feel the power of The Man and be afraid. The administration was out to get me right enough, and used the students as their tools. But the defense of snowflake students has been adopted by the military, this harnessing by adults of the young's self-righteous, self-centeredness, for the military's own purposes. It's the co-opting of a hard-left MO (students have the rights to an environment where they are not offended, and they alone can determine when they are offended) to further a hard-right agenda (no academic freedom and toe the party line).

The Naval Academy is clearly tired of the pretense of academic freedom and the protections of tenure and has taken the iron fist out of the velvet glove, using a technique from the left to further the aims of the right. I could see them upping the ante at each step and learning from their failures. Consider that it took them many years and my defense by the Office of Special Counsel to discover that they couldn't get away with punishing me for what I write. That must have been a shock. But they reconsidered and regrouped. In that case, they must have said, we'll get him for what he says in class. That produced the first Letter of Reprimand, but didn't shut me up. Hmmm, they must have said. We'll use student offense! The first attempt at this wasn't even with an offended student, and they botched it anyway. But you could see them learning from their mistakes. They got their MO down pat: we decide what version of that to interpret as we choose; no pushback, no cross-examination. (I was forbidden to have a lawyer at the hearings for the "investigation" they had to abandon, sparked by their view of what I said to the Asian athlete and run by the sneering history professor relishing her power, even though a JAG Navy lawyer was in the room to advise the Academy panel. This man told me as I was leaving—answering a question I had asked at the beginning—that, yes, anything I had said could be used against me.) Hmmm. More refining of technique. So hmmmm—enter the kid who wanted a higher grade. Gotcha!

Dean Phillips, himself a civilian but dependent on the superintendent for his contract renewal, repeatedly made the point at the MSPB hearing that the Academy was military and was run by military principles, not academic, and repeatedly compared senior professors to subordinate military members on ships. And, echoing Article 133 of the UCMJ, he repeatedly invoked the undefined offense of "conduct unbecoming a civilian federal employee." That apparently meant a professor answering student questions.

Seriously? Civilian professors, no matter whom they work for, operate according to entirely different rules than the military, just as doctors are doctors in the operating room whether they are at Johns Hopkins or the old Bethesda Naval Medical Center, now called Walter Reed National Military Medical Center. Our goal is truth, not imposing our will by force. And we have our own honor and sense of profession. The function of educational administrators is to facilitate the careers and productivity, whether with books or students, of faculty members. They are not senior officers whom we have to please.

The Naval Academy sees things differently. In his sum-up, this dean (whose son was given admission to the taxpayer-supported prep school and a place at Annapolis that he occupied for only one year, thus making it unavailable to anyone else, as we do not permit transfers into higher classes than freshman), asserted that he had "lost confidence" in my ability to further (his view of) the Naval Academy's mission. He further insisted (why is this relevant?) that officers who referred to enlisted military members the "disrespectful" way I did to midshipmen would be "relieved of command." (I jokingly called them "midsheeple" when they knuckled under to the Naval Academy's dispiriting system and failed to show individual initiative, and they always grinned—the point was to get them to [wo]man up, which their reaction showed they understood.) The Commandant echoed this position. But of course, he was told what to say, and as a mere Captain who wanted promotion, he had his career to think of.

All this was, I thought, simply ridiculous. Tenured professors aren't fired because an administrator has "lost confidence" in them. That's a military term, or one for political appointees in Washington. What fools they are. And how sure that they are right! USNA now clearly demands a subservient faculty, just as—I have repeatedly argued—they want subservient midshipmen. That's not the way to make an effective military, aside from changing the Athens-Sparta combination, with each side respecting the other, that once made the Academy so attractive to so many people, including me. But now all that has changed. Athens is dead. And Sparta is a joke. Meanwhile, the cost to you remains huge.

Data for FY 2010 put the price of the academies and their prep schools at $1.6 billion a year, about $2.25 billion in 2023 dollars, even if the expenses haven't increased, which they almost certainly have done (larger entering classes, for one thing). Sure, aircraft carriers cost several times this amount, but they last for a long time, and at the academies and their prep schools, the money goes to specific individuals each year. As a result, you might be more concerned about who gets your dollars. This is especially so as, of course, we have a conservative tilt in applicants since it's typically been conservatives who feel positively about a life in the military, presented as being based on self-sacrifice and sterling character. And typically, conservatives resist the government giving handouts, as in, to welfare recipients. How come they're the first ones to line up at the service academies with their hands outstretched?

But I don't blame you if you've never thought about their price tag to taxpayers. The administration doesn't make these figures widely available. When I started writing about this issue, I found data on our USNA website from the Naval Academy comptroller that showed the then-current comparative costs of the federal service academies; shortly after I began writing about them, they were deleted. So, you have to look outside the academies for information, and the official figures aren't recent. The GAO report from 2003, two decades ago, put the cost of FY 2003 for West Point (US Military Academy) at just under $365,000 per student, the Air Force Academy at $333,000, and the Naval Academy just under $300,000. That makes USNA half a million dollars now even with no increased expenses, and the other academies more.

Midshipmen can just leave without penalty during the first two years, though the Academy throws all sorts of roadblocks in their way in the form of negative "counseling" and many meetings with officers trying to talk you out of doing so. If you leave after the first two years and break the contract you sign after sophomore year, the Navy reserves the right to demand about half of this back, over $200,000. (At the end of sophomore year, students are asked to sign something called a "2 for 7," as in: they got two years of USNA free, now they are obligated to two more, and at least five years after that as a junior officer.) As far as academies vs ROTC goes, in the almost thirty-five-year-old 1990 official GAO report, the cost of a West Point officer was given as $229,000 (2023: $546,000), an average ROTC officer $53,000 (2023 $126,500), and an OCS officer $15,000 (2023 about $39,000). A more recent Navy Supply Corps study simplifies the math to ROTC costing on average one quarter of an Academy graduate and OCS one eighth (less using the above figures). The fees demanded in 2019 of foreign national students at all academies (we have about a dozen, from client states) was about $82,000 per year, not the full amount. So US taxpayers subsidize them too. (See also the paper for the International Society for Military Ethics by SUNY professor Stephen Kershnar, who documents costs and benefits of the academies, listed in the Appendix.)

I've always been suspicious of these figures because I think that in real terms, they have to be far higher. How about the fact that as members of the military, midshipmen can go to Bethesda Walter Reed Medical Center (or Brigade Medical in the Yard) with a cold, or to get the braces they had put off getting until they could do it at your expense, or to fix the knee they "blew out" (as they say) playing sports, address their sexually transmitted disease, or to treat their pneumonia—does this get factored in? How about the benefits and reductions they get in the civilian world as members of the military in uniform, which they must wear when they travel? The costs of the small ships known as YPs, Yard Patrols, that they learn navigation on? The trips to the fleet during the summer? The costs aren't merely classrooms and teachers.

Let me say it again: students at the service academies (except the Merchant Marine Academy) are actually in the military and can be controlled like military recruits. They are subject to the UCMJ, the Uniform Code of Military Justice. They are paid for attending class and pay nothing for healthcare, because it's all taxpayer supported. If that isn't Medicare for All, I don't know what is. Do you support that? Only for the military? But the military isn't just the guys and gals in the field. It's also the cadets and midshipmen, as well as (say) the members of the military bands. Granted, a certain percentage of the military budget isn't for fighting but for pomp. An old girlfriend of mine joined the Air Force Strolling Strings after the symphony orchestra she played in folded and, sadly, died of breast cancer. We went to her funeral at Arlington, where she is buried, with the horse and caisson and everything. She served too. By playing at military parties. I love military ceremony as much as the next guy, but the service academies need to admit that their utility falls in that category.

Still, we purport to teach things. And I'm a literature professor as well as a man and an athlete (and a human being). So over the course of my decades teaching literature, I've had to answer these questions: what's the point of reading (say) Shakespeare? Or Toni Morrison? Is the point different for future officers than for anybody else? If so, how? I don't think the point is to check the box through reading works by someone of a certain skin color or sexual orientation. There has to be a higher purpose. But teaching everything according to categories of race, gender, and sexual orientation is what has supplanted sexual assault training as topic A at Annapolis: hiring and teaching courses in gay, Latino/a, and African American literature focused on the experiences of recent immigrants to the exclusion of almost everything else, usually to emphasize how tough they had it. For example, two out of three upper-level senior seminars English majors could choose from in Spring 2023 were "The Queering of the Renaissance" and "Queer Communities in Film and Literature." We have courses in post-colonial studies, African American studies, and Native American Studies, and a "diversity" requirement. I guess we're really with the Zeitgeist!

Recent hiring emphasizes minority racial and sexual-orientation groups. And now the faculty get relentless "training" in DEI with newly hired administrators to enforce the rules—Diversity, Equity, and Inclusion. In our English Department, there is now a faculty committee to vet faculty syllabi to ensure that an acceptable number of works about and by nonwhite authors are taught. It's all intensely political, and usually with an edge of resentment: our kind didn't get or don't have as much as your kind! In fact, these kinds of resentment studies have nothing to do with being a good officer. Having a sense of what separates people, sure. How about what unites them?

This is our newest form of authoritarian imposition of left-wing causes on a right-wing institution. In 2021, the Academy issued a *Diversity and Inclusion Strategic Plan* whose lead picture has a black male midshipman standing as Brigade Commander in front of a phalanx of white males. A former military instructor in the History Department and USNA graduate J.A. Cauthen, in an article entitled "The US Naval Academy is Adrift" (echoing an earlier article by another instructor, Dr. James F. Barry, see below—these newspaper title writers love their metaphors!), objects—and it's hard to disagree with him that this plan "will erode the competency of future officers and imperil our national security." He quotes the plan as saying that the Naval Academy "will develop a diversity and inclusion checklist and schedule to inventory and assess all academic classes and training events," something I saw beginning as I was being forced out of the classroom. It will "partner with Academic Departments in conducting comprehensive curriculum review prioritizing the inclusion of marginalized scholarship and hidden histories within midshipmen education." And he asks a question relevant to my situation: "What will be the fate of those who will not comply, given their belief in, and right to, academic freedom?"

I can answer that question already. Academic freedom doesn't exist at Annapolis. And those who do not repeat the party line unquestioningly, such as (um, yes) your humble correspondent, will be relentlessly pursued and fired. Cauthen goes on with his quote: The Naval Academy "will develop a confidential process for reporting bias incidents"—for what it calls "nonpunitive informational purposes" to "identify areas for potential additional training." My experience suggests that "nonpunitive" is bunkum. Indeed, Cauthen points out that all of this comes with the whip hand of the UCMJ and quotes Article 917 as saying that "Any person subject to this chapter who uses provoking or reproachful words or gestures toward any others person subject to this chapter shall be punished as a court-martial may direct."

All this comes with something called the DPE Program, Diversity Peer Educator Program, including a confidential system to report "bias incidents." I've seen it all before with sexual assault training (see below). And he asks: "will a DEI agenda propagating woke ideology prepare future leaders to wage and win wars against our enemies? Those who believe so are either blind or worse." But of course, the service academies have long since moved on from preparing leaders to wage and win wars. Now they're about enforcing by military rather than constitutionally permitted means (even against civilians) the obsessions of a certain sector of society.

My generation—born in the late 1940s onward through the 1950s and '60s, baby boomers—learned the important lesson that skin color is not relevant to the individual. Only nowadays it has apparently become so once again. How is this not a step backward? What people have in common is far more important than the almost trivial differences that separate us. All of us are born, die, grow to maturity, usually pair up, at least for a while, typically reproduce, get old, wonder what it's about, and fail to answer any of the questions that have puzzled philosophers for millennia. And if you as an officer see yourself as radically different from people with a different skin color—and groups of your subordinates with different skin colors as lacking a common goal—military cohesion is torn asunder. This is military suicide, shooting ourselves not merely in the foot but in the head.

The theory is that you will be "sensitive" (see VADM Bucks's nonsense, above) to their differences. But how do you know what these are? Are we to assume that someone with a different skin color is "diverse" and individual, but that someone with (say) a single mother we don't know about, or an odd upbringing we can't see by looking at them, isn't? We are now told to emphasize differences. How about we emphasize commonality and deal with difference as it comes up rather than assuming it? It's insulting to say "I see that you have a different skin color, so I can tell you we have little in common"—aside from destructive of military cohesion. I never looked at the students in my class and announced who was "different." I treated all the same. Isn't that the goal of democracy? Certainly it is the goal of the military, all pursuing the same goal with the same leader. I guess we should let the (say) black students go in one direction in a charge and the white in another. What are they thinking with this insistence on differences being primary and immediately clear from skin color?

You can use force to compel people to do something in the short run, but in the long run they have to like you and trust you and want to do what you say. The service academies yell and scream and curse and punish to keep students in line. Few midshipmen respect the yellers and cursers and punishers. Some realize that this is an example of bad leadership and vow to be different officers than the ones back at Annapolis. Others think this is the way things have to be and act this way themselves when they are in a position to give commands. Some officers are good, but far too many are bad. Many of the latter come from the service academies.

ROUND ONE: RACE
AND RECRUITS

I t was the result of my year serving in the early-aughts as a useless rubber-stamp (I later realized) as a member of our Admissions Board that I began to understand what I had been seeing for the fifteen years before that. And that produced my first protests—as well as the first wave of revenge and retaliation by the administration. These waves grew larger and more violent, moving through denial of pay increase to the "Letters of Reprimand" to several exhausting "investigations" with no sign of due process (including a military "Command Investigation" defined by the UCMJ—to which I am not subject!—though it did not even follow UCMJ guidelines), and culminating in my firing in August 2018. Incidentally, though I was retroactively reinstated a year later, the dean, my nemesis who now thankfully has retired, "redefined my duties" to exclude teaching. Can't have Fleming poisoning the minds of midshipmen!

I volunteered for this "service" duty on the Admissions Board because at the time I was still a starry-eyed true believer. It was extra work in addition to my usual job of teaching, advising, and giving endless hours of tutoring to students in my office, called EI, Extra Instruction; now it carries a course reduction to compensate for the time it requires. Every

Wednesday afternoon we went to the admissions office and picked up a stack of applications, which we prepared that night into briefings of one minute forty seconds (!) each. The Board met in a room upstairs in Preble Hall all day Thursday, with a break for lunch. I sat on the side of the table that let me look out the dormer windows at birds flying by outside. There were over a dozen members, a mixture of civilian professors and Navy and Marine Corps officers.

By the way, the reference in the 2022 *Top Gun* movie to Tom Cruise "pulling the papers" of Goose's son is nonsense, as no such action is possible, aside from implying that Cruise was teaching classes on a several-year tour in the Leadership and Law department (now rebranded as Leadership, Ethics, and Law to look virtuous), highly improbable for a pilot like him, and was on the Admissions Board, where no one person has the power to "pull the papers" of an applicant. Besides, the kid could go to ROTC at a state university and end up at exactly the same place four years later. This is merely one more piece of evidence that the way the academies are portrayed in the popular media is completely false.

The format of the briefs never varied. First of all, the computer had generated a number called the Whole Person Multiple that gave points for academics, athletics, and club and student government-type involvement, the last called "leadership." This, please note, is the only place in the process where "leadership" played a role, and—see below—it was disregarded in the case of racial and athletic recruits. The result is that many students, about half the class, are admitted to Annapolis with no consideration of their "leadership" potential. Even the GAO report of 2003 fails to understand this point. Apparently accepting the academies' version of its admission process, it says (after raising the issue of lower-potential students being admitted):

> Under the whole person approach, the academies can admit some applicants whose academic scores were lower than might normally be competitive for admission, but who in their totality (academics, physical

aptitude, and leadership) are evaluated by academy
officials as being capable of succeeding at the academy.

Let me repeat: "leadership" (as defined by the admissions process
as being exhibited by things like participation in high school student
government or, in our not insubstantial number of homeschooled applicants, outside organizations) plays no role for about half the class let in
to fill teams or give us racial bragging rights, as I consider in a moment.
And the GAO report misses the point that letting in someone "capable
of succeeding at the academy," almost always at lower levels, causes the
rejection of someone capable of succeeding at higher levels, say a white,
athletic, smart kid who is not being recruited for the football or basketball team, the all-around student-athlete many people imagine is our
preferred student. And then we hire them all.

I called the noncompetitive applicants "set asides," because for them,
the sports and racial recruits, the Whole Person Multiple is set aside and
plays no role, and the 25 percent of the class sent either to the prep
school at your expense or to private prep schools largely on donor funding (Foundation-sponsored students) has no lower limit at all. Where is
the "leadership" in having a grandmother from Puerto Rico, especially
if you don't speak Spanish and grew up in Minnesota? Still, you can get
a slot at Annapolis to far lower standards. At taxpayer expense.

We started our briefing with the Whole Person Multiple the computer had generated for each student. Then we had to say whether the
applicant met (fairly low) standards for academic performance—what
we were looking for in the case of a candidate we would probably vote
"qualified" for USNA was As and Bs in high school grades. One C was
not disqualifying if it was early enough in high school. If their SAT
scores, still required but probably on the way out—and in any case disregarded for athletic and racial recruits—were over 600, we said, "OK"
and went on. (A score of 600/600 puts an applicant at about the national
75 percent level.) I bet you thought only really smart, athletic kids made
it into the service academies, right? Well, academically our average is
OK but not stellar. SAT or ACT scores of midshipmen are lower on

average than those of our state university, the University of Maryland at College Park, respectable but not outstanding—lower to mid-600s for SAT, not the mid-700s of Ivy-level colleges. The optional interview with a Naval Academy representative, usually but not always an alumnus/alumna, didn't count, nor did the usually rote "I want to serve my country" essay response to "Why Do I Want to Come to Annapolis?" If there were no arrests or other obvious disqualifiers, the briefer probably would recommend the student as Naval Academy–qualified. And the Board would undoubtedly second this, as the parameters for this had been explained to us. (This doesn't mean the applicant was admitted— only the brass could do that.)

Applicants got points for having a parent on active duty or a sibling at a service academy—the Naval Academy likes to reward its own. Sometimes whole groups of siblings, usually with military connections, go through USNA or USMA—it's pure nepotism at work, especially as actual admission to USNA is at the whim of the brass, not based on what the Admissions Board says or votes. I heard the children of high federal officials including a former FBI director recommended (and voted in) as "qualified" specifically on the grounds of their parent's position. And the children of USNA military (and civilian) administrators were regularly admitted for the same reason. Remember that this isn't just admission to a coveted place, it's a half a million dollar scholarship and guaranteed employment at taxpayer expense, so it's not like a civilian university smiling on the children of faculty over other applicants with their own money. They're using your money to provide cushy futures to its own. But because it's the military, the brass can do what it likes behind closed doors.

A particularly good essay (rare) also got points, and an egregiously loopy one, negative points. How many? A good Whole Person Multiple was something like 65,000–70,000, and 72,000 we joked "send the limo." A good essay or a sibling/parent in the military got 500 points, for reasons I never understood called a "rab." (But the bass could admit the one with military connections as they chose. I doubt anyone was admitted for a good essay.) Each member of the committee had a block, like two small cubes glued together, one red and one green, that we took out of a box in the morning and put back when we left. During the briefing, we would be turning the green face up to indicate approval or the red to signal a vote for no.

This was the morning. The afternoon session was devoted to briefings by the athletic representative and the minority representative. It took me far longer than it should have to realize that the pile of applications I took home every Wednesday were morning applications, which meant from white, nonrecruited applicants. And that was the beginning of my disillusionment. What I discovered led to the first article I wrote about the Naval Academy's loss of mission that infuriated the brass.

Applicants who self-identified as a member of a race the Academy wished to privilege—at the time I was on the Admissions Board it was African American, Hispanic, and Native American—were briefed separately to the committee not by a white member but by a minority Navy lieutenant. Briefings (to repeat: a minute and forty seconds per applicant, no more) ran through a number of factors quite quickly and offered a recommendation that we had been told was appropriate: "qualified" for USNA if grades A/B for white applicants (but not minorities, who needed only C grades), 600 score in each part of the SAT for white applicants (but about 550 for minorities who come to USNA without remediation), and Whole Person Multiple (points given for grades/tests, school leadership positions, and sports) of at least 55,000 for whites, no bottom for minorities. This is aside from the fact that 20 percent of the class could be sent to the remedial, taxpayer-supported prep school for a year, also with no minimum for scores. Other possible recommendations included a year at a civilian prep school that the Naval Academy Foundation pays for, where they also do a thirteenth year (the profile for this was white lacrosse players, not black football players), and USNA "pool," a sort of wait list for nonrecruited whites, who typically weren't tracked to NAPS or Foundation schools. The athletic department offered its list of recruits that were invariably deemed "qualified" no matter how low in scores, because many if not most to go to NAPS and only a few to USNA directly.

We also considered prior enlisted to these same criteria. Maybe a century ago this was heartwarming, with a particularly locked-on sailor or Marine catching the eye of his CO, who then said, "Son, how would you like to go to Annapolis?" That's inspiring stuff. Nowadays it's less inspiring, but it's still better than letting somebody in because his grandmother was Puerto Rican or came from Madrid. Nowadays, one important source for enlisted is people who in some cases had done less than a year at Nuclear Power School, people whose "military service" was sitting in a classroom (for the class of 2026, nineteen out of seventy-two). And some of these have told me in my office that they were told by the recruiter before they signed on the dotted line that they were almost guaranteed a slot at Annapolis if they went to Nuclear Power School. That's the tail wagging the dog too. But in any case, prior-enlisted were only 6 percent of entering plebes for the class of 2026.

Race in America is a complex question that we have no silver bullet for. We'd like to see everybody playing happily in the academic sandbox together, as well as elsewhere in society at large. However, in academic institutions with limited places, we have a problem—especially at an institution touted for academic rigor and that taxpayers fund for one specific job. Blacks, on average, consistently score lower than whites (who score lower than Asians) on standardized tests. The choices are simple. If you want students who look a certain way but tend to score lower than others, you accept the lower scores and stop talking about your standards. Or you go with the class that can meet these standards and stop talking about the way they look. The Naval Academy tries to square the circle by both bragging about its standards and letting in half the class to lower standards. No wonder they were furious that I pointed this out.

All educational institutions have this problem to some degree; the academies are just worse than others. And in 2023, the Supreme Court said we're legal in doing so, whereas all others are not. The top universities and colleges don't have this problem because they admit the top nonwhite applicants in the national pool. But because they don't have this problem, everybody else does. Whites are seven times more likely to score above 700 on either part of the SAT than blacks are, adjusted for their percentages in the population. The brand-name civilian schools tend to get these talented black kids. Who does that leave for the service academies? The other schools also usually offer them scholarships, so the cost to the students to attend is close to zero, as it is at Annapolis. This is part of the allure of the service academies, after all: "free college." And at other places, they don't have the service commitment at the end. At a civilian school, they aren't policed, can take what classes they like, can wear what they like, don't have to march in parades for tourists (which almost all the midshipmen hate and have no demonstrable defense value), and can't be placed on restriction or punished for breaking any of a million and one useless rules. What talented black kid would come to a service academy given his or her other choices?

Some do. I've had some brilliant black students over three decades, and quite a few really nice ones. I've taught classes at both ends of our ability spectrum—our honors classes and our remedial precollege English classes, which are almost all filled with black and Hispanic students, most of whom have just come from the remedial, taxpayer-funded thirteenth grade at the prep school. I usually love them as people, and the warmth I show them usually melts the ice when they heard they got Professor Fleming, the one who "hates the football team." I don't hate the football team. I just don't think we should be recruiting them to play Division I, which takes up slots better all-around qualified candidates (like your kids?) could have filled. But they got the offer, and here they are, so I'm going to give it my all, and hope to inspire them to do the same.

What we're doing by lowering standards for nonwhites for that reason alone was almost certainly illegal if we are considered educational institutions rather than military, The earlier Supreme Court decision of 2003 about affirmative action, *Grutter v. Bollinger*, was clear that race was only to be used as a tiebreaker between equally qualified candidates, and that schools could not do what the University of Michigan had been doing, namely run two columns or give a huge "bump" for race. The Naval Academy does both, as I discovered.

But now the sky's the limit, because of the 2023 Supreme Court ruling on its 2022 reconsideration of educational affirmative action, which explicitly exempts the service academies from its finding that affirmative action in educational institutions is unconstitutional. So the academies will continue as before, taking less qualified students of color over more qualified ones. The Supreme Court cases, declared irrelevant for the academies, were two cases, *Students for Fair Admissions v. University of North Carolina*, and *Students for Fair Admissions v. President and Fellows of Harvard College*. In the June 29, 2023 opinion for the conservative majority, Chief Justice Roberts wrote: "The student must be treated based on his or her experiences as an individual—not on the basis of race. Many universities have for too long done just the opposite. And in doing so, they have concluded, wrongly, that the touchstone of an individual's identity is not challenges bested, skills built, or lessons learned but the color of their skin. Our constitutional history does not tolerate that choice." Yet he specifically exempted the service academies, citing their "potentially distinct interests." These are conservative judges legalizing a liberal-backed practice, but only at conservative institutions. See the contradiction? The military can continue to discriminate.

So it seems to be official: we are not education, but military, despite the fact that USNA fought to get an email address of *usna.edu* to replace the earlier *nadn.navy.mil*. The admirals and deans are certainly popping corks as I write, as it happens on the very day the decision came out, because our admissions policies based on race rather than ability have been given the Supreme Court's blessing. But even if we agree that we have to have nonwhite midshipmen at any price (something many taxpayers would not agree with), we lie about that price by insisting there is no downside—no price at all. These kids may be lovely human beings, but they aren't very good students by and large—as the score predictors of many of them, hundreds of points in some cases below our average, would suggest. If we don't care about academics, fine. Say so. But we don't say that—quite the opposite.

The administration used to brag that we were like Dartmouth, an Ivy League university. But we're not in that league at all. Not even close.

We're like a mediocre satellite campus of an OK state university, only with uniforms, mandatory gym, and parades. Even these schools have a few standouts. Again, if you say, nah, we're not trying to compete at Ivy League–level, fine. Only we don't admit that fact. And we don't talk about who was rejected to make all this possible. I do, but it turns out that in the view of the administration that's not "professional" (as USNA's first retaliation put it). In other words, it's not the lie they want to hear from professors to prop up their hype.

I guess I don't get out much, because in addition to the two admission tracks, a higher one for whites and a lower track for non-whites and Hispanics, the athletic recruiting was also astonishing for me. These limited taxpayer-supported slots are supposed to be about sending the best officers to defend civilians, not about beating Memphis or Southern Methodist University before they become officers. Remember, we are funded by taxpayers for their own defense, not to make the brass feel important. And we're not like civilian colleges. We are like a Juilliard that guarantees slots in the New York Philharmonic to its graduates. Remember: we "hire all our graduates." All of them fill officer slots in the Navy and Marine Corps. If they are filling the slot, to repeat a basic point, somebody else isn't. Don't we want the best officers, not just a football team before they become officers? We've lost sight of our mission.

As one part of their application, they need a "nomination"—usually from a congressmember but also possibly from one of several other sources. There are presidential, vice presidential, and Secretary of the Navy nominations. The Academy will give you one of these last-named nominations if they want you for a specific reason, and you don't have a nomination already. Problem solved. A *USA Today* story found a high rate of generous contributions from the parents of kids who got in to service academies to the source of their kid's nomination. Your child going to Annapolis saves the parents lots of money, so some of what you saved can certainly be used to reward the congressperson who helped your kid get in.

And though I was on the Admissions Board for a year, to repeat the point I only understood after the fact, I never voted to admit or reject a single candidate: all we voted on was the meaningless "qualified" or "not qualified"—and there wasn't even initial agreement on whether this was merely "academically qualified" or all around, given that applicants have to take a physical test as well. (We decided: academically qualified alone.) During the one-minute-forty-second presentation of the Board member briefing the candidate, yes, the blocks were turned facing green or red, though because the parameters of what we were expected to do were so clear, there was rarely disagreement. But even so, as it took me almost an entire year to realize (I guess I'm a slow learner!), the actual admission was done by the administration. So "qualified" didn't mean you got an offer; conversely, a vote of "unqualified" didn't mean that you were rejected. If the admiral wanted you, or the coaches did, you were in. That's the military way: commanders like three options from subordinates, usually without a ranking. Then they exercise their "leadership" and choose one, a choice that cannot be questioned. "Leadership" ends up meaning: whatever I want if I have the rank.

I didn't know before I was on the board that taxpayers fund NAPS, the Navy's remedial school (the other academies have theirs too), where recruits of varying sorts go for a thirteenth high school year. They need no particular grades or scores to get in, constituting (again) about 20 percent of the class, with another 5 percent at private prep schools with Naval Academy Foundation funding, for a total of about a quarter of the class. This is where most of the football recruits and a lot of the racial recruits are sent and—for me the most defensible group—most of the prior enlisted. They only need a C average at the end of this remedial school to be guaranteed a slot at Annapolis, and the USNA superintendent can lower this as he chooses. Think of it! A C average (or lower) in a remedial thirteenth grade! We aren't skimming off the cream; we're running a machine whose results we know beforehand, because we are determined to get these athletic recruits and racial admits to Annapolis—and for many of them, drag them through the next four years to make them officers, something we have the power to do. The result is that we have an academic bottom quarter of the class that is very weak indeed, that typically takes the remedial precollege courses, and is frequently forced into the easier majors (like General Science) at the discretion of the administration. The *New York Times* reported in 2016 that the cost of NAPS to taxpayers was $14 million a year. In addition, that year at the prep school counts as a year in the military toward their retirement, and of course they get military Medicare for All, as well as food and lodging—just as if they were toting a rifle in Afghanistan. The four years at Annapolis don't count toward military retirement, but if they later get federal jobs, as many do, they do count for federal retirement. But one year at NAPS plus two years at Annapolis (and then leaving) makes three years in the military, which makes them eligible for GI Bill benefits. Taxpayers just can't shower enough benefits on these kids, it seems.

Even the GAO knows these students are at the bottom of the class—a ranking based not merely on grades but athletic and "leadership" factors. The report from 2003 about the academies noted that "Some groups (minorities, preparatory school graduates, recruited athletes, and students in the lower 30 percent of their class in terms of academic admissions scores) performed at lower levels on average in all categories than the class as a whole."

If you're a conservative, you probably shrug your shoulders at the football team—Division I, first Big East, then American Athletic Conference associate member. Everybody recruits a football team! If you're a liberal, you probably shrug your shoulders at the nonwhite admits: everybody recruits these kids! But once again, the service academies are not funded by private funds, but by your money, and they exist for the sole purpose of making officers to defend you in the military. You are paying for every slot at Annapolis and the other service academies. These are the people who will be in charge of your enlisted children, and there to defend you, barring attrition or being thrown out for misbehavior. (Very rare these days—why recruit them and pay for them if we only throw them out? Instead, we "remediate" offenses by sessions with an officer—the scuttlebutt is that mids get "one free honor offense." And failed classes are just repeated. It's almost impossible to flunk out of Annapolis.) This means that a large kid recruited to play football against (say) the University of South Florida and Temple who has trouble passing his remedial-level classes is given a slot that could have gone to a better, all-around performer. Remember, the kid who was rejected was probably a high school athlete too—just not one the coaches wanted to recruit for Division I. Academic smarts don't matter? OK. Stop asking for scores or touting them in hype. And remember that Navy football ends well before graduation day, which is when the purpose of the service academies kicks in. This is like Juilliard recruiting a football team to play Columbia.

The usual argument for athletic recruiting at the service academies is a version of the claim attributed to the Duke of Wellington that "the battle of Waterloo was won on the playing fields of Eton." Sports are battles writ smaller, that make better soldiers. Only we don't fight that many battles anymore, and we could have sports without the recruits. There are certainly virtues to playing sports, such as encouraging commitment, teaching young people to deal with failure, encouraging them to keep going, and so on. But walk-on teams or less concerted recruiting would field teams with the same benefits to the students. Most colleges in the US have teams, and so do most high schools (and middle schools), so we hardly need the service academies for this. And most of those others who play sports do not enter the military to fight at Waterloo, so perhaps the value of sports is not just to the military. Besides, who says you can't learn these lessons elsewhere, not just on the playing field? Really acing an academic project, for example, or practicing the clarinet really hard? True, older men like seeing younger men crash into each other. That's a fact of life, but it doesn't mean taxpayers should be filling slots at a federally supported program for people whose chief skill is that they play football. (Navy had some successful football years about a decade ago, but now even with the most strenuous recruiting by the coaches, the results are pretty lackluster. Who wouldn't rather go to South Carolina than Annapolis?) Recently the Secretary of the Navy has been willing to waive the service commitment of the rare Navy football players recruited by the pros. So no payback for them at all. We take football seriously at Annapolis.

I sometimes look at the team pictures from bygone years that line the walls of Ricketts Hall, where I use the weight room. They are melancholy in the way the pictures Robin Williams shows the boys in the movie *Dead Poets Society* are melancholy—look into their eyes, he says. They are all long dead, the USNA football team of the class of 1894, but here they are in the bloom of youth, looking just like my students of today, all of them with the life force passing through them. All are white, of course, and wear the leather head protectors of yore, more like wrestling guards for ears than today's motorcyclelike helmets. But what is most startling to me is how normal their bodies are—they are not the massive behemoths of today's college football but pretty scrawny guys. After all, this was even before weight rooms. And back in those days, and even much later, Navy had a fighting chance in the big time, before everything became monetized: Roger Staubach, Joe Bellino—the good old days. And yes, these names adorn parts of this building. But the sport has become commercialized and needs a specific extreme body type, as it did not back then. We should have given up competing with this, saying, that's not our purpose.

But it's America's sport, and it's rough, and it's tough, and it has big guys, and we're going to play it. The NAAA, the Naval Academy Athletic Association, has deep tentacles into federal finances at the Naval Academy. They built the weight room in this building. They own the stadium that the Naval Academy rents for things like graduation (you may have thought the stadium belonged to the school, but no). The coaches make about twenty times what I make, with NAAA help, and the taxpayers bankroll the slots for the coaches' recruits, who go on to become officers if they graduate.

However, being recruited for sport X or Y at Annapolis and filling a scarce student slot doesn't even mean you actually play it. There are plenty of kids on the bench who are taking up a midshipman slot denied others. If you're injured, that's probably the end of your playing time, but you continue in a slot as midshipman that was denied another applicant—and the taxpayers pay to have you fixed up at Bethesda/ Walter Reed. If you just decide to quit the team, there is also no penalty, and you also continue to fill the slot that was denied someone who probably had higher predictors than you. This is the Catch-22 of pretending that all midshipmen let in are the "best and brightest," and will therefore make the best officers after graduation, rather than recruited athletes to fill teams until graduation.

And nobody ever justifies, or tries to justify, the way we do all this. Ours is "not to reason why" as Alfred Tennyson's famous "The Charge of the Light Brigade" poem has it, about the slaughter of a brigade in the Crimean War due to the higher-ups' blithering incompetence. When I was on the board, I asked, without getting an answer: Why the push to give taxpayer-supported education to applicants to the Naval Academy based on their self-reported race? Was it a form of reparations? I had white students whose parents came from South Africa who got in as African American. And who's to say they aren't? What of applicants whose parents had come from Nigeria where they had been in the upper crust of society? What were they owed by America? For that matter, was giving slots in the military and at Annapolis a way to pay back something at all?

This was perhaps plausible in the case of self-identified Native Americans, who were given special treatment and admitted to lowered standards, except for the small problem that we couldn't ask what percentage Native American they were or ask to see their tribal affiliation card. We were told that DOD regulations required us to accept self-identification, which came with enormous benefits. I had a student some years ago who said that he had checked Native American because he was born in the USA—hence a native American. He did it out of ignorance, he said. I'm not sure I believed him, though he laughed ruefully as he told the story. But clearly this meant that had Elizabeth Warren applied to the Naval Academy, yes, she would have been given preferential treatment. How you like them potatoes? If you're a conservative supporter of the military, probably not much.

That wasn't a huge problem during my year of giving and listening to briefs, at least not one that I remember, as there were, after all, relatively few applicants who self-identified as Native American in whatever sense (only five were admitted for the class of 2026, though these were part of a group of thirty that listed this as one of their two or more races: that's getting specific!). The larger issue was self-identified Hispanic applicants. This was problematic because there were more of these, and it was much harder to argue for the sympathy vote: what did America owe people whose parents had come from Central America? Hadn't they already won the lottery by being here? (All applicants have to be citizens.) We tried to discuss the rationale for this special treatment but were told that wasn't our business.

I've had students whose parents came from Barcelona who entered (they told me) as Hispanic, because they grew up hearing Catalan, or what we call Spanish and the Catalans call Castilian (but didn't necessarily speak it). They were white. Does Hispanic mean racially brown? What about white Mexicans? White Chileans? And here's one we discussed at the board without getting an answer: if you are the child of German immigrants to Argentina who then made it to the US, you got special treatment at Annapolis to lowered standards as Hispanic. If you were the child of German immigrants to Brazil who made it here, or for that matter brown or indigenous Brazilian, you did not. Remember, it says Hispanic—not Lusophone, though "Hispanic" is a designation invented during the Nixon presidency and still much debated. (It's equally unclear what Latino/Latina, usually written by the initiated now as Latinx, means. Is it racial? Linguistic? Cultural? Up to me?) By the way, I speak Spanish pretty well, French and German perfectly, and Italian better than Spanish. Do I get to choose my designation? If your (grand)parents came direct from Germany, even as Jews fleeing Hitler, you got no preference.

Some cases posed problems. We had an applicant with a Scottish last name who had gone to a flossy private school in Texas—the same school the George W. Bush twins had gone to, a Texan officer on the board told us—who got special treatment because he checked the Hispanic box. Do Hispanics have to be poor and brown to get a free slot at Annapolis? Why are we doing this? We didn't know and couldn't discuss: this being the military, we were just supposed to do what we were told. In any case, there was no effort to make a holistic evaluation to achieve class "diversity"—at the Naval Academy, everybody is supposed to do the same thing, not learn from each other, as civilian schools frequently say. It was to get certain racial groups into officer slots. And this push to enroll non-white students has only intensified since I was on the Admissions Board. For the Class of 2026, 49.6 percent, half, of the entering class self-identified as Hispanic, Native American, African American, mixed race, or Asian. Between 20 and 25 percent of the class of the class scores below the usual minimum for non-minority applicants of 600 on the (required) SAT (or ACT equivalent). Six hundred on the SAT, again, is about the national 75 percent level. Best and brightest? Correct skin color or ethnic background.

It is quite true that the enlisted ranks in the military contain many black and Hispanic soldiers and sailors; in 2016 African Americans were almost 20 percent of the Navy enlisted and Hispanic 16.7 percent. It makes sense to want to have black and Hispanic officers. However, the military can get these elsewhere than from Annapolis—for example, they have expanded ROTC in heavily Hispanic areas of Texas precisely to do this. Even if we say that we have to have black and Hispanic officers from Annapolis, the most prestigious commissioning source, the problem is that we have to lower the standards by a lot to get them. What is it worth to the taxpayers? Or to the military? And what of all those officers from less prestigious commissioning sources than the Academy? Apparently, standards to be an officer don't actually matter—if you can walk and talk and are the right color, you're good to go. And remember admissions is a zero-sum game, and at Annapolis admission means that the admitted plebe will almost certainly enter the military four years later as one of the officers whose job is to defend you, the taxpayers. (USNA's recent official rates for graduation in six years, i.e., including NAPS and those students who fail courses and have to take an extra semester, are given at over 90 percent, an improvement over the closer to 80 percent of past decades. Remember, we own you because you're in the military: we can force you to repeat the class, go to summer school, go to tutoring in the Academic Center, and knock on the professor's door and ask/expect him or her to re-teach it to you one on one.) If we let someone in with lower predictors because s/he isn't white, and whom we drag across the finish line so that s/he ends up as an officer, we reject a more promising candidate for that slot, someone who probably would have grasped the material faster and better. But maybe it doesn't matter? Then say so: admit by lottery, or by throwing a dart at a board.

The usual argument at civilian schools for giving prestigious slots to minorities we want to encourage is that they serve as role models for aspiring whatevers: doctors, lawyers. Only, the problem is that in the military, the enlisted whom the minority officers will command don't move up a ladder to become officers. They remain enlisted—except for the handful we send to Annapolis, where they get in as prior-enlisted to lower standards anyway, mostly via NAPS (for the class of 2026, forty-six out of seventy-two).

Is the argument that black troops will more readily follow a black officer? There is no evidence this is so, and if it is, why isn't the converse true: that white enlisted will more readily follow a white officer? Should black enlisted be segregated with black officers and white with white? Of course, we need a certain number of officers of color if there is any substantial enlisted group of color. But any given sailor is not guaranteed to have a commanding officer of his or her own skin color. What happens then? Do the percentages of X officers have to be the same as the percentages of X enlisted if the experiences of any individual depend on the luck of the draw? Besides, one nonwhite minority isn't interchangeable with another, and we treat all nonwhites as equivalent. There is no evidence that a black sailor will feel more comfortable with a Hispanic one than with a white one.

Let's say we want a black officer, but it turns out he is a Nigerian immigrant whom African Americans resent, or we want an officer who seems "Hispanic" enough but is from a different country than other "Hispanics," say a white Italian immigrant to Chile put in authority over largely indigenous Guatemalan- or Mexican Americans. troops. Or what if it's a (black) Rwandan Tutsi immigrant who doesn't get along with black Rwandan Hutu enlisted, or an Asian woman from

New York put in because she's female who doesn't jell with white female recruits from Georgia? Anecdotal evidence over three decades indicates to me that sailors respect people who care for them and who don't get them killed.

The military forces policies on its people from the top down, like the most disastrous Communist five-year plan that is sold in rosy colors and never achieves its goals—only no one is allowed to say that. Usually, the goal sounds good on paper, but there's no attempt to see how it actually works out in practice or determine whether it actually helps things rather than making them worse. And like General George Patten, the military typically only goes forward with such rammed-down policies, never back, even if it turns out its policies are disastrous.

Oral arguments in the Supreme Court affirmative action cases presented in Washington on October 31, 2022, show this rosy "top-down-ism" from the military with respect to filling scarce slots in the officer corps and service academies/ROTC based on racial criteria. US Solicitor General Elizabeth Prelogar presented the rationale of the military for its draconian affirmative action policies. This argument was apparently successful, with the Supreme Court deferring to the military: the academies were (to repeat this important point) exempted from its finding that educational affirmative action is unconstitutional. And as things stand, and will continue to stand, the military can promote anyone it wants for whatever reason in the military itself, including a desirable skin color. This Supreme Court ruling doesn't affect this promotion process, nor whom it enlists into the military, which apparently includes induction to the rank of "Midshipman 4/C" or not—that apparently means admission to USNA (or to the other service academies at a comparable rank) is a decision internal to the military.

A pro-affirmative action article in the *New York Review of Books* ("When Diversity Matters" by Sherrilyn Ifill, January 19, 2023) quotes Prelogar's arguments and adds commentary:

> Preserving racial diversity in service academies and ROTC programs, Prelogar argued, is "critically

important" for the military to ensure that the enlisted officer corps [enlisted officer corps? what is this?] reflects "diversity [which presumably means skin color/race] in enlisted service members." When in the past the corps failed to reflect that diversity, she noted, "it caused tremendous racial tension and strife." She warned that "when we do not have a diverse officer corps that is broadly reflective of a diverse fighting force, our strength and cohesion and military readiness suffer." (Ifill, p. 26)

This sounds super. Of course, we want a strong military, and we want the enlisted to be happy—especially given our all-volunteer force and the fact that the services are currently far behind in recruiting goals. Only this level of vague "what we want to achieve and here's how we're going to do it" is worse than Mao's Great Leap Forward campaign. How far in the past are we talking about by referring to "strife"? What kind of strife? Complaints? Sidelong glances? Mutinies? Does Prelogar mean that black and brown soldiers refused to follow white officers for that reason, or did so at half speed? (Many enlisted follow officers unwillingly for a slew of reasons, starting with being subpar officers, but they don't mutiny.) Is there any evidence that this is a problem now? Give us examples, and show that they were or are caused by (say) a black sailor having a white officer—which presumably is the issue. (I don't actually believe these examples exist, or if they do, are more than a handful.) Why, in any case, is this worse than the "strife" that forcing people into leadership positions based solely or primarily on skin color causes with those passed over, and with the enlisted who have to follow a subpar officer clearly put in place because of skin color? (And we shouldn't kid ourselves that the enlisted don't figure this out.) What of the negative aura that this casts on the competent black and brown officers now assumed to be there because of their skin color?

In short, does an officer's skin color trump competence for soldiers and sailors? My experience is that members of the military aren't racist that way. And where is the acknowledgment that skin color becomes a big problem if—to call a spade a spade—a less competent nonwhite midshipman or officer is placed in a position a more competent white officer or midshipman is passed over for. But it's not a problem if the black or brown officer is also stellar. And that's the real meaning of this "Great Racial Leap Forward."

It creates resentment in the ranks—lots of it. What I saw at Annapolis was that nonracist white midshipmen became resentful at realizing that leadership positions were awarded to less competent midshipmen on the basis of skin color, and that they themselves, if they noted this out loud, were punished for not being with the program—which increased their resentment. And I hear anecdotally that the same is common in the fleet. All promotions or preferences are individual ones, and "broadly reflective diversity" is bought at the individual level by preferring a less competent individual with the desired skin color. If they are equally competent or more competent, the problem disappears. Does the Solicitor General really think the enlisted military doesn't notice these things? Or the other officers? The military shows all the problems of any top-down totalitarian state, and its members can be court-martialed for resisting.

Bottom line: Annapolis is and will clearly remain a racist football school with a handful of smart kids, some ultraalpha physical performers who generally hate the place, and lots of others who generally hate it too. But they aren't going anywhere, because mom and dad and their high school guidance counselor are thrilled they are there—it's free, remember—and they'll look like quitters if they leave. Not to mention, they're giving up the guaranteed employment and the prestige. Plus, all you have to do is keep your head down, and you'll graduate. That makes them passive and listless and saps their youth and resolve. It's the way the Academy turns hard-charging young men and women into draggy-assed, sad-faced adults just waiting for it to be over that hurts me the most.

Still, the brass insists that the Academy produces "Leaders to Serve the Nation," as the line under its name on its website had it for years.

Its financial campaign asking for yet more money from civilians is "Called to Serve, Daring to Lead." But while Academy graduates are put in charge of enlisted sailors, few people would describe this situation as other than low-level management, a fact of life in the military where enlisted are under the orders of officers, the lowest rank of which Academy graduates enter on their commissioning. (At one point, Academy graduates received a different type of commission than ROTC graduates, but no longer.) The junior officers don't make up their own orders; they get them from senior officers.

These junior officers are initially mostly undergoing training—and it's difficult to see leadership here—say, as a pilot; for that matter, where is the leadership in flying the airplane when they finally get their wings, in a cabin with one other pilot, called an NFO, a Naval Flight Officer? Or they are training for some other specialized work, or serving as one cog, the lowest, in the complex interlocking web of a huge ship. The Marine Corps, which has recently commissioned about a quarter of Academy graduates as 2LT (Second Lieutenant) rather than Navy Ensigns (because they were needed in Afghanistan), comes the closest to what people think of as "leaders" because junior infantry officers frequently lead platoons on maneuvers—marches, weapons drills, and so on. And this is true of West Point graduates as well, as Army is still more land-based than Navy. But there are many other billets in the Marine Corps than infantry: air (pilots), logistics, intel, and so on. So, what is this "leadership" taxpayers are supposed to pay for? The Naval Academy graduates not one thousand leaders a year, but one thousand officers, and that is because they have the power to proclaim them such. Almost all are bitterly disillusioned about the Academy, I have found, and ecstatic at leaving. Has their experience at Annapolis made them better officers than all the others? Show us the data. Or as I say to midshipmen in class: Justify that assertion.

By the way, the mission statement of USNA says its purpose is to "graduate leaders who are dedicated to a career of naval service." But many people will be surprised to hear not only that this bit about "leaders" is questionable, but that, given the mission statement about a "career," they only have to be in the Navy for what is usually five years, more for pilots. And in fact, a large proportion of each year's class leaves the military after its initial commitment. For those who were sent to the prep school, that's five years education for five years as a junior officer. And the GAO has found that about half of all naval officers (regardless of commissioning source) leave at some point between five and ten years; and only a small proportion make it to twenty years, the military's definition of a "career." There are many articles about the military's problems with retaining officers, especially in the Surface Warfare (ships) community, which for most people defines the Navy: about a third of these officers make it to ten years. Anecdotally, I have heard this is also related to the new "wokeness" of racial and gender promotions, and the assumption that any sexual problems are the fault of individuals rather than the unrealistic expectations of celibacy.

Surface Warfare Officers (SWO), those on ships, are the backbone of the Navy's fleet. But the sea service is struggling to retain them at the end of their contracts, and women are leaving at especially high rates, according to the GAO report. One lieutenant quoted in a *Navy Times* article (see Appendix) about retention problems in the SWO community starts off positive, but then punctures the myth that being a junior officer on a ship is "leadership." The article considers her situation:

> For one Navy lieutenant, there are certain aspects of life as a surface warfare officer, or SWO, that can't be beat, such as globe-spanning deployments and pulling into exotic ports.

> "People join the Navy to see the world," the O-3 with eight years under her belt told *Navy Times*. "But that's only nine months of your entire cycle on the ship."

> For SWOs at her level, even those nine months deployed are full of endless paperwork, assorted busywork and zero sleep, in addition to the manning shortfalls and

frenzied operations tempo that plague surface fleet sailors of all ranks.

"It's a shitty job, to be honest," said the lieutenant, who requested anonymity because she was not authorized to speak about her experience. "You see these pilots who get to fly, and they love flying. COs [commanding officers] love driving the ship. But me, as a middle manager on the ship, I don't sleep. And the CO sleeps less than that."

Still, I can see why the brass are so fond of claiming "leadership." It is a squishy concept that's hard to pin down, it seems to differentiate USNA from other institutions, and the military can define it as they wish. But very few Academy graduates end up as head of a Fortune 500 company—to take one metric of "leadership" after the military. West Point, to be sure, has four such Fortune 500 heads in the top thirty institutions, but that's the same as New York University or the University of Miami, whereas Annapolis isn't even listed in this group. Lehigh University, Bucknell University, Michigan State, and Stony Brook University all have five, Harvard has twelve, and the University of Wisconsin has fourteen. So maybe we don't produce "leaders."

I was so shocked by what I had discovered on the Admissions Board that I wrote an op-ed about all this for that well-known subversive magazine of the US Naval Institute, *Proceedings*, objecting to the misuse of taxpayer funds to compete with civilian colleges for athletic recruits who wouldn't get in otherwise and to produce a class that was the right color. Apparently, nobody had ever thought about how the sausages were made, and I told them. It ain't pretty. The result was hundreds of emails from students (until they were ordered not to contact me—yes, they can be ordered not to contact a professor, and I can be ordered to have no contact with them—the administration took this step again in 2018). The vast majority were positive and supportive, though with several death threats mixed in from anonymous, self-identified midshipmen.

A few days later, an official letter came from the then-superintendent fuming that writing this op-ed was not "professional." Funny to claim that a professor writing an article was not professional! In fact, I found it so funny I immediately contacted newspapers, and CNN ran a segment on it (Appendix). Besides, the superintendent harrumphed, a tenured professor should have exercised "better judgment." Remember, this is a Navy officer with no academic credentials telling a professor what professors do. Oops. I forgot. He's showing "leadership."

There was no acknowledgment that this was all behind the taxpayers' backs. But then again, the military brass does a lot of things it doesn't want you to know about. And they used these same words, and same arguments, almost fifteen years later when I was fired. I guess I was the dumb one to think they'd stop.

The administration responded to the CNN reporter that first round by claiming that the recruited athletes and racial recruits still make officers who can function. Not a very high bar. One Hispanic female athlete interviewed by CNN said she could "take care of [her] people." Nobody questions that having somebody in the slot of a junior officer is better than having nobody, as a large portion of the job of a junior officer is merely filling the chair and office, being the person the enlisted go to and who passes on orders. But since we're talking about admissions, which is a zero-sum game—more admits of X means fewer other admits as the number of slots is capped—the proper comparison isn't to nobody at all, but rather to the more qualified applicant who was turned down.

At no point was the howler addressed of the equivalent of a college president, then a pompous and sad old man poetically named Rodney Rempt, telling a professor to self-censor because the administration found his revelations unwelcome, and at no point was there any attempt at rebuttal of what I was showing to be true. Their response was to assert that "Professor Fleming thinks academics are the only things that matter!" I heard this often, a talking point the administration concocted and encouraged students to repeat. The superintendent claimed to CNN that I had a narrow academic view whereas USNA wanted "leaders" rather than people with the qualifications we say are at our academic minimum—thereby acknowledging that we give away slots to academically less accomplished students, but not admitting that "leadership," as I had discovered, plays no role in recruits.

The admiral's official letter accusing me of not being "professional" was the first volley in their decade and a half battle to take me down. Clearly, at first, they thought that an old man waggling his eyebrows would do the trick. It works in the military, after all. Take cover, the Admiral is seriously displeased! Command in the military consists largely of gut response and dangerously little of rationality. It was my first lesson in the fact that at Annapolis, the professors are seen as being there to carry out the whims of the military brass, not to be professors. Hindsight is 20/20, and I'll admit I did not see where this would end up. I thought this letter was just the temper tantrum of a ridiculous old man (he was obsessed with the sailing team and made the student body sing songs on the parade field) who had heard "Yes, *sir!*" so often he couldn't imagine any other response. But um, what was he doing being the head of what passed itself off as a college if he didn't know what he was doing or where he was?

I don't think there is a defense for using taxpayer slots designed for future officers to recruit a football team when they won't play football as officers. That is, assuming there is any ability to predict who will make a good officer or leader. I'm willing to say there may not be, but if that's the case, there is absolutely no reason to give the military billions of dollars for these institutions, or even select candidates in the first place. The brass and the alumni want a football and a basketball team, so we'll make taxpayers (who didn't go here) pay for it, in so many ways. And pretending that we have solved one of the toughest American problems—race—by providing students who have lower predictors and lower performance with a constant stream of remediation that still doesn't get them up to the level of the people we rejected and then putting them in the same jobs the better-qualified candidates were rejected for is a lie.

Again: we're a job-preparation institution. It's all about what happens after. What we do is like music schools graduating violinists based on their eye color. If the music doesn't matter, admit it. But we don't.

Being on the Admissions Board was an eye-opener, and I've never been the same since. I know as a result that most people who have views about the service academies are dead wrong, going on century-old and outdated myths and the current hype the administration pays to have ad agencies spew out. The academies have one of the most efficient hype machines on the planet and are in total control of the message they emit—until somebody like Fleming starts writing. And if they can characterize me as an outsider and a mere civilian who "just doesn't get it" (as Rempt said after my first article about USNA hit the headlines), then they can continue as before with no oversight. Who will question them? Most civilians are caught in the myth and are afraid to question the brass, who bristle and get fierce if somebody gets too close. There are plenty of people who know what I know, but they don't speak out: the service members aren't allowed to contradict the party line in public, and after they are out of the system's grip, their prestige is determined by keeping the hype flowing. Besides, the military teaches you to just say, "*Sir, yes, sir*" or "*Ma'am, yes, ma'am.*" For most people, it gets to be a habit.

A few people have tried to speak out. There was a man more than twenty-five years ago named Dr, James F. Barry, a civilian but former military man teaching at the Academy, who wrote a big article for the *Washington Post* that the paper entitled "Adrift in Annapolis," about how USNA was all smoke and mirrors—about looking good rather than being good. It's spooky to me now, reading what he wrote when I was still starry-eyed:

> Over the years, I have come to see that the academy promotes exactly the wrong environment for creating the kind of moral leaders the Navy needs. It is run like boot camp, only worse. Marine drill instructors will tell you they spend one week breaking recruits down and

12 weeks building them into a team. In contrast, the leadership of the academy—administrators, faculty and eventually the midshipmen themselves—spends four years motivating by fear. The result is graduates who are often left emotionally crippled, unlikely to question, think, or express themselves.

Barry quotes one Academy graduate saying then what I say now:

"We live the lie of denial here, which is perhaps the strongest lie of all; we are like an alcoholic family that denies to itself and outsiders that there is a problem. The Naval Academy family must come out of this denial and engage in open, honest and productive communication."

In fact, I could quote the whole article, which I had not reread until I started writing this book, so eerily does Barry prefigure my own thought, conclusions, and suggestions:

We must stop expecting midshipmen to act like 40-year-olds while treating them like 4-year-olds. We should give them the respect we give sailors; if we treated sailors like we treat mids, the sailors would mutiny. We must teach leadership to mids as the highly motivated students they are. They must be allowed to fail. By doing so we will create a system where midshipmen's performance as future leaders is based on their ability to think and develop their judgment in a safe and supportive system. The importance of this cannot be stressed enough. The current academy paradigm is leadership through intimidation and fear. This leadership model has been continually found to be ineffective.

Midshipmen will learn leadership by assuming it. We should put them in a role where they have to take responsibility for their actions, not just survive a fat rule book. Part of this will be accomplished by giving them back ownership of the Honor Concept. We should make mids responsible for making it relevant and then seeing that it is obeyed—and they should do it because it's their duty, not because it's a punitive tool of the administration.

We should de-emphasize varsity sports by moving them to a lower collegiate division. There are too many instances where athletics detract from the academy's mission.

Barry quotes from student journals that say what I have heard from midshipmen for thirty-plus years:

"All the things that I believed were true turned out to be completely untrue. I don't believe in this place. I got suckered in by the brochures, photos and the image and the glamour. It never really occurred to me what I was getting myself into."

"In the old days the Honor Concept was owned by the students, they were proud of it and proud to live by it. Now, people look at it as another obstacle that you have to overcome to make it here."

"What do I learn from any of this, other than that these are people I don't want to emulate? Should I stay or should I go? I'm so out of place here. This place reeks of hypocrisy."

"I think back to plebe summer and I realize how much different my outlook was. I was green and starry-eyed.

I was proud of my uniform and what it stood for. I was proud of my country and willing to give my life for it. Those feelings boiled inside me with such passion that it seems ridiculous that they would not be here today."

Barry sums up his attempts to fix these problems (oh, why didn't I take heed?):

Every day I see evidence of the decline of this institution, and no evidence that the administration even realizes there's a problem. Certainly my own attempts to raise the issue have been met with silence. [A] Middle States report [our accrediting body]...said, "A significant number of faculty members reported morale and communication problems to the team....The problems seemed to focus on leadership, communication and trust. They [faculty}are concerned about dissent, and being typed as uncooperative. Many believe, rightly or wrongly, that taking an opposing view in discussions with the administration may lead to retaliation."

The retaliation against Dr. Barry arrived swiftly. He was ripped from his classroom the next day (just like me). Dr. Barry had a temporary position with no tenure that the brass had given him in the "Leadership" Department (which he quotes people calling the "Leaderless" Department), now "Leadership, Ethics, and Law," so they must really have felt betrayed. The then-superintendent excoriated him publicly by name in a meeting (just like me!). Needless to say, Dr. Barry was not rehired the following year when his contract ran out. I guess they figured they'd use the same playbook on me. Their take-no-prisoners methods in dealing with criticism for any form of loyal opposition are clearly meant to discourage others. (I wrote an article for *Proceedings* called "Loyal Opposition Isn't Disloyal," which of course fell on deaf ears.) These jackbooted methods usually work. In any case, they are apparently the only methods the brass know.

A LITTLE BACKGROUND
ON THIS RACE BUSINESS

Why do we use taxpayer money to admit students defined by race? Some people would say, we are making up for our sins in the past. I say: let's talk about that, because that's what professors do. The USNA administration says: no, you will simply do what we say and not talk, especially not with future officers. You will toe the line and say, "*Sir, yes, sir!*"

Um, no.

Born in 1954 in Salisbury, on Maryland's Eastern Shore, I lived the first phase of the Civil Rights Movement. By the '60s, times were a-changing for Salisbury's (white) Main Street and the "colored" Main Street that continued in shabbier fashion on the other side of the Wicomico River, over a bridge. The Salisbury merchants had figured out which way the wind was blowing and had signed off on serving anyone regardless of skin color. In Cambridge, thirty miles to the north-west, they hadn't been as prescient. The result was riots that burned a large portion of the downtown and the subsequent bombing of the courthouse.

The Eastern Shore is the South. Frederick Douglass was born about twenty miles to the north of Cambridge, outside of even further north Easton. Harriet Tubman operated part of her Underground Railroad north of Salisbury, near Cambridge; the highway by Cambridge is now dedicated to her. Maryland wanted to join the Confederacy and was only prevented from doing so by the Union troops that Abraham Lincoln (who could not allow Washington, DC to be surrounded by two Southern states) sent to Baltimore. This is the event memorialized by what until 2021, following Black Lives Matter protests, was the Maryland state song, "Maryland, My Maryland." It was sung to the tune of "O Christmas Tree" and begins with the claim that "the despot's [Lincoln's] heel is on thy shore" (i.e., the Southern city of Baltimore). *Shore* rhymes with the "patriotic *gore* that flecked the streets of Balti*more*" in the next line; the wounded locals who threw rocks at the soldiers. A subsequent stanza refers to Lincoln as a tyrant chaining the state and says that "Virginia should not call in vain"—meaning that Maryland should join the Confederacy.

In the '60s many things changed. I was all for this. With two college professor parents who taught at Salisbury University, formerly a State Teachers College, then a State College, then a State University, which was the white college—the black college was nine miles down the road, what is now the University of Maryland Eastern Shore—I was acutely aware of racial injustice. It probably helped that I was co-raised by a black woman, Mrs. Amy Lee, known as Miss Amy (in the South all women are Miss X, white or black), because my mother had a full-time job teaching music at the college. My mother was a professor like my father, with three degrees including a doctorate from NYU, and earned the same salary. So, I was a "no-duh" feminist, I guess you'd say, from the cradle. I grew up insistent that people be judged as individuals and not by their skin color, sang "We Shall Overcome" at a summer camp run by the National Council of Christians and Jews (NCCJ), and followed with horror the well-known events of the '60s, from the assassination of Martin Luther King Jr. to the political antics of Strom Thurmond and George Wallace.

I graduated from a Quaker college (Quakers hate discrimination of any sort and were some of the earliest abolitionists) and more than a decade later when I arrived at Annapolis, had just spent two years teaching at the National University of Rwanda, in central Africa. The thing is that in Rwanda, all the students and all but a handful of foreign professors were, by American standards, black, in a country where having dark skin simply meant you were a human being. The president of the country was black. The supreme court justices were black. All shop owners were black—but so were all employees, prisoners, laborers, and students. Skin color meant nothing, and that it was an American obsession became clear to me when civil war broke out three years after I left between the Tutsis and the Hutus, all by American definition black. We all know skin color is the most fundamental divider, right? My two years in Africa, in a country that erupted into a war of what we saw as black on black, made me unsympathetic to this all-too-easily accepted American left-wing mantra. The paradox is that it has infected even the right-leaning military—probably worse than in civilian society, because what the military brass says goes and isn't to be questioned. I somehow hadn't gotten that message.

Of course, whites were remarked in Africa, where people don't mess around: they speak of "black and white," "*noir et blanc*," or "European," which is another word for white. The educated people, of course, know that white people exist and let it pass. It's a fact but not an astonishing one. Not so for the ragged, barefoot farm boys or goatherds I'd pass along the rutted unpaved road from the small university campus of one-story brick buildings in the shadow of the volcanoes, the road where I went running. I'd say, "*Mwiriwe*" (good morning) to the women walking barefoot by the side of the road, who responded, "*Yego* (yes)." They were interested, but modest and not nosy. But the little boys came running as fast as they could to see a white person—there weren't more than a handful at the university, and I was the only one who went running several miles out. So, it's possible they had never seen one up close. "*Mzungu! Mzungu!*" They'd yell both at me and to summon their friends. White person! White person! I'd smile and wave, and they would dance up and down excitedly. I'd made their day. I ran every day, so maybe they were looking forward to seeing me.

People get used to what they see. And in the hinterlands of Rwanda, they didn't see many pale people. After a while, neither did I. One trip

115

to Paris during a vacation, I arrived late at night (I was staying in the empty apartment of a friend—he was in Senegal, where he taught at a French lycée) and got up the next morning to go to the Louvre. The subway ride seemed surreal, and I simply couldn't concentrate on the pictures in the Grande Galerie. All these bleached people around me!

But those were simpler times. A few years later, the Rwandan Civil War broke out because the country was invaded by the descendants of the Tutsi monarchy who had fled to Uganda after the country attained independence in 1962. They wanted to retake what they saw as their country, and attacked in 1990 with the aid of the Ugandan president (actually dictator, still in power decades later), a darling of the West because he was better than Idi Amin, who had preceded him. Little did I know in 1987, as indeed as little as anybody else in Rwanda, that they were already plotting to invade. Their country cousins, cattle herders rather like the Maasai in Kenya to the East, had remained in Rwanda, apparently with no revanchist tendencies. Few People in the West took the slightest notice of the Tutsi invasion of 1990; the cameras started running only in 1994, when the Hutus struck back with slaughter of Tutsis, usually by machete.

Such killings were, of course, terrifyingly beyond the modern pale and certainly something Westerners were appalled by. (The invasion with modern arms by the uniformed Tutsi army seemed apparently less horrifying, because more modern and unexceptionable.) Yet some journalists have argued that the Tutsi invaders allowed the killings to proceed, knowing their propaganda value in the West (see the book by the Canadian journalist Judi Rever entitled *In Praise of Blood: The Crimes of the Rwandan Patriotic Front*—the Tutsi invaders). The local Tutsi who stayed in Rwanda, who were mostly the target along with Hutu supporters, do not in retrospect seem to have posed much of a threat. But the Hutu fear of being once again controlled by Tutsi overlords was real, as events made clear. And that's how it ended. Rwanda is once again a Tutsi-controlled country with a Tutsi dictator, the successful invading general Paul Kagame. In best Orwellian fashion, it is now illegal in

Rwanda to speak of Tutsi or Hutu: the story is that all are Rwandans—now that the Tutsis have won.

These killings were, to repeat, horrible (far worse than slavery; see below). But the problem is that this is where the Anglophone West picked up the story, which it saw in its own terms: a majority beating up on a minority. They had no paradigm for processing the fact that the ruthless minority had lorded it over the majority for centuries. What if the white minority of Rhodesia had invaded Zimbabwe to take it back? I doubt the West would have risen to their defense as they did to defend the Tutsi invaders. The situations were comparable. Of course, the Tutsis spoke English, rather than French, having spent several generations in Uganda, and to Western eyes are simply more attractive—being tall and thin with thin noses and lips, the same group of people who produced the Somali supermodel Iman, who was married to David Bowie. What chance against them had the shorter, more "Negroid" Hutus, speaking French and Kinyarwanda, the local language, in the Western propaganda wars? Reading the nonsense about Rwanda in American news outlets in the early 1990s gave me a lot of sympathy for the view that our media are biased and parochial.

Americans have a view of race that is the result of our history, but that has no relevance for most of the rest of the world. And that means it's not a debate about race, but just about our own local view of things. And this goes as well for the latest wrinkle on our obsession with what we call race, namely insisting that race (like everything else) is a "social construction." That makes it malevolent because we created the concept. But dark skin color, so important in America (but equally so in India, for other reasons, and in Latin American countries, for something of the same reasons), obviously is a nonissue in Africa. In precolonial Africa, black was simply the way people looked, as indeed the paler skins of Europeans was simply what people looked like in pre-exploration Europe. So, skin color is not "diversity" in Africa. Of course, there are other things that are, in fact, issues. In Rwanda I heard from Tutsis that "it's all about the nose." Tutsis have thinner facial features. Perhaps this is what Freud called (translated) the "narcissism of small differences," as skin tones themselves may be.

Slavery has been a part of human history until the modern West, as has torture and unspeakable barbarity toward other humans. Read both the Jewish and Christian Bibles, or study classical history. Slavery persisted in the Ottoman Empire until its dissolution after World War I and in China until the twentieth century. But the US abolished the trade in 1807 (no new slaves as of 1808), Britain abolished slavery itself in its colonies in the 1830s and America in the South in 1865. The serfs in Russia were owned, like slaves; serfdom was abolished in 1861.

Slavery was always part of the fabric of Africa, including in the Great Lakes Region of Africa, where Rwanda is located; the most accessible work documenting this trade is by Paul E. Lovejoy, called *Transformations in Slavery*. The distinction between owner and slave was unrelated to skin color in Africa—and indeed almost all other places in the world until the modern age in the West—when Western countries finally abolished slavery. Africans had kept Africans (a meaningless label inside Africa, as Africa was a patchwork of countless chiefdoms and power centers that regarded most of the others as enemies) as slaves for millennia. Typically, slaves in Africa were the fruits of conquest and war by one tribe/people or kingdom over another, which was continuous. Before the Portuguese arrived, they were used locally. Or they were taken to Muslim North Africa or the Middle East by Arab or black-skinned Muslims, who usually castrated the boys to use them as soldiers or eunuch guardians of harems; women were preferred. The castration, with rusty knives and no consideration (or knowledge) of bacteria, is estimated to have killed a large proportion of those subjected to it. Many others died in the trek across the Sahara. in what are estimated to be vastly greater percentages than the numbers that died in the Atlantic trade. Black on black plantations (note: not an invention of the Americas) were worked by slaves. Slaves were also bought inside Africa to be sacrificed (ceremonially killed) at the funerals of the rich and powerful.

What Americans (and other outsiders) nowadays call "Africa," to repeat, is actually a world with hundreds of tribes and peoples that have fought each other since time immemorial, taken slaves and prisoners, and yes, sold some of these slaves to lighter-skinned outsiders who wanted to buy them. They themselves had slaves. And captives were secured precisely to be sold, a market that made many of the local kingdoms rich and underlay their power. Slavery in Africa, again, had no correlation to skin color—except in Arab countries, where the lighter-skinned Arabs had Negro slaves. De facto and even legal slavery existed in Africa until the modern era; Mauritania only outlawed it in the 1980s. The fact that the Arabs were some of the biggest slave traders in the continent makes it grimly amusing that during the civil rights era in America, some black people converted to Islam and learned rudimentary Swahili, the patois of the Arab east coast, apparently believing that Islam was more pro-black than Christianity.

Some African kingdoms were bigger slavers than others: two of the most active were the Buganda kingdom that borders Rwanda in what is now Uganda and the Kongo kingdom covering what is now Angola, whose capital Luanda was the single most active slave port to the Americas. It was Western countries that put an end to their own slave trade, and then via colonial control, some of the African, where slavery continued for a century longer than in the West. I visited the so-called *Maison des Esclaves* (House of the Slaves) on the island of Gorée in Dakar harbor with the French friend I was visiting (and whose apartment in Paris I borrowed) when I lectured in Dakar. In fact, all the houses on Gorée that were built along the Atlantic had prisons in their cellars from whence the slaves were embarked onto ships, but this one was chosen to stand in for them all. As we stood in front of the house, my friend remarked: *Ce n'est pas nous qui avons inventé l'esclavage, mais c'est nous qui l'avons aboli.* We weren't the ones who invented it, but we were the ones who abolished it. It's true. Go us!

Slavery is not, as I sometimes read, the "original sin" of America. Or if it is, it is also the "original sin" of almost every country or tribe or civilization that has ever existed, including the African. Is it the original sin of the Hebrews of the Old Testament? Of the Greeks and Romans? Of China and the Ottoman Empire? The Russian Empire? Britain and France? Of Germany? Of Russia? Of all of Africa? Of the pre-Columbian tribes such as the Mayans and the Aztecs, that took captives to sacrifice them? Of the ancient Greeks and Romans? Of the Persians?

It was Western Enlightenment thought that caused people to come to see both slavery and torture as abominations, violating Immanuel Kant's formulation that people are ends in themselves, and the insistence of the American Declaration of Independence that people are endowed by their Creator with the unalienable rights of life, liberty, and (departing from John Locke, who thought property the third right) the pursuit of happiness. Slavery was unexceptionable in the premodern age, but it couldn't survive the Western Enlightenment, with its emphasis on the rights of the individual. If each individual has rights, slavery won't work for long in the larger scheme of things (a century is not long by those standards)—saying OK, equality, but not for slaves.

Of course, slavery wasn't going to go away all at once—millennia of practices assumed to be normal don't disappear that quickly. But remember, America stopped importing slaves shortly after independence, Britain did away with them on its sugar cane islands shortly after that, and more than half of America—the richer part—outlawed it. The miracle isn't that it lingered and was defended. In the context of history, the Southern slave owners (and initially, Northern as well) were the norm and not the exception, the status quo that had merely continued the way things were before. The miracle is that it was abolished by countries with largely free white populations. So: if slavery was the "original sin" of America, a theological term, how about the fact that America abolished it? Surely (to continue in theological terms) this was America's redemption?

Want to beat up on America because of the Constitutional compromise that slaves counted as 5/8 of a person? It was the slave owners who wanted to count them as a whole person, to bolster their population numbers and get more representation, and the slave-free North that wanted them not to be counted at all on the grounds that they were ill-educated and poor and not free agents. (Remember that initially only landowners could vote in the United States, and women could not until after World War I, so the denial of rights we now take for granted was not limited to slaves.)

What about financial reparations nowadays, from whites to blacks in America? Let's talk about that. First, why are we just talking about America? Surely this is a moral issue for the world. Are current Greeks to pay reparations to other Greeks because Aesop was a slave? Too hard to track, and not visual enough because all are white, too long ago. Do Gulf Arab states pay Uganda (or the still-extant kingdom of Buganda?) for centuries of slaves from central Africa? Except that it was Buganda which enslaved and sold them. Hmmm. Complex. How do we count the slaves? Or know what current country they came from? Should we start pressuring the other American countries that had slaves to pay reparations too? Brazil and Cuba only abolished slavery in the 1880s; perhaps we can start with them? But how do we force sovereign or even enemy countries to follow our lead? Moral pressure? This is very confusing.

OK, just American slaves. And not historical ones. Reparations? One group of today's Americans pays another group of today's Americans: it's a wealth transfer. Let's say we do extensive research, and if you can prove an ancestor was a slave you get $X. Two ancestors gets $2X? Just in America, mind. How about if they were slaves under the British before independence? Does London pay? And when does the US start? 1776? The Treaty of Paris? The ratification of the Constitution? And how about the British naval actions against slave traders? Who gets compensated for that? Who pays back the descendants of white Union parents for the loss of their sons in the Civil War?

Many blacks in America (about 10 percent overall, but about half of the black students Harvard admits—see Appendix) are recent African immigrants or their children, whose ancestors back in Africa may have owned and sold slaves. Are they to get a check? Or to pay? Some American slaves undoubtedly had slaver family members back in Africa—remember, it was all about who won what battle. What if you were a slave here but ancestors back home bought and sold slaves?

What if black people had a free ancestor in the North? Do they get as much? What if they are mix of white and black? Do we require DNA testing? Is the white part assumed to be the result of rape and if so, does the part-white black person get even more money? Does Barack Obama get a check? Do the children of more recent interracial marriages where one partner is, in fact, the descendent of slaves?

So: who pays? And how much? My English ancestors, my father's side of the family, came to North America long enough ago that they could have owned slaves. Most were so poor that it wasn't an option, but I can't be sure that some of them didn't. What percentage? Does one slave-owning great-great-great grandfather mean I pay the same reparations as someone from both sides of slave owners? Do I get a discount because most didn't? How about the Germans on my mother's side, who arrived after slavery was abolished and, in any case, lived in the North? Is 50 percent subtracted from my bill right away because of them?

The wealth of American blacks, even if the descendants of slaves, is clearly higher than the average per capita wealth in, say, The Gambia, the home of Alex Haley's fictional Kunta Kinte, to whom there is a memorial at the Annapolis city dock, where he is supposed to have landed, with a statue of Haley reading to children. Do American blacks pay current Gambian ones? Clearly, they too have benefitted from American slavery. These questions do not go away if we say that the funds will be more generally collected and more generally allocated. A transfer is a transfer: one of us gets more, one of us has less. And what I now have used to belong to you.

Even the logic is unclear. Are we trying to repay you for something your ancestor suffered? That doesn't make sense—I guess you would want them to have suffered more, or more of them. Why do you get rewarded for this? Answer: It's not a reward. It's an attempt to make up for past injustice. OK. Are we making up for any other past injustices? In the US, we're lucky that we started so late that we avoided most of the injustices of the last two millennia, assuming we think only of this recent country as decoupled from Great Britain. I'd like to see treasuries deep enough in Europe to make up for the Thirty Years' War! Or do we do that too, as immigrants to America came from the countries that fought it? Do some Americans with English backgrounds owe others for the Wars of the Roses? What if their genealogy is mixed with other countries'? What if they don't know whether their ancestors fought this, and if they do know, then on what side?

It's quite true that post-war Germany assumed the responsibility for the atrocities of the Third Reich and paid reparations to the country of Israel and to individual Jews. But these were a relatively small and well-defined group, thanks to the Nuremberg Laws. Because of the lack of documentation and the fact that the US didn't want to eradicate black people, we don't have any way to establish as clear a group of victims. Usual answer: All white people have benefitted from the "structural racism" of slavery. So: haven't some blacks also benefitted from structural racism? Wasn't the point that the whole society profited from slavery? Is it just whites? In any case, it's always individuals who pay and individuals who are paid to.

So, to return to Annapolis: are we paying back past injustices, giving a form of reparations by giving a slot at USNA to a black applicant about whom we know nothing more than self-identification as African American, perhaps a recent immigrant from Nigeria? This is a slot that otherwise would have gone to a white applicant about whom we equally know nothing else. It's all skin color. And here's a category that makes even less sense: Hispanics. Applicants with a Puerto Rican grandmother? A Mexican mother? A Mexican mother of Spanish descent, but white? Who don't even speak Spanish and have Anglo last names because dad was a non-Latino?

The "black is black and goes in this line, white is white and goes in that" way of dealing with admission using taxpayer dollars at the Naval Academy is enough to drive you mad. Or at least make you mad, as it did me. And still does. I wrote an article for *Proceedings* called "Separate Water Fountains" describing separate facilities, bathrooms, and water fountains, for example, for "colored," because it all brought back my childhood on the very southern Eastern Shore of Maryland. Do we really want to go back to that? But what do you think a Navy admiral looking at retirement knows or cares about Rwanda, or a Marine colonel who was sent to Annapolis for three years before retiring or moving on? Or about world history? Or about American parochialism? Or about the left-right divide? All he wants is for that infuriating Professor Fleming to shut the eff up, or be made to do so.

There have been developments since I was on the Admissions Board. Apparently to respond to the fact that we were simply unable to get African American numbers above about an acceptable percent, despite lowering standards, and were sucking air on Hispanics, the administration came up with a creative solution: redefine Asians as "minorities," despite the fact that most of the people on Earth are Asians. (When I was on the board, African Americans were at about 5 percent. Now they are closer to 10 percent, which makes me wonder what they had to achieve this.) Besides, even if we limit our consideration to the US, where Asians are still minorities, most aren't downtrodden, and it can't be argued that we exploited them through the evils of colonialism. Asian immigrants to the US come by airplane: Indians (South Asians), many of whom are doctors or in IT, are the single most successful immigrant group, and other Asians are increasing in number. If Harvard was accused of trying to keep them out, we decided to invite them in.

And so, the numbers of Korean and Chinese American midshipmen shot up, despite the fact that there are few sailors or Marines in those categories—many of them recent immigrants with language problems, like the English-challenged recent Asian immigrant athlete whom the administration used to jump-start one of their "investigations." The Class of 2026 has as many self-identified Asian Americans as Hispanics, 180 out of 1184, about 15 percent, each almost twice the number of African Americans. But if there is no clear reason for having more Asian American officers in a Navy whose enlisted corps is not bursting with Asian Americans (in 2016, according to official Navy data, 5.6 percent vs. 19.1 percent African Americans and 16.7 percent Hispanic), this was a stroke of accounting genius on the part of the administration. See how diverse we are? Nearly half the class!

7

ROUND TWO: MEN, WOMEN, AND KING KONG

I f race and recruits were behind my first major run-in with the Naval Academy brass, and my first evidence that USNA in its current form was going in the wrong direction, the botched integration of women into the military in general and the service academies was behind my second major run-in. Or was it actually the third or fourth? It depends on how you reckon them up, as they come in all levels of harassment ranging from bad to worse.

I'm not even counting the late-night phone call from the then-dean, the predecessor of the one who fired me, who threatened the English Department and the sabbatical system (I was on a semester-long respite from teaching to finish a book) if I did not withdraw an op-ed that was due to run a few days later. At that point, I still played the game of letting them know as a courtesy that an article they would have to respond to was coming. After this round, I stopped giving them that courtesy— since I am not obliged to get clearance from the military of what I write as a civilian professor. (Want to bet they will soon make a rule saying we do have to get this, as if we were part of the CIA?) They must have figured that if they couldn't stop me writing, then they would stop publication. When they realized they couldn't, they later decided to punish me after the articles appeared. I merely said to my late-night caller that I had no idea what to say, and that was that—it was about ten o'clock, and I was reading in bed with my wife. The English Department chair later suggested to me that the dean was told to call by the superintendent, but in any case, I heard no more about it.

And I don't count the hour-long talking to I got several years later from a tubby little Marine Colonel who was the then-Division Director. These Marine Colonels have posed no end of problems for the civilian professors they think they are in charge of. The almost biological reaction of a typical Marine Colonel to being in a situation he doesn't understand is to turn up the volume and bellow louder—namely at an educational institution where he is told he is "in charge" of troublesome civilians with advanced degrees (Marines make jokes about how dumb they are). Still, I'm sure the administration puts a Marine Colonel as the so-called Division Director of one of the hotbeds of civilians of the Academy, Humanities and Social Science, precisely to keep us in line. (Now they have been promoted to "Dean—!—of the School—!—of Humanities and Social Science." Give me a break.) I actually took time to go to the retirement ceremony of this one, whom I liked better than most of the other clueless and out-of-their-element incompetents that they had sent us before him. I mean incompetent in education—but what that's where they are, in education, not at Parris Island. At the ceremony, this little guy joked that being Division Director of Humanities and Social Science with its PhD professors was like herding cats, and showed a video of a cowboy on horseback brandishing a whip and dispersing cats. Needless to say, that killed my liking for him.

This talking-to by the cat herder was about answering the midshipman's question, "Sir, what does it mean to have sex change surgery?" to which I initially responded, "You're kidding? You don't know?"—hormone therapy, the mechanics of male to female or female to male body reconstruction. But in fact this objection hadn't even come from a student. This was before they had begun harnessing student objections to punish professors, or rather to punish one professor: me. Instead, it came from an adult woman, a civilian secretary to whom another student, not the one who asked, was recounting her day. I imagine the student saying, "And oh yes, Professor Fleming explained a sex-change operation." "He did *what?*" I imagine this easily shocked secretary saying, starting up from her chair. And she went straight to the Marine colonel with her discovery. Clearly, we had to put a stop to that!

The scandalous charge that I had once again addressed the subject we now call "gender reassignment surgery," a key part of the then-current opposition to trans individuals serving in the military, and hence of interest to a new group of midshipmen who apparently had also never been exposed to such stuff before, came up ten years later as part of the "investigation" that culminated in my firing. Not so hilarious that time. That Fleming just keeps dispensing information!

At the deposition prior to the hearing that reinstated me, the lawyer for the Naval Academy asked, in a tone of deep disdain and thinking he had me on this one: "Is the subject of transsexual surgery on your syllabus?"

I said, "I don't remember what stories I read that semester [by this point years before] but it could have been, as there are stories about many things in the anthology I use, and I write the syllabus."

This last one floored him. "Nobody checks your syllabus beforehand?"he asked incredulously.

"Of course not," I said. It was topic A in newspapers at the time, and the students asked; I answered. Literature is about all of life—I try to make as many tie-ins as possible. Maybe the subject in the story was outsiders of one sort, and that suggested other current examples? Who knows why they asked me about that? Anyway, they wanted to know. Professors answer questions. That's what we do. Now, however, the push is to have oversight over professors' syllabi to make sure they include texts by groups the current orthodoxy wants to forward. So much for academic freedom, or even decision-making power by professors, or authority over their classes. Can't have midshipmen talking about things the administration doesn't want talked about! And conversely, we have a party line to deliver. So, deliver it! Take that, you presumptuous professors. Don't you know who's in charge here?

The reason I liked the tubby little colonel well enough to go to his off-putting retirement ceremony was that he took an eye-rolling "this is pretty ridiculous" attitude to his lecture. He said that this woman had "thrown a grenade into a room and run away from the door." But it wasn't a dressing-down. In this, it was completely unlike the reaction of the tall, thin colonel a decade later who pronounced me morally unfit to be around midshipmen because I said the greased obelisk they climb half-naked was a phallic symbol. The Marine Corps has standards, and so does the Naval Academy! I'm reminded of the acerbic response of Winston Churchill to a mention of the "traditions of the Royal Navy"—these traditions, he countered, consisted of "rum, buggery, and the lash." At Annapolis, it's half-naked boys wrestling in lard on a greased obelisk. And then this Marine colonel retired mere days after his recommendation that I be fired, a recommendation he may have been told to make, and that the dean carried out in August 2018.

So how many times did they harass, "investigate," and punish me? Half a dozen or so in an increasing scale of severity as the years went on. These started small and crescendoed to my firing, before this last one was overturned by the judge. Probably I shouldn't count the outrage caused by my very first personal essay about the Naval Academy, even before the Admissions Board one, about taking a group of poetry students to read at our sister military academy, West Point. After this appeared in the *Antioch Review*, an offended female West Point cadet who had read her poems read the essay and complained to her chain of command, that called ours, about the fact that in one of the interactions I described, she would have been identifiable to people standing by hearing our conversation (if there were any such people) about putting mayonnaise on a spot on the table that a tea bag had made. (Of course, I did not name or otherwise identify her.) In the essay, I had given my thoughts about her too, saying that I thought she was both an attractive woman and had written a bad poem (the students had read their work aloud). It was the "sexist" combination that galled her: I was identifying her to anybody who might have overheard us talking as an incompetent but hot bimbo, and this was as apparently if I had said this very thing to her face. In any case she was offended.

I listened to my then-department chair say with sad tones and shaking his head, "Bruce, I wish you hadn't done that." Clearly, he was the Naval Academy ideal of a team player. Done what? Write an essay for a major literary magazine? (It was later reprinted in the academic journal *Lingua Franca* and the core of my first book about the Naval Academy, called *Annapolis Autumn*.) Write about the inner workings of these strange institutions for the taxpayers who fund them and for whose defense they exist? I can't say in an article not aimed at anyone in particular that a poem (not quoted or the title given) was bad? The woman (not otherwise described) was attractive? I guess it would have been OK if I had said her poem was good. Or was it that I'm not allowed to even think that a female student, not one of mine, is attractive? Maybe that was it.

Sure, it would have been inappropriate if I had said to her face, professor to student, that she was attractive. But writing thoughts in an essay that wasn't aimed at her at all and uses no names is not addressing a remark to her. How odd that people think writers are talking to them, rather than about them. It's the difference between serving a restaurant meal that a specific person has ordered, where the diner is well within the normal bounds to object if it's not to his or her liking or not what they wanted, and a buffet: if you don't want it, you don't take it. You don't criticize something you don't want. And you don't blame the chef.

Writers set out buffets that people can pick and choose from, and so do professors, or anybody speaking or writing publicly. But nowadays, everybody seems to think that a public utterance was prepared just for them. In retrospect, I see that this was the first faint warning sound of the tsunami that has crashed against the shores of our society and crashed even harder in academia: the notion that what counts is how something is perceived or felt. Especially if the perceiver is anything but a straight, white male—there's no arguing with an offended party. She's always entitled to her reaction of being offended, which means somebody is going to pay. If there's a victim, logically there is a perpetrator.

Guilty. This woman knew she was the one I talked to about the mayonnaise, even if no one else did, and that's all that mattered.

Certainly, I should count, when totting up all the harassment the Naval Academy threw my way before their Hail Mary pass that fired me in 2018, the first punishment by the same dean who fired me. He hadn't been at USNA for many months before he took the (to me, at that point, still amazing) step of denying me a merit pay raise that was voted by my department—and then unwisely saying before a witness, whom I had had the foresight to bring to my meeting with him, that, yes indeed, he had done this because I should not have published another op-ed he disapproved of, one that highlighted Naval Academy actions I took to be illegal. If I had suggestions for improvement, he insisted, I should have submitted it up the chain of command, as in the military, with the end effect that it would be quietly quashed. He was still saying the same almost a decade later. I guess I'm a slow learner.

So let me return to this seminal incident. To repeat: federal employees who speak out against waste, fraud, and abuse in the federal system are protected against retaliation by the Office of Special Counsel, the OSC. My allegation was that USNA's action, more precisely that of the academic (!) dean (!!), constituted what is poetically called a PPP, prohibited personnel practice (that is, a federal policy and law being violated by a federal institution). So, I immediately contacted the OSC, and they defended me. It was suggested we go to mediation, and at the time I didn't see why not. (Now I do.) The USNA representative began by handing out a sheet with his biography—a retired Navy captain in, if I remember correctly, from the "Leadership" Department. We were somehow supposed to be impressed by his various deployments, completely irrelevant to the matter at hand. Still, I am told this is what newly arrived commanding officers do—they hand out what are called "brag sheets." And then he made clear that USNA demanded my total capitulation. Some "mediation." The lawyer from OSC sat with her mouth open while the Naval Academy representative made clear that they were offering precisely nothing except disdain for faculty members. So, I got up from the table and left, the OSC continued its efforts, and the matter was resolved so that I did not have to pursue it further. (I'm not supposed to say whether I won or lost.)

From this, I should have learned the following: USNA plays hardball. It thinks it's right. And it does what it wants within its own walls, with no apparent regard for legal norms or any others and with no apparent consciousness that the Navy purports to be running a legitimate academic institution, or that all members of the military swear an oath to defend the Constitution that lists my rights, such as those of the First Amendment. What I learned the hard way is that they aren't running a legitimate, or even legal, institution, certainly not a legitimate academic one, though that is the way they sell it to the outside world and to unsuspecting students. Maybe they just assume they can get away with it? They did for a long time. And I believed them for a long time too. So, probably, do you. Why not? We respect the military, and we don't want to believe they are up to no good.

But all these harassments seemed in some way silly; stupidly, I thought them ridiculous rather than threatening, because they were so clearly out of line. Things got more serious when two women complained about my comment about gender issues and my criticism of the military's disastrous response to sexual assault, the SAVI/SAPR program. (The same program changed names from the first to the second after a few years. SAVI stands for Sexual Assault Victim Intervention and SAPR stands for Sexual Assault Prevention and Response.) Their complaint was not made the way the regulation in force at the time (since changed to give the administration total power) governed the process of student complaints. Namely, by speaking with the professor directly, or if that person was too scary, with the (usually civilian) department head. No, they went directly to the military head of SAVI/SAPR, a female Navy commander.

In retrospect, this seems to have been the logical next step in the Naval Academy's riding the larger societal and academic wave of female or minority offense. Of course, this was only to control civilians, as they already controlled the military. Think about it. If lower ranking military members can complain about an order they don't like or the attitude of a superior, the military, which is based on force down the chain of command, becomes impossible. So, this wave was ridden only with respect to civilians—whom the military, I have also learned the hard way, generally despises. I heard with increasing frequency that Professor Fleming "just doesn't get it." He's a mere civilian, not one of us.

This clubby insider mentality is encouraged at Annapolis—we hear it every year at graduation. Annapolis graduates, rather than being the most fortunate people alive, are the best and deserving of more. The graduation where it finally became unbearable for me to hear this was in 2017, when the speaker was then-Vice President Mike Pence. He praised his boss, then-President Donald Trump, and assured the military that the president was going to take care of them financially. President Trump was the best thing that ever happened to the military: he's got your back. The military exists to serve civilians; I silently objected! It's not a special interest group! But apparently it is seen as such and sees itself the same way. These are dangerous waters, with currents that take us out to the deep blue sea of military juntas and banana republics.

That semester, I was teaching two sections of a creative writing class—one of my favorites, as I get to encourage otherwise stifled students to talk about things that matter to them. I even love the room I typically taught it in, a small room with a big oval table that reminded me of seminar tables at Haverford and the University of Chicago, where we could all get more personal with what we write and talk about. They couldn't lapse into the disengaged lethargy that is their default in larger rooms where they can settle down behind individual desks. They have to lean forward onto the table, and I have them stand to read their works to give a bit of formality to the undertaking.

I loved teaching this class. The fact that they are reading what they themselves wrote means it is closer to the bone, also because usually it is about them. Of course, I have to make it clear that in opening themselves to me and to others, I am not setting up an ambush. We don't discuss whether or not we "liked" a piece, but asked what worked and what didn't, and this only after characterizing it: Dialogue? No dialogue? How did this function? Details? Showing or telling? It's all as analytical as possible. "What works, what doesn't?" was the phrase that one class years ago put on the cake they had made for our final in-classroom party. They wanted it to be a prom, so I wore a tux, and they dressed up as best they could. The girls had fancy dresses, but the guys threw together things from their collected closets—seniors are allowed civilian clothes.

I love getting to know them through their writing, if only for a semester. The whole experience is like what I call "rent a kid"—I get to know who is from where and things about their lives from what they write, watch them come in excited or cast down and ask why, and have them bring treats for the others on their birthdays. I take care of candy for major holidays. And then it's over. Typically, I never see them again. Bam. And it all starts again the following semester. It's both exhilarating and sad. I get to be an active part of the life force, but the life force always moves on.

You may be wondering, why creative writing at a military institution? As I tell them, they have to know who they are before they can be there for others—in a year or less, the others will be their enlisted, who come to even young junior officers with problems, even though the enlisted may be twice their age. I've had students write back to me about how strange this is. One young woman, by then a junior officer, wrote about how a man older than her father, an enlisted man, came to her in tears because his wife had left him. "Ma'am, what do I do?" he said. My former student, his officer, was flummoxed. "What do I say to him?" she asked me. "You listen," I said. "What else can you do?" I've had students who broke down reading about the death of one of their parents. "Want someone else to read it?" I would ask. "Want us to move on?" They shake their heads vigorously. This is part of dealing with it. And they are growing up, something the Academy tries to deny them, and that I know they have to do.

I am very fond of them. Some classes I'll have half a sports team that all signed up because of me—several times it's been the lacrosse team. (Both my sons played and still play lacrosse.) Is that love or what? And then when it's over it's over. But that's OK. It's not them as individuals

I love—it's their youth, their striving, their lives. And I get to share and guide it. Call me the luckiest man alive!

So sure, I can answer what future officers should be doing spending taxpayer dollars in a creative writing class. They should be getting in touch with their demons, their angels, or whatever else usually is silenced, because once they are in positions of authority, they will have to deal with problems from the enlisted, not their own. You have to get over your parents, your relationship with the opposite—or same—sex, and the demands of the military before you can be there for others. And the best way I know to encourage them to deal with their demons, or their angels, is to take my creative writing class. It's been very popular at USNA over the years.

That year, the semester had barely started in this class. We alternate discussions of published authors' poems, usually contemporary, with discussion of their assignments. This particular day it was the turn of a poem by the former poet laureate of the state of Missouri, William Trowbridge, called "Kong Looks Back on His Tryout with the Bears." This author, in fact, has a whole book of King Kong poems, but this is the best. It was in our writing anthology.

The poem is a corker, and especially useful with midshipmen in that it is a commentary on the newly "woke" Naval Academy position on how lethal men inevitably are. In this poem, King Kong is imagined at the end of the classic Fay Wray movie with him on the top of the Empire State Building about to be taken out by planes: the "Air Corps" from the Army as they were then. Remember several guys are swatted down to their deaths by his massive hands so it's not just fun and games. RIP, gentlemen.

But the poem is inside Kong's head, not concerned with mourning the pilots doing their job. He was recruited to play football in Wisconsin. Why? I ask the class—why a giant ape? Well, he's hyper strong and hyper fierce. Hyper masculine maybe? So, he seems a natural fit. But it turns out that he can't be controlled—and his sexuality takes over. Besides, he's rather dumb. He storms the field, then the bleachers, literally eating the women (who taste of fish, ha ha), and as a result is captured and put on display. And here he is now, at the top of the Empire State Building, ridiculous (as he knows), with a "bimbo" and himself become a "panty sniffer," an apparent reference to the deleted scene with Fay Wray where King Kong takes off her clothes (widely available on the internet).

But Kong is only an ape, so he's baffled. He thought that's what they wanted, more force! Yet he didn't know when to quit. Since my job is to find literature that helps students process their lives, and in a world where the phrase "toxic masculinity" is much used, I thought this poem was pretty good. In the discussion, I suggested that this is the problem with masculinity in our society. Football and SEAL movies encourage men to be more aggressive, but then it turns out that the feminist SAPR/SAVI indoctrination at the Naval Academy thinks they are responsible for all ills. Is this a paradox?

I think it is. And so did a lot of the male midshipmen in these early years of the SAVI program, who said in the privacy of my office that they were all being treated like rapists. (Note: the *V* in SAVI stands for victim. How can you have a victim without a perpetrator, and where does that leave the assumption of innocent until proven guilty? And yes, I know, this term is used in the civilian world as well, only it's worse in the military with the power of the court-martial.) No surprise, as the women involved with the program threw around such modish terms as "rape culture." Rape culture is what we see in Kivu province, eastern Congo, bordering Rwanda, where soldiers rape and impregnate women as a means of terrorizing and control, not in the West where lone women can go running by themselves in most parts of most cities before or after sundown without fear of being molested or attacked. Look outside your bubble, people. Nobody is surer of herself than a newly empowered twenty-year-old woman. Probably the men are just as bad, but I know how to control those by turning up the testosterone. If you want fanatics, search among the young. Think that Mao's Red Guards who dragged scholars from their libraries and humiliated them for insufficient love for the revolution were an exception? They say the child soldiers in Africa are the best: amoral, ruthless, and drunk on their own sudden power.

These two women who complained about this discussion, one in each section, didn't bother speaking to me, though that was what the then-current regulation said they had to do. That, after all, wasn't the point. The point was to make me pay for views that diverged from theirs. That's why they went directly to the female commander in charge of the SAPR/SAVI program to complain about what Professor Fleming was saying in class. (By the way, this woman was subsequently promoted to captain to reward her for her role in the USNA program. To her credit, I should say that she refused to take the complaints against me by the two women any further. That's why the administration picked it up and ran with it.) Academic freedom? Ha. Professor Fleming was saying *what*??? The Academy barred me from the classroom immediately and forbid me contact with students. (I should have learned from this that this is always step one for them. Want to apply for a job there now? Think it would be a cool place to teach? Think again.)

In doing so, to emphasize the point, the Academy had to flagrantly disregard its published policies that students with beefs with professors had to go up the chain of command, which started with the professor—the chain of command being stressed repeatedly in the pseudo-military theatrics of Annapolis. This they clearly didn't want to do, knowing that what I said about a poem would have been sanctioned as part of my job as a professor.

One of the two women told subsequent faculty "investigators" out-right that her goal was to get me fired. That was clearly the goal of the administration as well, though it took them years. One of these women was so disrespectful in class (very bad at Annapolis) I wrote her an email saying that she had been over the line, at which point she apologized. When I filed a conduct violation report for them jumping the chain of command, something professors are supposed to do (ignoring a mis-deed is held to be condoning it, and this one matters), the administra-tion slapped me with the first of two official Letters of Reprimand, this one for "retaliating against a complaint." This put me on probation for two years, during which any action they disapproved of would have been held to be grounds for firing. They didn't have the nerve that time, but on the second Letter of Reprimand in 2018, they did. The hapless civilian department chair was told to sign the one in 2018, which was handed to me in front of the lanky Marine colonel—I was ordered to appear to take my punishment. And shortly thereafter, I was fired.

Apparently, any female making any accusation about anything, even comments in class, is golden and cannot be questioned. That was my point about the hugely destructive SAVI program. No, I wasn't being accused of sexual harassment—nor was I ever. But the administration had realized that that sort of complaint from students that a male civilian wasn't on board with the new orthodoxy was the way to whip me into line. Yes! they must have thought. The gods have smiled. That's how we'll get rid of Fleming. (This will be the way accusations of "racial bias" in the newer DEI program will work, too. It's the way the military does things.)

You think that at the Naval Academy people have to be accused of actual offenses, told what they are accused of, and be confronted with their accuser, right? Hey baby. You ain't seen the military. In the military, it's all about what the people in charge disapprove of—and making sure they squelch dissent. Don't feel sorry for me. Feel sorry for yourselves, because you are defended by a military that is unable to self-correct and instead simply compounds its mistakes, since it's made clear that disagreement will not be tolerated. It happens over and over.

This round set the tone for future attacks against Fleming. They didn't tell me what the accusation was, or why the complainants could jump the chain of command. Instead, they sent a faculty committee to take over my class the next day while I was barred from the classroom and from contact with students. Sound Kafkaesque? That's what I thought. But this is the Naval Academy. Why not?, they must have thought. That's what they do with midshipmen.

Why not? Because I'm a civilian tenured professor and federal employee, that's why not! You stupid fools. At the time I thought it nothing but exasperating. Silly me.

The faculty committee of course found nothing wrong, and I returned to the classroom, where these events were all the students wanted to talk about. So, we did. Great learning experience, I thought. The military at work. Right?

Wrong. The result of the faculty investigation that nothing had happened that I could be punished for wasn't what the administration wanted. And they definitely didn't want the students to see how badly they had botched it. Time for a second swing at the Fleming piñata. They took things into their own hands, having the Marine colonel who was head of the Division of Humanities and Social Sciences run a UCMJ "Command Investigation." This particular Marine Colonel was neither the tubby one nor the lanky one, but an utter fool who showed pictures of his dogs at his introductory briefing we were required to attend. Like we cared. I bet he still has no clue what a blithering idiot he is.

A few more substantial problems here. First, I'm not subject to the UCMJ. Oops, but no problem. Who is Fleming going to complain to? We've got him.

Second, a Command Investigation according to the UCMJ (look it up) is not to try a person or determine guilt, innocence, or what happened. It's to find out why an incident we all know happened—such as a ship accident—happened. But of course, this was set up for the purpose of arriving at a different conclusion than my colleagues, so it did. Fleming was guilty of "discussing a conduct allegation with students" (who had seen the whole thing, realized it was a violation, and explicitly asked me if I had filed an allegation of a conduct offense) and of "retaliating" by doing his job of reporting the alleged conduct violation. To be clear, filing an allegation doesn't automatically mean there is found to have been a violation. The brass decide that, so they could well have just said no. But they knew there was a violation, so they punished me for reporting it. And by the way, I had discussed beforehand whether I should do this with a Navy captain in our department; he completely agreed I should, and showed me how to do it. But that's not what the administration wanted to happen. So: an official Letter of Reprimand. Loss of merit pay. Very bad boy. I still (somehow) found it all ridiculous. I guess they vowed to show me ridiculous.

Let's take a moment to disengage from the increasing stridency of the campaign against Fleming and consider the larger issues about male behavior I was trying to discuss with midshipmen—who, after all, are "future leaders."

Most fundamentally, men see themselves as actors, not acted upon, so legislating their behavior from without by people who don't understand them is the least effective way of achieving the goals almost everybody wants, namely some control over male excesses. This control can only be achieved if we accept that a good deal of male behavior is not excessive and is merely the way things are. Much derision is piled nowadays on the phrase "boys will be boys" because this has been taken to justify behavior we all want stopped, like rape—which is already illegal and punished. But just because the extremes are culpable, this doesn't mean all male behavior is. Kindergarten teachers differentiate between inside and outside voices and encourage outside voices outside. As a result, children are able to keep outside voices for outside. Nowadays we simply forbid yelling, and then are surprised when this doesn't work.

Men, at least straight men, at least straight white men, don't see themselves as a marginalized group. In fact, they don't see themselves as a group at all: each man is his own Rambo. So, the men aren't listening. Still, what they are told is that everybody is part of a group that defines his/her/their essence (which most men do not accept), that being a man is an illusion or a way to enforce power because "gender is socially constructed" (which men do not accept either), and that everybody gets to choose his/her/their "gender"—which apparently means that men who think that God or nature got their gender right are simply wrong. My nuts were not added on to me. They *are* me. This means nobody is getting through to men, who simply turn off the sound and walk away, because there's virtually no one expressing maleness as men see it. Feminism in all its various iterations, after all, is about women saying what women are and demanding that men listen—why should it be any different for men?

This telling men things they know aren't true makes the problem worse, and is actually very bad for women, because men won't do what women want them to do if they are approached in the wrong way. And women have a slew of beefs with the way men act these days. Sexual assault is topic A on virtually all college campuses, or was until it was replaced more recently by race-based DEI, and much scorn is heaped on the idea that male behavior is simply genetic. Of course, there is bad behavior by men, but nowadays this isn't seen as being bad behavior by men, but rather as intrinsically male behavior that needs to be stopped. This is not effective, and it infuriates men. Want to try a different way?

This situation has been made so bad in the service academies by the military acting like a lapdog to clueless civilians. And it's been horribly destructive to morale, because men are assumed to be guilty by the system. I found my lawyer through a student who told me one day he might no longer be in class, as a former girlfriend with whom he'd had sex had accused him of sexual assault, and that he had been slapped with a restraining order and was probably going to be thrown out. He had retained the lawyer, later mine as well, who showed that it was the woman stalking my student, not the reverse. He graduated late, but he graduated.

Congress has mandated yearly reports on sexual assault in the military and biennial reports on the service academies. Politicians are convinced we have a huge problem (a tiny faction in less than 1 percent of the population), and that they are going to do something about it. The kickoff of this sense of panic at what the press called an "epidemic of sexual assault" in the military was the Pentagon report for fiscal year 2012, released in May 2013. Epidemic? What epidemic? Only in the eyes of the beholder. There were fewer than 1,600 reported cases that were found to have merit, among about two million in uniform (including reserves), and these were far below the number reported four years before (though more than those reported two years before). The most important issue of the questionnaire was the perception of those reporting "sexual assault." What percentage is satisfied with the response of the "victim advocate"? (About three fourths.) That's what counts. This questionnaire was sent out to a small number of service members (one hundred thousand) of whom about a quarter chose to respond. (Any sociologist can tell you that voluntary responders aren't a representative sampling.) So, any extrapolations to the entire military are going to be speculative. Yet the newspaper reports of this survey headlined a "sharp spike" in reports of "contact or penetrative sexual assault" (see below for the contact thing). But the estimated percentages have varied between 4 percent and 6 percent since the reports started. Highlighting yet another 4–6 percent report (when this is all so approximate to begin with) merely serves to create headlines.

For the military, "sexual assault" is in fact a range of crimes; in each instance even the alleged attempt to commit one counts as a case. To quote from the 2012 report, and also subsequent ones, "The Department [of Defense] uses the term 'sexual assault' to refer to a range of crimes, including rape, sexual assault, nonconsensual sodomy, aggravated sexual contact, abusive sexual contact, and attempts to commit these offenses, as defined by the UCMJ. When a report is listed under a crime category, it means the crime was the most serious of the infractions alleged by the victim or investigated by investigators. It does not necessarily reflect the final findings of the investigators or the crime(s) addressed by court-martial charges or some other form of disciplinary action against a subject." So, it also includes cases where the alleged perpetrator turns out to be innocent. And it includes many things that most people wouldn't think of as assault.

When we go to UCMJ Article 120, we find the following things included as offenses (presumably those referred to in the passage above—a good deal lacks citation in the report), starting with the things most people assume sexual assault means; rape is at the top. Then we get to things like "wrongful sexual contact," which carries this definition: "The term 'sexual contact' means the intentional touching, either directly or through the clothing, of the genitalia, anus, groin, breast, inner thigh, or buttocks of another person, or intentionally causing another person to touch, either directly or through the clothing, the genitalia, anus, groin, breast, inner thigh, or buttocks of any person, with an intent to abuse, humiliate, or degrade any person or to arouse or gratify the sexual desire of any person." It's not pretty, but it's not what most people call sexual assault. If someone thinks you were getting intentionally close in an elevator, for example, we are looking at an accusation of sexual assault under the UCMJ definition.

Nobody condones rape, but the UCMJ definition of "sexual assault" is so broad as to incorporate a lot of behavior that is going to take place so long as men usually make the first move sexually—a kiss the woman doesn't want counts as "sexual assault" and can land the man in military prison. Some of the actions defined legally by the UCMJ as "sexual assault," despite advocates' universal denigration of such reasoning, are things that are excusable because "boys will be boys." Boys don't typically rape, but they do typically make the first move even when they're not sure of the outcome: this is normal male behavior, but advocates seem to think this is going to be stamped out, or should be. The fact that so much normal behavior is caught in the net that seems set for actual crimes such as rape has alienated almost everyone.

A key component of the 2012 Pentagon report is uncited "civilian research" that turns under two thousand substantiated reports into a conjectured twenty thousand: most alleged assaults, all advocates insist, go unreported. Probably that is so, but the precise number is a guess and produces the current push to get accusations and prosecutions, at any cost—narrowing the gap between those reported and the iceberg of what are asserted to be unreported. One tenth reported? Why not one half? One one-thousandth? No justification for any figure was given.

This methodological sloppiness continues to dog more recent reports. The Pentagon report released in 2019 offers about seven thousand reports of "sexual assault," though it notes that these are not necessarily by military members, or during military service. Once again, it performs the impossible task of guesstimating how many "assaults" do not get reported and once again guesses at about twenty thousand. So, we have the new "statistic" that about a third of assaults get reported.

The push to get more reports of sexual assault has led to a poisonous situation. Sex anywhere on the Naval Academy is grounds for court-martial, or for discipline—the latter usually by what's called an Article 32 that can (but need not) lead to a court-martial. So women

whose voluntary sexual encounters later come to light are being counseled—I have heard from numerous sources—to report these as sexual assaults so they can enjoy the amnesty for sex in the Yard that the
administration offers to those who allege sexual assault. One story I
heard involved a hand job in a public place that was periodically inter-
rupted as people walked by—something that can't be coerced. The man,
of course, is immediately on the path to an Article 32 hearing, and possibly a court-martial. The woman goes free.

The very focus on this issue makes clear that it cannot merely be
a crime of the normal sort: there is no comparable "murder awareness
month" like the military's "sexual assault awareness" month. Advocates
insist that "it's a societal problem"—which makes it unclear why the
military is being targeted. The military can't decide whether it's pursuing malefactors or trying to persuade people, which is to say men, to
modify their behavior.

Rape in the military isn't zero, of course, and must be prosecuted
like rape anywhere—and of course there may well be resistance to doing
this as there may be everywhere. But this more general campaign is
an ideological war that advocates can win through Congress because
Congress can force change on the military, and the military can force
change on its people. This is the problem with the military's response
to sexual assault: it's intellectually unjustified, it's imposed from the top
down based on force, and it brooks no opposition. That, more generally,
is the source of many of the military's problems nowadays. The solution
is to demand more rational discussion—which means disagreement,
something the military loathes—and less policy by fiat.

How does this play out at Annapolis? Take, for example, the prosecution of one of the three male midshipmen accused of sexually assault-
ing a female midshipman at a 2012 party. Against the recommendation
of the naval judge of the Article 32 hearings that transfixed much of
the American military community during two weeks in late summer
2013, the then-superintendent sent the cases of two of the three, all of
them football players recruited to play for Navy, to court-martial. (We
heard that the superintendent told his staff that he had nothing to lose

by insisting on a rape trial and would be seen as soft on sexual assault if he followed the legal advice he was given. That's called showing "leadership.") One case was not forwarded for court-martial for undisclosed reasons, and another was dropped because investigators had failed to read the midshipman his Miranda rights.

The military defense attorney for the alleged assailant mounted a strong defense of their client. The issue on which guilt or innocence rests for crimes covered by Article 120 of the UCMJ is that of consent of the alleged victim, so what they argued is that the woman consented. Consent or its lack was more difficult than usual to establish: the woman had been so blotto drunk from (underage) drinking, itself a punishable offense at the Academy, that she had no memory of any sexual relations she might have had that night. In fact, she only learned she may have had them via her friends' postings in social media the next day. Thus, there was unclarity about whether or not she consented, although drunk (as one defense attorney noted, "drunk sex is not sexual assault"). Moreover, the argument was made by the defense that oral sex, which she performed, implicitly implies a degree of consent that other forms do not. The man was drunk too. The verdict of this lengthy trial was that the man was found not guilty of rape or sexual assault. The woman was not punished for underage drinking or anything else, because she had brought the allegation of sexual assault that the administration was asking for, but the man was expelled from the Naval Academy for "conduct unbecoming." Military justice at work.

This case, precisely because it is so far from most people's understanding of what constitutes sexual assault, showed how convoluted, conflicted, and downright destructive the response of the Navy and the rest of the US military, the press, and, to some degree, the country at large was to the "epidemic of sexual assault" in the military. The alleged victim was so far from being a poster girl that the case was an insult to women who have been assaulted for real. And the case showed that the military is making things far worse by giving a botched response. Pushed by politicians, the military is carpet bombing its own people where it should engage in surgical strikes and, in the process, is causing untold amounts of collateral damage—to itself. And that means to civilians, because the military exists to defend civilians.

Though the court decided that there was no perpetrator, and hence no victim, the Navy, to underline the point, had been using the term "victim" for many years in its mandatory training of personnel in a program that, remember, was called Sexual Assault Victim Intervention. The revamped mandatory training for 2013, and then its recycled version for 2014, that I underwent as a civilian employee did (to be fair) encourage the self-identified "victims of unwanted advances" (legally counting as cases of sexual assault) to speak to those doing the advancing and, as a next step, to seek help within the system. However, the emphasis was on the colossally wrong-headed "bystander intervention," one of the military's panicked responses to outside pressure, and an insistence that all cases ranging from a little bad to very bad indeed be treated as if they were all the same. To be clear, the military doesn't make up this stuff; it hires outside advocates. At the 2013 rape trial, the prosecution offered as an "expert witness" someone based in Boston with no specific knowledge of this case who testified that there was a huge gap between reported and unreported assault cases—and that we were therefore to assume that any accusation was justified. The judge, having gone to law school, dismissed this argument.

And this pattern has continued, with the Academy pursuing losing cases to look tough. Another midshipman was found not guilty of rape in 2014, another in 2019, and another in 2022; another midshipman was acquitted in 2022 of having posted tweets the administration disapproved of. The USNA administration clearly thinks it gets points by showing how on board with current programs it is.

The video we watched in 2013 showed three scenarios, all of which involved men coming on to women, where the objection by the woman in two of the three cases stopped the behavior. But this wasn't our take-home point. The video instead focused on the third party in each case who felt bad after the fact that s/he did not intervene: accompany the subsequent alleged victim home, walk her back to the hotel, or object to the man being familiar with a woman who did not object. If that isn't infantilizing the woman, I don't know what is. Somebody else has to solve her problems; she clearly can't do so herself.

The key concept, again, is consent, so if it's welcome or accepted it isn't assault—only whether it is or not is sometimes unclear to both parties. So why don't we work on encouraging people who don't want the advances to do something about them? Oh, I forgot: that's "blaming the victim." Saying men are never to take the initiative simply contravenes the rules of normal male-female interaction. No wonder sexual assault "training" seems so other-worldly to men: they are being told things that simply do not jibe with reality. And in the program of bystander intervention, we all become snitches and third wheels on each other, accosting people even before there are any visible problems, and assuming that what we see is always the sign of something bad. Most social situations do not end in problems: apparently, we're supposed to police them all, put a stop to all male-female interactions we see.

That's demeaning to women. And also infuriating to men. That's why male midshipmen subjected to countless hours of SAPR training objected to the overall assumption (they told me) of "men are potential rapists" in the sessions, usually led by female midshipmen like the two women who objected to my views in class, who had the power to keep the men there until they hear the responses they want. Specifically, the men objected to the fact that parallels were always drawn between normal life in the military or at USNA, and horrific gang rapes, which the midshipmen have to say loud and clear that they abhor, before the trainers (their fellow midshipmen) will let them go. Who isn't against gang rape? But what does this have to do with a bunch of drunken libidinal midshipmen willingly at the same party that gets out of hand?

An even newer video we had to watch involves a male police officer telling the story of having been raped at gunpoint by other men. Those men: they'll do it to anybody! Still, SAPR insists this is not targeting men; assault is a "human problem." (If I were a gay rights advocate, I'd be apoplectic at this new wrinkle.) This is nonsense. In fact, the training makes the men out to be always 100 percent responsible, and the woman never, to any degree, responsible or complicit. Men raping women, men raping men. It's always those men, at it again. That the man is always completely responsible is especially untrue at the less objectionable end of the spectrum, which is to say all but a few cases—as the Naval Academy's rape trials showed. At the suggestion that the "victim" could bear some degree of the blame in cases such as the drunken midshipmen at a party—far more common than real rape or assault—"victim's advocates" grow apoplectic. They're thinking of violent rape. The problem is that most of what gets reported as "sexual assault" is closer to the 2012-13 "nobody comes out looking good" Naval Academy case than it is to the clear, black-and-white cases of the training. The military personnel are aware of the divergence; the brass don't seem to be.

Of course, the military is fertile ground for this paranoid policing of sex within its ranks. The military has never condoned anything remotely sexual, which made sense when the ranks were filled by men assumed to be straight. But adding women and the lifting of the ban on homosexuals have changed all this. The pressures are immense, and the military has responded by holding the top of the pot down more firmly as it boils more vigorously. This can't go on forever: at some point the military will have to narrow its definition of impermissible behavior and the times and circumstances under which it is impermissible. Say, when it is clearly aggression and clearly impacts unit readiness. If not, shrug and look the other way. You don't have to police everything.

But the military has always seen itself as policing the whole person—character rather than actions. That too has to change. Many prosecutions for sexual misdeeds in the military take place not just under Article 133 of the UCMJ, the so-called conduct unbecoming article, but also Article 134, the general article, forbidding any activity that is a "breach of custom of the service," "brings discredit" on the service or is "prejudicial to good order and discipline." Typically, these have been understood to mean no sex on base, no fraternization (sex between officers and enlisted) within the chain of command, no adultery, and of course until recently, no same-sex sex. But they all come from the presupposition of an all-male, no-gay-sex world. Women change things.

Lifting the ban on gay service members changes things. Admit it and change the rules.

Prosecutions are based, to repeat this fundamental point, on the commanding officer's personal views of how much "discredit" has been brought or how much "good order" has been compromised (Article 134) or how "unbecoming" (Article 133) the actions have been. Specific sex acts (such as adultery) are deemed worse than others, and the UCMJ still contains prohibitions against "sodomy" (defined as all nonvaginal intercourse and including oral sex with married heterosexual couples), though attempts are being made to remove these after the lifting of the ban on gays. The military's response to the "epidemic of sexual assault" takes the form of unfocused carpet bombing because it disapproves of all sex, an attitude left over from the old days. See where the Marine colonels got the idea that it was up to them to use their personal views to police what a professor said in class?

This is all a big mistake—not to mention ineffective, as well as crazy-making and infuriating to the men. We need to encourage people who feel sexually aggressed to speak up and ask for help. Anyone who feels actually threatened must ask for assistance, as we all do from police. We also need to distinguish between "unwelcome but controllable" on one end of the "sexual assault" spectrum and "violent" on the other, and not treat them all as if they were the same. Most men aren't rapists, but most men will take the sexual initiative. Unless our real purpose is to declare war on men, we need to make a distinction between these. The training must stop conflating the two radically different approaches of male sexual initiative, which is good and makes the human race continue, with the clearly criminal extreme of sexual aggression.

The training has to make clear as well that we know that men and women are sexual beings, welcome this, and welcome the appropriate exercise of this deeply human activity. We're not wise to tell a room full of military men as if they're hearing it for the first time that rape is a no-go. But we can explain why fraternization is so destructive of military morale, and give them the woman's POV, which many have simply never heard before. For instance, that sometimes women go out in short skirts just to look nice for girlfriends: it's not always about the man. Sympathetic female PhD psychologists—not female midshipmen or sailors the same age as those they are hectoring, and not advocates out to change "the culture"—can open male eyes to the puzzling ways of women. And the reverse: men aren't bad by nature, and most of what they do can, in fact, be explained to women. If the training were like this, most of the male members of the military, now after ferocious recruiting of women about 80 percent of the Navy (92 percent of the Marine Corps), might be with the program. Now, constantly lectured about being potential rapists, they aren't.

I'm so tired of hearing the phrase "toxic masculinity" I could spit: it's not masculinity itself that's toxic, only some extreme actions by men. So target these actions as exceptions: don't attack men. They won't listen to you. Besides, more fundamentally. masculinity, associated with decisive, forceful action, is the lifeblood not only of the military but perhaps the world at large. But it has to be controlled by rationality. It's great that men are expected to be decisive and forceful when they have thought things through and know what they are doing, but not so great when they haven't. The problem is not the action, but the lack of justification behind it.

So, I speak about it in the classroom, sometimes in connection with Chinua Achebe's much-read (and much-misunderstood) novel *Things Fall Apart*. Contrary to general belief among English professors or the high school teachers who like to assign it to have a non-Western text on the syllabus (only it's written by a Christian Nigerian in the colonial language of English, for Anglophones, and was published in London, so it's not clear how non-Western it is), this is not an anticolonialism screed. In fact, it's far more nuanced. The ultimate hero benefits by the arrival of the English and many of the grislier aspects of pre-colonial now-Nigeria go away when the English are in control, such as the custom of killing all twins (held to be evil spirits) and sacrificing hostages handed over in judicial settlements.

The main character Okonkwo suffers from what I call "testosterone poisoning." Not "toxic masculinity," which suggests that masculinity itself is potentially toxic. Testosterone is great, but too much can be bad for you—and others. It describes a pattern like a Laffer curve of giving increasing results until the curve begins to fall, and the results alter and become negative. Of course, "testosterone" is used here in a metaphoric sense. Okonkwo is a caricature of what his society (and ours) sees as male virtues—strength, fortitude—which initially raise him up and, ultimately, bring him down. He is strong and resolute, planting three harvests of borrowed yams (for the Igbo, his tribe/people, yam planting is a man's business) before he is finally successful, subsequently taking two out of a possible three clan titles, and along the way, keeping his wives in line (as a man is supposed to do in his society—Achebe is clearly not faulting him for this). But he goes too far. The problem is not the strength. It's unguided and excess strength. That's not a problem with masculinity itself, but with how it's expressed and applied.

Okonkwo goes too far, not in beating his youngest wife, which (according to his society and apparently according to Achebe) he should be doing, but in doing it during the Week of Peace, when wife-beating is (exceptionally) proscribed. Worse, Okonkwo (we are told) is afraid of appearing weak (since he's ashamed of his ne'er-do-well father, now dead), and so he personally kills the hostage in his care, who has grown up as a member of his household and who calls him "father." And he is unable to use words to any effect and thus always resorts to his fists.

This isn't a problem with masculinity. It's about how King Kong, or a human version, can fit into the normal world. We want men who can take the sexual initiative, but not men who rape or who ignore clear signals that their advances are unwelcome. We need more situational awareness. Okonkwo needs more thought, less blind lashing out. He needed my English class at the Naval Academy where we learn to reason out an action and justify it, as I joke to midshipmen.

The solution to an Okonkwo is not to have females tell him that his very masculinity is toxic. It's to have a fellow alpha male who can use words show them that force and strength are good—if rightly guided. And then guide them. Not to attack men for being men, but to show them that they have to be able to package and sell this commodity in order to be effective in the world. And men will only allow themselves to be guided by someone who doesn't denigrate their masculinity but who instead exemplifies it. You want to rein in men? Women telling them they are defective won't work.

MEN AND WOMEN IN THE MILITARY

Some version of this chapter is what I would say to all midshipmen, male and female, if the administration were more effective and actually had the welfare of the military and its members at heart, rather than their own careers or their retirement.

So here it goes. Hold on to your hats (in the military called "covers").

The Naval Academy is not gender neutral. The military is not gender neutral. This doesn't mean that women have no place in it and, in any case, the train of including women in the military has long ago left the station. But it also doesn't mean that millennia of societal assumptions that men do the fighting are simply nonsense, or alternately, that the military expresses the male desire to keep the good things full of cool actions for themselves. Including women doesn't necessarily mean that women should do absolutely everything in the military, that the military should be 51 percent female, or that women should be mixed with men. It's a political decision to change something, and another decision about what form that should take. Fine. Justify that. You can't just assert it and insist that we believe it because you say it. This is a skill I have to teach repeatedly in class, where the self-righteousness of youth, one-sided political upbringing, and the military's reliance on rank rather than rationality make the students think that a loud assertion of their point of view will carry the day.

The military, to be sure, has dealt badly with the integration of women into its ranks, and the service academies have dealt worse. Anecdotal evidence from dozens of conversations in my office suggests to me that the women who are most disappointed by the Naval Academy are the ones who had brothers who supported them and fathers who came to their games, kissed their boo-boos, and encouraged them to follow their dreams. They get to Annapolis and find favoritism for women (chosen by the military staff at disproportionate numbers to be things like company officers, what are called "leadership positions") and annoyance by the men at this favoritism, as well as at the fact that the conduct rules are bent for women and that men are punished at far greater proportions and more harshly. This was corroborated statistically by in an article for the Annapolis *Capital Gazette* of May 17, 2009, entitled "Academy Justice Was Tilted Toward Women." Its author, once again, was Earl Kelly, a lawyer and a former military guy, whose final career was as a journalist. He wasn't about to put up with the brass's hype and bullshit, and of course he didn't buy into the worship of the military the brass sells as a protective screen.

It's probable that some of the old-school animosity toward women at Annapolis is still floating around, but it's certain that the administration makes things far worse by this blatant favoritism that they apparently think goes unnoticed by the men, who in any case can't complain. (If they do, they are punished.) The men were almost universally attracted to what they assumed would be a masculine environment. Almost all love the association of the military with muscles and strength—male muscles, male strength. Many midshipmen are self-declared Catholics, though I discover they know nothing about Catholic doctrine (try getting them to define transubstantiation or the Last Judgment). They made up almost half the class up to about a decade ago, and now there are a sizeable number of home-schooled evangelicals. Many of the Catholics went to single-sex schools, and are used to a religion that sees both God and their Savior as male, and in the Catholic church, allows only men to be priests. (It's arguable as well that these religions make people comfortable with being told what doctrine is. End of story.)

The military encourages this focus on male authority and on the male in general with its multiple weight rooms, disproportionately patronized by the men (women don't typically bulk up), I use these weight rooms too, sometimes working out with them if they ask me to. Then there is the (male) midshipmen bodybuilding team. The mascot Bill the Goat (note: not Nanny) has huge horns and, in the drawings, huge pecs and arms that he shows off the way the Marines show off their "guns" by rolling their sleeves above the biceps. Watch the hype recruiting videos—they highlight sweaty muscular men, and physicality is one of the three divisions of our mission statement: we aim to prepare "midshipmen morally, mentally and physically."

The military churns out reams of male-oriented physical propaganda to lure in men eager to bathe in a testosterone-saturated world. Is the idea that women can do this too? Most women don't want to. But that has been the way of the military—to insist that women can be as loud and as strong as men. It's certainly twice as hard to be a woman in the military as it is to be a man, and not because men resist—but rather because the very structure of the military, from the uniforms and parades down, was made by men for men. You think women would ever have invented this system of standing rigid with their chests out while another woman barks orders in their face? The uniforms that hug the body and emphasize the muscles? The idea that hardness and dirt define the soldier? The military prizes strength, and most men prize strength.

But what I've discovered over three decades is that many of our male midshipmen have daddy issues. American society being what it is, with half of all marriages ending in divorce, many boys lack fathers or deal with stepfathers, or develop a vision of what a father should be that their biological father, even if present, cannot satisfy. Probably this is made worse by all the movie depictions of hypermasculinity, almost always associated with the military. Indeed, for most of us, the military is the one place where men are encouraged to be men—that is to say, strong, physical, muscular, forceful—the opposite of the "female" virtues of kindness and compassion.

Most of our male students are chasing what I call the "Big Hard-on in the Sky"—an absolute ideal of strength and courage that society doesn't offer them. That's probably why Naval Academy SEAL candidates do better than ROTC candidates at BUD/S (and are given twice as many billets), the grueling screener for SEALs where finally they go a week without sleep and are constantly on the move in a challenge called "Hell Week"—and you don't understand SEALs if you don't understand that this is said with pride. We get the ones who want to be challenged to be tough and "take it like a man." They are also for this reason the ones who are the most disappointed because they discover that the Naval Academy is a ladies' teetotaler society version of the military—all about looking spiffy. It's not what they thought, which was "are you good enough for us?" It's about putting on a show.

I remember reading years ago an article about a man who volunteered in his son's kindergarten class. He said that he could always tell which boys had a father at home and which ones didn't. The ones who wanted to climb over him—to use a real man as a jungle gym—lacked a father. Many of the young men who come to us are looking for that smell of the man they never had. And they are disappointed, because that's not what we're about. We're window dressing for the military, nothing more. Neither the women nor the men find what they are looking for, so they are almost always bitterly disappointed. And then they become officers.

It's quite true that Annapolis, and arguably the whole military, botched the integration of women. They should have known this would require major changes in fundamental structures, but none were made. As a minor but illustrative example, in my building I even found urinals in the women's bathrooms in the 1990s, decades after the arrival of women—I had taken my young daughter in after hours with no one around. They changed the sign on the door, but left the urinals, which stayed until the building was renovated a decade or so after that. That's a metaphor for the way women were admitted to Annapolis. You want to play a man's game? they seemed to say. OK. Then play. Nobody thought of changing the game to make it more accommodating to women. In fact, everybody denied that changes would be necessary. Were men physical with men? Sure. OK, now we can be physical with women. And when the (it seems to me inevitable) way women were treated got out, the outrage in civilians who thought adding women to a quintessentially male environment would be unproblematic produced a strong swing of the pendulum to the opposite side. A woman has only to twitch on the thread of claiming that a man has sexually harassed her (even if she was drunk too, or consented, but later decided she didn't mean it) for him to be immediately engulfed in a net of restraining orders and expulsion. And she assumes the mantle of victimhood.

There's no question that women were, in fact, treated horribly in the service academies when first admitted, though given that no measures were taken to accommodate them or change the institution that their presence was sure to change, this seems more predictable than not. Some years ago, I asked a married couple of graduates—a couple in which the wife came from my hometown and had married a boy from her Annapolis class, both by then done with their time in the Navy— to speak to one of my classes. They had graduated in the first several years of women, though not the first year or two. Still, the woman had horror stories of having to keep a sawed-off broomstick by her bed to fend off the men when, not if (as she said), they came in her room late at night to throw themselves on her. She was still naïve enough that she complained to the commandant. His response: What did you expect from red-blooded men at Annapolis? But, of course, the men weren't prepared to find women in their dormitory either. Was it really fair to either the women or to the men?

I'd almost be ready to say that the current hounding of men serves males right, only two wrongs don't make a right, and it's not the same men, and the problems this woman and others faced could have been addressed more directly. As it was, the attitude of the Naval Academy was passive aggressive: we didn't want you, so you deal with the consequences. This ought to make us 100 percent supportive of the women who "just wanted the chance to serve" along with the men, as we some-times heard (actually, to get the same outrageous government handout, but why not?). But I say hmmm. We should have been clearer that there is, in fact, value in things that are all male. Women see that as excluding women. Men tended to see it as including men: the exclusion of women wasn't the point. We may decide that it should be given up because the good for women is so huge—a sort of utilitarian argument, the greatest good of the greatest number. But why be surprised if the men resist? They have lost something they valued. All-male brotherhood is not chopped liver, as New Yorkers say.

Only it's increasingly threatened these days, as well as derided, if not outright destroyed. The only places you can find male brotherhood are in the rugby or football team locker rooms, or in Marine infan-try. And who knows how long it will survive there? It wasn't men who pushed for female inclusion at the service academies and in the military. It was women. And no, that doesn't mean these men are Neanderthal pigs, just that men (unsurprisingly) see benefits to all-male groups that women (understandably) do not. Let's say that because of the force of history, we see no alternative to including women at the service acad-emies (Virginia Military Institute tried to set up a female "leadership" institute at another college but was overruled). That doesn't mean it will be without a price, one we should be open about.

All these issues are central to James Webb's mistitled article "Women Can't Fight" that has raised so much Cain since its publication in 1980, the first year women were to graduate from the Naval Academy. (Webb is a novelist, a Marine, and a former Secretary of the Navy, as well as sub-sequently a senator from Virginia.) It got a bad title (writers don't title their stories, typically) because it doesn't argue that women can't fight, rather that they change and weaken the male bonding so important in combat situations—such as in Webb's Marine experience in Vietnam. Is the weakening so much that the combat effectiveness is compromised? We don't know, but suggesting that it does is not merely Neanderthal resistance to letting women do the good stuff. Me personally, I say sure, let's get all the Marine infantry to be women. Maybe the other side will do the same, and if not, probably our really cool gadgets will make up the strength deficit. I don't think any guy should die with a bullet in his gut. If women want to, let them. It's the Marines that have resisted longest and hardest the full mixing of women into all units. That's because they are the closest to what you think of as being the military—the Navy is safe in ships, and pilots are above it all. Hand-to-hand violence is usually seen as male; women get their dragons to do their incinerating and never muss their hair—at least to believe *Game of Thrones*.

Oops. I forgot. Male aggression is a "social construct" and with proper gender-neutral upbringing we can get them to let go of that. But I'm confused. Is it Barbie dolls for boys and trucks for girls? Barbies for all? Trucks for all? Let them choose their toys as well as their gender? Will we raise the women to be the aggressive ones? Nobody? Everybody?

We men typically like the fact that we are large and strong and hairy. So there is in fact a connection between our liking ourselves and the connection of masculinity with the military. At any rate, you can't assume there isn't. Prove it: justify your assertions, as I say in class. Don't think I'll be convinced merely because you assert it.

Webb is usually taken as the quintessential male chauvinist pig, but what he says in his article is the simple truth. Men do have a tendency to protect women. (Through nature? Nurture? It's there at any rate.) And they also act out to get female attention. Men interact differently with men than they do with women—duh. Even feminists who assume that men are all potential rapists, such as the late Andrea Dworkin (whose book *Intercourse* I enjoyed, as she gets a lot of male-female relations right and uses literature the way I think it should be used, to comment on life), agree that men treat men differently than they treat women. Webb's article, however, is really about how women would change combat when they are thrown together with men. He knows. I bet you don't. If you say women and men are exactly the same under all circumstances, you're the one who has to justify that.

There is clearly a scale of relations between men and women from one extreme, where we are simply identical humanoids, to the other extreme where we are almost completely different. At the first extreme are things like who takes care of the pet bird or the fish, which don't care about our gender, or what white-clad masked, gloved, and bonneted surgeon performs the operation. But if you are choosing a psychiatrist to talk to, you might well have a preference for a man or a woman, or maybe you would like a male or female gynecologist, urologist, or sex therapist. We might not care whether it's a man or woman flying the plane, but we might well care whether our platoon lieutenant was male or female. Violinists male or female? Irrelevant. The more the job is a specific action as opposed to a type of person, the less we tend to care about gender.

How about the model for underwear? Usually, we want a man wearing the brief with the pouch in front and a woman in the bra. There the particular body matters. Singers? You can't swap a bass for a soprano. Trapeze artists? In theory, the woman could catch the man, but it would be an exception. Heavy lifting? Sure, one woman out of perhaps a thousand could do it, and everybody gets dirty doing crappy work, so why not. But typically, we get two guys to move the couch, not two women. There's a reason, aside from prejudice. Actors/actresses? We are big into what is called blind casting these days, which means putting nonwhites into roles meant for whites and never the reverse. But by this we don't usually mean gender-blind casting: it's far rarer when an actress does a man's part—almost always this rather than the reverse, which is reserved for comic effect, as in *Mrs. Doubtfire* or *Some Like It Hot*—like Glenda Jackson playing King Lear, or Sarah Bernhardt as Hamlet. (Tellingly, sometimes the point of this is to make fun of the male, like Melissa McCarthy playing Sean Spicer.)

The military has this entire scale ranging from "gender is essential" to "it doesn't matter." So, let's talk. There are situations where a separable skill not involving the whole body means it doesn't matter who does it. But the more it's the whole person involved, including the body, the more it matters. And the military, unlike an office, is to a much greater degree about the body. Not as much as a sports team, but more than a sales force. For the Marine Corps in the field, it's about the body. There, Webb is right.

We men are willing to countenance the possibility that women need to see women in positions of authority and sometimes (always?) need or at least want to have women making the decisions. And racial preferencing of nonwhites usually includes the justification that people of X need to see people of X in positions of authority, and that people of X will understand people of X in a way that people of Y will not. So, we also would need to accept that sometimes, men need to see men. Of course, we should be leery of reaching these conclusions too absolutely because this will produce problems. What happens when we don't have an X to X match? What happens if we do, but it turns out that other factors override the assumed congruence?

How about if we stop categorizing people by the rubrics we think they can be categorized by? This is a possibility that is irrelevant to an organization like the military that follows orders. Once the principle of racial or gender tracking is established, it won't be questioned, at least not until there are major changes at the top. The military relies on orders, which means from the top down. But there are degrees of rigidity in these. We need to encourage more discussion and questioning at all levels, when it's possible to have discussions. At Annapolis, it is always possible, as nobody is shooting at us, and it's also possible in the vast majority of military situations that are not actual warfare.

All of us want inclusion, sure, but inclusion of whatever group by definition means change of the status quo. We need such discussions to talk openly about the fact that this comes at a price, and that resistance is not just the resentment of straight white males angry at seeing their unjust "privilege" (the newest buzz word) challenged. High time they got pushed off their unearned pedestal! Is not that simple, because it's not true that people in the military are gender-neutral robots—they are men and women, and that makes things complex. It's great to open slots to groups that hitherto were denied access. But does that mean we should force members of these groups into slots that are therefore denied to individuals who arguably could fill them better? The military has a purpose, even if the service academies don't, so we diminish the effectiveness of the military if we insist that it merely look the way we want it to look. Even if we can agree on what, ideally, we'd like to see—men and women, whites and people of color, gay and straight, trans and "cisgender"—all playing happily together, that doesn't mean it's a good idea to flip a switch and demand that this be achieved now under pain of severe punishment. And what is achievable, or even desirable, may well be something different.

Feminists claim that society is set up by men for men, though this is not the way it seems to most men. All it lets men do is compete, and most lose. But few people would contest the assertion that the military was set up by men for men—to possibly take a bullet for the team. Do we get any credit? Nah. Feminists deny any reason for this other than merely the old one of privilege. That exasperates many men. We're doing this shitty thing for you! You could at least appreciate us. But it's undeniable that the military is still seen as a male undertaking—which is precisely why many women want to enter it, to show that they can succeed in the big leagues. Is this the result of good reasons or bad? According to contemporary theory, all reasons are bad as we only "construct" differences between men and women. But the push is always to get women into formerly male situations, not the opposite. Hmmm. Guess there's some point to what men do after all.

The popularity of the insistence that "gender [and practically everything else] is socially constructed" is presumably meant to show that we can remake the world as we wish, because what is constructed, rather than presumably natural, can be deconstructed or reconstructed. But it's so widely used that it's lost its bite. It's like saying that all perceptions are subjective. OK, but we can learn to filter out those that are more subjective than others—like when we are drunk or if we are blind. Then we collate the others in Venn diagrams where we agree to call the overlap—are you ready? Objective! (Both Immanuel Kant and Arthur Schopenhauer would beg to differ, but I don't think many military members read either Kant or Schopenhauer.)

The three little pigs all constructed houses, but one house actually kept the wolf out. If you tell me all colors are optical subjectivities, fine. (That's Kant and Schopenhauer again.) You still haven't showed me that red is blue. And anyway, how do you know absolutely every-thing is man- (oops: woman-) made? In fact, what you mean is that you want to change a specific set of circumstances, so you start by denying theoretical legitimacy to them. Now we are supposed to sit back and let you tell us how you will reconfigure the world. It's all about getting the power position.

Feminist theory assumes that men are plotting against women, but the fact is that a lot of the time, women are not uppermost in most men's minds. Men are usually more interested in their relationships with other men—or at least have to figure these out, so it's incorrect to say that their self-definition is based on what they are not. What's like them is what defines the group with which they operate. Runners don't com-pete with pole vaulters, and certainly not with couch potatoes. They worry about, and compete with, other runners. The Naval Academy is built on male-male relationships. Though some male midshipmen do have sexual relationships with female midshipmen (not "midship-women"), this is frowned on and called "dark siding." Mostly they have friendships with other men.

The female students are clothed to be desexualized, with the uni-forms flattening their chests. and the flat shoes and trousers making them look like men from a distance and their hair short or in a severe bun. Many female midshipmen, in fact, have told me they feel as if they are cross-dressing when wearing the made-for-men uniforms. Uniforms for men, by contrast, are flattering to the men, as is their short hair and the rims of the military covers shading their eyes like a state policeman who has just pulled you over for speeding in South Carolina backcountry.

You think the men don't know this? Ha. They are all about who "looks like a stud" and who doesn't. And the Marine Corps, 92 percent male, is all about showing off for other men, including rolling up the sleeves on the digi-cammies (camouflage made as if with pixels) to show off the biceps: the "guns." Think it's chance that biceps are called some-thing that shoots? As my students say: sun's out, guns out! Short sleeves show off your biceps! To the other guys, of course.

We are aware of other men because that's what we are and what we compete against. Being a man is red in tooth and claw: think we're all about making sure women can't compete? We can see that it would seem so from your perspective. But that perspective is not ours. Want to talk with us? Ask us how we see things. And oh, you want us to compete against you? But you're not a man! Sorry, we momentarily forgot that gender is "just a social construction," and we just have to get over it. Have you gotten over being a woman? No? Oh, it's just men who have to change. Think we'll sign off on that? Would you?

Even the hats ("covers") worn by women have gone male at the service academies, in going from the so-called bucket hats for women (smaller rims in front and back, little on the sides, flush to the head rather than towering above it) to male covers for all, though it's clear that these V-shaped male covers were made to flatter the male torso by giving it an extra-inverted pyramid on top of the V of shoulders and pecs. The body V is emphasized by the buttons on the parade uniforms (tight waiter jackets), and the double-breasted suits in black that the Navy insists are "navy blue." (I hear that, at least originally, one thread out of every cluster of maybe a dozen black threads was blue, giving the cloth a faint blue sheen. If this is still the case, I can't see it.)

One day a student asked me, "Sir, have you heard of the eighty-twenty rule?"

"No," I said. "What's that?"

Answer: "That a uniform makes a man look twenty percent better and a woman eighty percent worse." Everybody knows this to be true and almost nobody says it, that military uniforms are made to cleave tightly to the musculature of the male body. Women now wear it too, and they're not flattering given that "female" clothing emphasizes curves, softness rather than muscle. The military has not solved the problem produced by the fact that it wants men to be masculine (and you can write that in quotes if you like) but does not want women to be feminine (also quotes?). Including women means allowing in those women who are willing or eager to act like men. Don't like that? You'll have problems.

But uniforms can only go so far in making a woman gender-neutral; she has to assume sober body language, not curvy or flirty "female" gestures. Some women go too far with the nonfeminine body language: I've seen female Navy members who swagger with their legs open John Wayne-style and emit gruff male verbalisms. But that's not what we're after here either, as the men note it as overcompensation and smile to themselves.

Men can be as masculine (or "masculine") as they want, turning up the volume (which energizes other men), but women have to turn down (not up) the volume of who they are. I am leaving aside the fact that, as I hear anecdotally, butch lesbians are drawn to the military precisely because they don't have to act "female" at all. The woman who told me this was the vice president of an association of gay Naval Academy graduates, back before DADT was repealed. Sure, it's all unfair to most women. Why can't a female officer wear short skirts, high heels, and low-cut blouses with her hair down if she wants? Because the men wouldn't accept her orders, unless they were into dominatrixes with whips and black high-heeled boots, which most men aren't. Everybody knows this, yet somehow it's a punishable offense in the military to acknowledge it. We should, so we can deal with it, which means saying it's a problem and discussing ways to respond—rather than pretending (as we now do) that it isn't true.

EDUCATING FUTURE OFFICERS

W hat do I hope to impart to future officers to improve the military and the defense of civilians? I take that responsibility seriously. It's not a matter of shoving factoids down their throats. People who don't know what really goes on inside the service academies speak knowingly of how important it is to "teach the cadets/midshipmen" X or Y, including this or that subject in their mandatory curriculum, or giving them training in A or B. They don't realize that cadets and midshipmen regard the classes they must take, by and large, as intrusions on their day and a waste of time. You can lead a horse to water, and at Annapolis or West Point we even shove its head in the water and punish it if the tongue doesn't go up and down. But what students don't want to take on board, they won't, and at the service academies, it's a rare young man or woman who wants what s/he is being forced to drink.

Our daily reality has all the worst aspects of socialism, with its relentless dumbing down to the minimum of effort and outcome. And because midshipmen aren't paying for it, and have no control over it, most resent it or at least don't take it seriously. They may have wanted to come to the Academy (at least as they believed it was) but once there, almost everything is mandatory. It's something they have to put up with, not something they are actively seeking. Their four years as midshipmen or cadets are not something they are doing, but something done to them. A course can be more interesting than expected, but all will graduate if they keep a relatively clean record and do a minimum amount of work, and all will be hired by the government—the work they came to get credentials for. There is no winnowing. If you know that your effort makes no difference, as under dictatorships and planned economies—and I'd say the academies are both these things—there's no reason to exercise your individual initiative. So most midshipmen don't even try. They just let the current carry them along. That's sad.

Sure, there is some competition—your rank in class decides the order you get to pick some things, higher going before lower. And a tiny handful of the best students get graduate fellowships that they are allowed to follow up immediately after graduation—though the Navy can forbid you from taking it even if you get it, as it happened recently to a young woman in my class who was accepted at a major university for defense studies. Nope, she had to go to the fleet. The few Navy football players who get drafted by the NFL, by contrast, are almost all at the bottom of the academic pecking order and regularly (to repeat, because it's not OK) have their service obligation forgiven by the secretary of the Navy. We love our football players!

Plus, you don't always get to take even the classes you want to take. Though the institution has always discouraged majoring in anything but engineering or science, the push for women made that difficult. At first, so-called Group III majors—English, History, Political Science, and Economics—were limited to 20 percent of the class. Under Ronald Reagan's Secretary of the Navy John Lehman, who had a PhD in history, this permission for 20 percent of the class to major in nontechnical subjects was increased to 30 percent. The idea seemed to be that 30 percent could major in frivolous materials like English without the Navy and Marine Corps suffering irreparable harm. Then they removed the cap on nontechnical majors. With the numerical cap on majors like English and history gone, the proportion of students in nontechnical majors crept perilously close to 40 percent. Clearly that could not be tolerated. So, if a student with the slightest aptitude for anything other than, say, English, declared a desire to be an English major, the chain of command swung into action to convince him/her of the folly of his/her ways—more so if it was a he. (As a result, the percentage of female English majors was always substantially higher than the proportion of women in the student body, the Brigade.)

Even now, the Academy reserves the right to force you to major in something you don't want. It also reserves the right to force you into a service selection (job after graduation) you didn't want. You have to put down three choices of service selection, ranging from aviation to ships/surface warfare officer (SWO) to Marine infantry to nuclear submarines—only loosely correlated to your major—and you can be made to do any of the three. Or the administration can even, albeit more rarely, put you in one you hadn't listed at all.

Being too worried about student majors doesn't make much sense to me. Regardless of major, all students take a technical core of calculus, chemistry, and Naval engineering, along with Naval history, western civilization, and a slew of other courses—though most say they forget what they were force-fed soon after the course is over. The Navy will teach it to you all over again anyway in a post-graduate specialty school for all new officers including ROTC graduates, who probably didn't follow this curriculum at their schools. Besides, when midshipmen take most of the courses, they don't know whether they will end up after graduation as nuclear power nerds, or leading men as a Marine infantry man, or flying a helicopter or plane, or walking the deck of a destroyer.

However, USNA solved what they perceived as the problem of too many (say) English majors the same way they solved the diversity problem, by redefining. They created an economics major with more math, called Quantitative Economics, and moved it from the column of Group III to the technical groups. That gave them the numbers of technical majors they could live with, and by and large they left the non-technical ones alone. That in turn meant that the students who wanted to major in English, regardless of gender, could do so. Proportionally more women than men choose the nontechnical majors, but because there were so many more men than women in the Brigade, that meant that a fairly even mix of men and women could be English majors without endangering their futures. So my classes felt normal to me, co-educational.

And here's some good news: At Annapolis you can be an English major and not be condemned to a future of flipping burgers! You are commissioned into the Navy or Marine Corps just like all other graduates. If male, you may take guff from your buddies about choosing a "bull" major—but if you are strong, you can pull it off. (The term "bull" was still in the student's book of facts they had to memorize, called "Reef Points," when I arrived. I was the one who objected to it, and miraculously, it was removed: this belonged to the same generation that referred to all foreign languages as "dago," as in "what dago are you taking?")

Most of the students I have taught at Annapolis weren't English majors, who chose to take the upper-level class I was teaching. Two out of my three classes every semester were almost always (with rare exceptions) the required freshman classes of two semesters for plebes. I long ago realized I had to directly face the fact that plebes didn't want to take these classes in freshman English, which includes both literature and writing exercises. Otherwise, they just sit there and withdraw.

So, I began by saying, "You guys don't want to be here, I know." They would look around with guilty smiles. "Hey," I would say, "I've been here twenty-nine/thirty/thirty-one years [or whatever]. I know you don't."

"No, sir," they say.

"So, ask me why you should be here in English class," I counter.

"OK," they say, "Why should we be here?"

And then I tell them.

I say: You should be here because this class teaches you to synthesize data and arrive at defensible conclusions, and to learn to be able to justify those conclusions. These are essential skills in the military and in life. Plus, it helps you figure out who you are and how you relate to other people, the characters in literature, who may be very different than you. Knowing who you are is essential to being in the military, because if you don't know who you are you can't deal with the problems of your enlisted who don't know who they are.

Not only do Naval Academy plebes not want to be in a required English class, whose utility for their being officers they deny, but also many of them see no point in being in classes at all. (I've had students tell me they didn't realize they had to take college classes at Annapolis.) So, I play a game with them. I ask, If I had the power to give you your commission as an ensign/US Marine Corps (USMC) 2LT now, would you take it from my hand? Most say, "Hell, yeah, sir!"

So, then I say, "Let's talk about this. I have skills to teach you that you don't have. You need them before you are officers. You should refuse to take the commission. Literature has, as its point, self-knowledge. Self-knowledge is essential to a leader. You need these skills."

I already get points for being able to tell them, correctly, that they don't want to be there. And more points for being willing to talk sometimes about what they really want to talk about—not the short story or Act III of a play. Usually that means the absurdities and frustrations of the US Naval Academy, or problems in the military at large. They are most interested in the Academy itself, which overshadows anything we might talk about in classes. Not talking about what bothers you makes it worse. And these plebes have three more years of this place ahead of them. Best to come to terms with it now, or decide that they are going to leave (some do).

I also get points by dressing nicely for them. The judge who reinstated me called me "fashion-conscious," which I suppose comes from my several years as a print model in the D.C. area, and also from my realization that military uniforms are largely about men looking sharp for other me—as well as from my own sense of having always to live up to my own expectations for myself, to put my best foot forward. It's a fact: men want to see a superior who looks great. They themselves have to look snappy, so the person in front of them is supposed to show the self-respect, and respect for them, of doing so too. They spend a lot of time on uniforms at Annapolis. The midshipmen are issued everything ranging from regulation gym gear, to hot weather short-sleeved shirts, to their double-breasted "navy blue" suits, to the waiter jackets with gold cummerbunds of mess gear, like the Ken dolls they are treated as. During the introductory boot camp of plebe summer before freshman year, they have uniform races to see who can change the fastest, and at any time, they can be punished for having the wrong uniform, or for looking sloppy. And so, given also how much time the midshipmen spend obsessing about their clothes (that's the Naval Academy's show over substance in a nutshell), I figured I have to put out too. I know I have the substance, so I vowed to give them the show too.

My experience has been that they are appreciative of the trouble I take to look spiffy for them, and very, very interested in the gear. They want to know what my jackets are made of (cashmere, say, or a silk/wool combination—I even have a jacket made of bamboo, which they liked), and if they want to feel the material, I take it off and pass it around. (I take it off for pushups anyway, which we do if they are sleepy.) I explain about tailoring, and the fact that worked-out men need to have the waist taken in, as US suits or jackets are made with a six inch "drop," the difference between chest and waist—far too little for athletic males, as all of us in the room are. They are interested in my cufflinks—I explain that today's, say, started life as earrings in India in about 1850, and in my stable of watches—they like the Rolexes, and ask me to pass them around. I compliment them when they are wearing their SDBs, the double-breasted suits, which makes them look very adult. They tell me if they like something I'm wearing. This takes two minutes at the beginning of class, then they have a few minutes to tell me what's new. Or tell a joke or two. Then we get down to work. It's an investment in bonding that is always worth it.

The judge who reinstated me also noted that I am a "workout fiend," which gives me something else in common with my students. I'm lucky I like the clothes, and can do the pushups. (I start the semester with a set of one-armed pushups, which of course is showing off, but it always gets them, every time.) What I have learned from this is that if you're self-assured and not defensive, you can establish a relationship with people you want to guide that is more personal, because they will never mistake it for loss of authority. And that makes everybody happy.

In short, I play the cards that I know will work with them. I can't talk to them about Schopenhauer or Kant, or the books I write, and since it turned out I had these cards that I discovered appeal strongly to young men (and women) at a military academy, that's what I play. They have little intrinsic interest in the material or the skills I am offering, so the next best thing is to have them interested in pleasing me. And that means impressing them—and to a certain extent, putting on a show. So I do. I suppose it's demeaning if you get high and mighty and tell yourself they ought to be more interested in the material. But they aren't, so you go with Plan B. And that's what I learned to do. Most professors at Annapolis don't have the option for such a Plan B, which is why the midshipmen sleep through other classes, if at all possible, and tell me sheepishly that this is the one class they look forward to.

Elsewhere, playing these cards to get students to pay attention would be useless, and even counter-productive. This is so partly because the students at civilian universities aren't all issued multiple outfits they have to wear at different times of day, and don't have to take gym and pass a physical test each semester. But also, it's probably because they may be interested in other things—like the subject matter of the course. One day I happened to mention to a friend who teaches at an Ivy League university that I did one-armed pushups for the students. He was silent for a long moment, as if unsure how to respond to such a ridiculous statement. Then he said, in a voice he was clearly trying to keep as neutral as possible, "I can't think of anything that would impress students *less* at [X University] than doing one-armed pushups."

"Yes," I said. "I probably would have thought it odd at any of my colleges as well. But it sure works at Annapolis."

Dealing with literature is a skill. And responding to it, another set of skills. Prime among these is, can you justify your assertion? Midshipmen, like freshmen everywhere (with the exception of a small handful of students), are sloppy readers. They read quickly, if at all (I have learned to keep texts short, because otherwise they won't read them) and tend to fill out the details from their own preconceptions. So, what I teach is that they have to actually pay attention to what they see, not go with what they want to see. That, I tell them, is a useful skill in life and essential in the military, where they could conceivably be called upon to make judgment calls in dicey situations. Drawing on a scene from the movie *The Hurt Locker*, where the EOD guy has to decide if the man apparently selling pirated CDs from a cart up the street is only doing that, or whether he is an enemy who has to be countered, I tell them that gathering clues from what you see is necessary to making an informed decision—not necessarily the right one, but at least the best one under these circumstances. And it's useful that literature is almost more subtle than the obvious things they might get at first glance—like a guy selling CDs.

To make this point, I sometimes start the unit on poetry with a poem by James Dickey that is widely anthologized, called "Cherrylog Road." They read it in class preparation beforehand. I tell them: read it three times, the first to get the gist, the second to see why that is in fact the gist (what data are they given?), and the third to appreciate things like word choice and repeating patterns that may mean something. I tell them to apply the Santa Claus rule—making a list and checking it twice: if you see something happen in the poem once, it may not be all that relevant. But if you see it again, you should be on high alert— as if the man with the CDs makes that same odd movement twice of reaching under his cart. And if you see it a third time you can be sure it means something.

Midshipmen typically hate poems, because those they read in high school were read under duress and with teachers they felt no connection with, teachers who told them to look for "deep meanings." In fact, there is no such thing as deep meaning; all you can do is pay better attention to the surface—unless the phrase "deep meanings" is shorthand for just paying attention. I draw a schematic bunny rabbit on the board (a circle for the body, a smaller one for the head, and an even smaller one for the tail, with ears and whiskers) and then make the universal cross-out circle and line meaning No. Then I say: I bet your high school English teacher (whom I refer to generically as Miss Smith) let you go around in circles for forty-nine minutes, then pulled a bunny rabbit out of the hat in the last minute that you didn't see coming and had no idea how to get yourself. Right? They agree that this was so. No bunny rabbits here! I say. This means I want to teach you how to see the data, synthesize it, and draw conclusions yourself. It's meant to show them how to be active responsible adults in understanding the world, not passive onlookers as they largely are at Annapolis, passengers in a roller coaster they do not control. By the way, no administrator ever asked me why I teach the way I do, or what I had discovered about the students. Ask a civilian? Pah!

"Cherrylog Road" seems on a cursory reading to be about a young man who meets his girlfriend in a car junkyard to have sex, arriving and leaving on his motorcycle. Because sex is all but impossible for plebes (it's forbidden in Bancroft Hall for everyone, but the upper class have loads of it in the Hall that the administration punishes when it finds out), they like the idea. And so, invariably, when I ask them what the poem is about when I open the discussion the next class period, that's what they tell me.

Poems are always about something, even poems without a plot, and you have to be able to justify your assertion. I tell them I have had many students who say, "Sir, you can say anything you want because it's just a poem"—so much bad high school teaching! (I also tell them they don't always have to start with "Sir." Once or twice per hour does it.) Or perhaps, given the pro-military and athletic nature of my students, it came from so much teaching from teachers whom they did not respect or want to emulate. I say it's definitely not about why Mickey has three fingers plus a thumb on each hand, right? When they say "right," I explain that with poems there are some things you can say about poems with 100 percent certainty, like whether it's about Mickey, and then some you can be pretty sure about, because the poem gives you repeating patterns that suggest something strongly. But at some point, the sidewalk ends (most have read Shel Silverstein). That's where you can begin to get fancy about reminds-you-of and can-also-be-applied-to. Simply because literature trails off into individual associations doesn't mean it's completely in this spot all the time.

In that, I say, it's certainly different from engineering, where it's black or white, true or false. But it's much closer to life. I ask them to consider going on a first date. Did he/she like me or not? You list the evidence through pros and cons and usually have a feeling which way it tilts. But certain things may remain unclear, and finally, you may not know. If you go on another date, you may get more information, but what if you are ghosted or turned down? You're in the same position as with a poem, which can't talk to you. All the evidence it will ever give you is right there. You can pay better attention, and so be aware of more, like Sherlock Holmes, but the crime scene isn't going to change. And I'm not going to pull a bunny rabbit out of the hat. The evidence is there so what I can do is show you how to see it—and as a result, you can justify your own conclusions. You can be active about figuring it out and don't have to wait for the teacher going "whah-whah-whah" like in Charlie Brown.

So, I ask them to justify their conclusion that the boy arrives on a motorcycle and has sex with his girlfriend, whose name is apparently Doris. They show me the passage—it's in first person, and he says he thought he heard her. She then is described as stealing car parts to serve as a reason for her father not to beat her unmercifully—the imaginary scene is described in lurid and sadomasochistic detail (and note that this is a boy with a vivid imagination—we'll come back to that in a moment, class!). The list starts with things that already take time to pry off or out of old cars, such as (certainly rusted) spark plugs (and I tell about my adventures changing all that in my first car, a 1966 Studebaker), then goes to the even harder to remove headlights—but it's what comes next that clinches the deal. Bumpers. Not just one bumper but more than one? And I explain that in the old days, bumpers were separable but firmly bolted on and very heavy (the Studebaker again). So, there's something fishy here. And that noise of tapping ascribed to Doris? Grammar matters, and if you look at the subject of that sentence, class, you see it's the sun—which makes sense, as the metal heats up.

And then the sex scene, where the words get more and more frenetic until the money shot of many words in quick succession that start with the explosive letter "b." How would you film it if you were making a movie? What would the camera see? The poem tells us that someone would have seen the car door closing inexplicably from within. Closing, but inexplicably, with no agent. What sense does that make if Doris opens it from outside and gets in?

Silence. And what did she do with her bumpers?

And now let's go back to what the boy has been doing. With 100 percent certainty, he's been getting into these old cars, which are referred to as being dead—which suggests that cars were once actually alive (start thinking about patterns of words related to death, class), pretending to be their long-gone owners. In one sort of *Driving Miss Daisy* car, he pretends to be not (as we might expect) the male driver but the old woman in the back, which seems a bit odd for a horny young man about to get laid. He lives in fantasy; it's clear, fantasies associated with death, including what the kudzu is held to have done to the cars and the last line that seems to indicate a death wish on the part of the boy, to become wreckage like the cars.

So, something about death. Doris, in all probability, is imaginary—but yes, there's something sexual for him about this junkyard described in terms of death as well as his image of a Doris (clearly a big girl if she can stick several bumpers under her arm or pry them off to begin with), and probably he masturbates, alone in the car with his imagination. The money shot is pretty clear. This is no longer 100 percent sure, but over 50 percent probable, they agree.

And if no Doris, what is he doing there at all? He no longer seems the swaggering muscular stand-in they wanted to visualize. Is his ride a motorcycle or a bicycle—the poem calls it the latter, but one that's powerful (or is he the power?—that's a defensible reading too). It isn't clear which it is, though the students imagine the more manly motorcycle. Yet suddenly the bicycle seems more likely, now that we see him more as a weedy masturbatory adolescent drawn to death and other people's lives, themselves long dead. What percentage of probability, class?

There's a range, and no right answer. Somewhere upward of 60 per-cent I'd say—only how old the boy is falls in the same category as that famous New Critical question of literary theory from the mid-twentieth century, how many children had Lady Macbeth? How many children is not in the text of Shakespeare's *Macbeth*, so we can't say. And it's not relevant exactly how many, just that Lady Macbeth knew what it was to "have given suck." Here, we don't have to know whether the boy is a weedy fourteen or fifteen, but that range is far more plausible than a worked-out twenty-one. And so, I imagine him with pimples and liter-ally a bicycle, destined for no great things if he spends his time jerking off in a junkyard because it has the smell of death, living in fantasies. Or destined to be a poet? Also possible.

So there is a point where the pavement ends. Can we even say the junkyard is real rather than imaginary? Unless everything is a dream and then you wake up (a classic young writer's trope), the junkyard seems real enough. A male arrives on some two-wheeler in a junkyard, imagines things, and leaves: that's close to 100 percent. Then things get dicier. But they get dicier in a pattern, and we can follow the clues to say what is certain, what is probable, and what is beyond the end of the sidewalk. Just like life.

One last question, class—we have five minutes. You see that what you started with (real sex, real girlfriend) is contradicted or at least made very improbable by the evidence of the poem—and no bunny rabbits! Assuming what we have now is a defensible summary of the evidence (and if I'm wrong, show me—silence), what's the point of writing a poem about imagination and death and sex and youth?

Admittedly this is a stretch for my students. They are not typically weedy aesthetes who might appreciate this. At another school, where the students are not so uniform, and not in uniform, someone would have seen all the death (if not the bumpers) and begun to draw some conclu-sions, or used that as the dangling thread that, pulled on, unraveled a good deal more. But that's the reason why I have them read this poem at the Naval Academy. I'm pretty sure they will see it as they do, namely as their own fantasy. Which means they have failed to understand what was in front of them, like the EOD guy getting the wrong read on the man ostensibly selling CDs. And that can be fatal. So yes. I've set them up, laid a trap I'm pretty sure they will fall into. In my first years, I couldn't have said this, because I didn't know them well enough. After a decade or so, I did. And for two decades thereafter.

There are unforgivable misinterpretations—this poem is not about why Mickey has three fingers on each hand—and there are forgivable ones. Dickey has set the poem up so it's in the imagination of this young man, and this young man is clearly imagining Doris, so it's forgivable for readers who read too quickly to think she's flesh and blood rather than imaginary. And even the imaginary Doris is a lot more plausible than the other imaginary (dead) people evoked in the poem, and the boy's motivation for (so to say) calling her into life more accessible.

And the sex seems real, if probably solitary. The poem does seem to have a money shot: the passage with all the alliterative, even onomatopoetic "b" sounds—so Dickey is responsible for my students' error—that's the point of the poem, to some degree: that imagination can be almost real, or realer than real. But if you pay attention to all the evidence, you can figure out what is merely blurry, and what the reader adds. That's an important distinction in life, I tell them. If you want to believe so desperately that your date is into you that you ignore cues, that's bad. But if you really can't say, that's another. Conspiracy theories are spun by people who desperately want to believe what they have no evidence for. In the military, as in life, you have to resist doing that. Or even with this this sexual assault business: gentlemen, you have to be sure she consents. Look at body language. Ask. Even a "yes" can mean no if you've forced it, or if it seems hesitant. Evidence is a bear, but it matters.

I am pretty sure that midshipmen will fall into the trap Dickey and I have laid because I know the type of kid they are—and it is a type. Even a state university has a type, and elite private schools definitely have a type. But less tied to type are the problems with one of the most-cited poems in English, Robert Frost's "The Road Not Taken." Students everywhere almost invariably say it's about being your own (wo)man, taking the road "less traveled by," which "has made all the difference," because it's read in a lot of high schools and that's what they are told, and so what they take on board. Namely, that the poem is what midshipmen call "motivational." (At Annapolis everything is either motivational or not.) Be your own (wo)man!

Yet it's not titled "The Road Less Traveled By," but the much more regretful "The Road Not Taken," so that already calls in question the "motivational" reading that imbues the last line, "and that has made all the difference," with braggadocio rather than rue. And it's set in the autumn of a "yellow wood": in Western literature familiar with four seasons, autumn means incipient death and dying, and the narrator is "sorry"—hardly a motivational beginning. (In Rwanda, a few degrees south of the equator with no seasonal variation, the students were stumped by this aspect of the English poetry I taught.) Instead, I start by focusing on the question, is the road he takes, in fact, less traveled by? At first, the narrator seems to think so—the roads diverging in the yellow wood, he looks down both and takes the one that "wanted wear"—but then immediately concedes ("though as for that") both were covered in leaves that "no step had trodden black," so he couldn't actually say which was less traveled by. And anyway, the paths curved away and were lost to view.

So why does he say at the end that he "took the one less traveled by"? Look a couple of lines further up—and consider a timeline, I encourage the class. The narrator is how old now? And how old when the roads diverged? Maybe forty for now, twenty for the roads diverging? So, what's up with the end? How old is he imagining himself being? Sixty to seventy? It's "ages and ages hence"—which is a pretty unmotivational way of summarizing a lot of life, to put it in Annapolis terms. And he will be telling it "with a sigh," which sounds pretty sad. What will he be saying, an old man? He imagines, at perhaps forty, that he will be bragging about himself when he is seventy as the staunch loner who succeeded. So, he knows about the lies of old age.

Alternately, it's possible this is literally true. We don't know whether the difference is good or bad. And anyway, each of us travels a road of one—our own. Sure, it makes us different. But it also is necessarily so—not a choice but a logical necessity where each of us travels his/her/their own path.

So, what is the poem about? The fact that we never see where our paths lead? The fact that we have to sometimes just blindly pick one path? The fact that whatever it leads to will define us (our path) as a human? That we may lie about it to the young to make it seem much more chosen than chance? The fact that all of us are alone? That we are lost in an autumnal wood that reminds us of Dante Alighieri's wood? The sidewalk ends at some point. But with 100 percent certainty, it's not about why Mickey has only three fingers plus a thumb.

Because I know my audience after so many decades, I can pick and choose works that I can be pretty sure they will be interested in. Younger professors at less job-oriented schools don't have that luxury, because they don't know their students. Still, the young, such as many college students are, tend to have similar interests, and if you know what these are, you can find works that speak to their situation. These interests are typically, sex and finding their way in the world, as well as a combination of fear and assertion about their own success—at any rate, it's a completely different stance than the position of much older people, and also different from the middle-aged, who are dealing with the reality of having achieved their goals, or not.

If I were teaching at a civilian university, I probably wouldn't have the same list of essential works—but some would remain. The sonnets of Shakespeare are essential regardless of what you do when you graduate, at least some of them (73, 29, 130, for instance—the last about the allure of Barbie dolls and GI Joe). Maybe the troubling stories of Heinrich von Kleist that show the chaos lurking under our surface of order, or George Orwell's *Burmese Days* about the mask of command we assume when we conquer another people.

A good part of the situation of traditional college students is that they are young. And libraries are full of works that are unlikely to resonate with the young. For example, I remember that I completely failed to get the point of Gustave Flaubert's *Madame Bovary* when I read it as a late teenager. It's about fantasies and how they give way to reality, or rather should give way, but in the case of Emma Bovary do not do so, as we pass important milestones—in her case, marriage and motherhood. At that point in my life, I was still sure I knew how things were going to turn out for me. But of course, they didn't.

Unlike Madame Bovary, I coped with the fact that reality didn't end up being like my dreams—that actually were a lot more realistic (?) than Emma's to begin with. Or maybe not. But anyhow, if you'd told me at age twenty I would end up teaching for decades at an institution that is as fundamentally anti-intellectual as the Naval Academy, I would have said you were crazy. If I knew that I would be divorced from the woman I loved and who was meant for me, but where the love turned to its opposite, with her two daughters I had adopted completely estranged, then my own daughter turning out to be autistic, then a second marriage with two boys, or that my brother would die from AIDS—no. Of course, it's good we don't know what the future holds.

But that's precisely why I feel it necessary, or at least a good idea, to read and discuss *Madame Bovary* with plebes, as well as "The Road Not Taken." I have had pretty good success with *Madame Bovary* precisely because I know what the young won't get about it. I didn't, after all, and I was far more attuned to things literary than they are. So, I can anticipate their objections. Most of the men say Emma is just a slut (well, she is) who should have made a nice home for Charles. I counter by knowing what their dreams are—starting with the Naval Academy and moving to glory in battle—and ask, would you give these up? Should you? That quiets them down fast, and they grow thoughtful.

Though I almost always taught two sections of plebes, my third class (again, at USNA we teach three a semester, year in and year out—more than at research institutions, but less than at a community college) was upper-level. Because my background isn't narrow, and I've taught in Europe, India, and Africa, I've been able to teach almost all the courses in our curriculum: courses in poetry, the nineteenth century novel, Romanticism, Modernism, drama, and many others—including a go at a Marcel Proust–James Joyce–Thomas Mann course (difficult because the texts are long, a deal-breaker at Annapolis). As special topics courses,

I taught literature by Indians and Africans in response to the colonial experience, as well as the Academy's first Middle East literature course, which included Persian poetry, tales from the *Thousand and One Nights*, the Koran (in translation, which is called an "interpretation" because the angel Gabriel is said to have dictated the suras of which it is composed to the Prophet in Arabic, and language matters), and contemporary works by writers such as the Nobel Prize–winner Naguib Mahfouz. I taught a course in Indian classics in translation (there is no standard text of these in any language) including the *Ramayana* and the *Mahabharata* (whose famous conversation about the role of the warrior, known as the *Bhagavad Gita*, is essential for future soldiers).

It turned out the administration didn't care about any of this. Criticism of the way they run the Academy was the deal-breaker. Loyalty meant not commitment to the mission but individual support of the brass. The semester I was ripped from the classroom as a "danger to the students," I had put together a course in Romantic to Modernist French and German literature—*Faust* I, Friedrich Schiller's *Mary Stuart*, some classic German novellas, Gustave Flaubert, Émile Zola, up through Albert Camus and Christa Wolf. On February 1, I was handed the letter barring me from the classroom and from having contact with students, or they with me. And I never saw them again. If you're reading this: I love you guys.

Here's what I know: some works just aren't for young men, the majority of my students. I decided after trying a couple of times that there just wasn't any way I could teach Jane Austen to a group of largely male plebes: I could probably teach it to ten older women in an elective course, but it's just too female, too oriented toward marriage, and sees men from too distanced a perspective to be palatable to young men who didn't see themselves in those terms. That was a bit sad, but I accepted it, because I too had had a "huh?" reaction to Jane Austen at their age. It was only later that I came to see that the agonizing constraints of her world—women sit still and watch as men pass briefly by, having to grab a likely one based on insufficient information that condemns them both to a lifetime of unhappiness—are generically the same as the constraints on my world, or on anybody's. And anyway, it's not just women who are limited in this way in Austen's world. The same is true for the men, like Mr. Bennet in *Pride and Prejudice*, who find themselves married forever to ninnies who once were young and hot: the man was thinking with the wrong head for sure. But that's how the young think. Are mistakes inevitable? Maybe. But a world before divorce! It all seems so foreign to our world of hookups. Class, discuss!

I had to get older to see myself in Jane Austen's heroines. And eventually I did, knowing that we are all in prison cells, even if we don't see them. But that is a realization of age. The midshipmen were simply too young, and too male—and even the women weren't focused on marriage—and didn't see the traps that life had set for them. I had to learn the hard way. And so would they. Unfortunately, the chances of their trying Jane Austen at forty are pretty slim. I joke and tell them we need the twenty-year reunion course. They laugh. I'm serious.

If I can see myself in Elizabeth Bennet, or a black character, then black kids don't need a black professor, literature by black authors, or a novel with a black heroine. Why not, sure. But they don't need it any more than I need novels about a middle-aged professor at a military institution. OK, there isn't such a thing as classic or canonic literature, so the old farts should stop saying that, because the black lesbians have their cue to say, "But it's straight white men! Not black lesbians!" Which is quite true. But if I can see myself in a black lesbian, they can also see themselves in Virgil's Aeneas. Or his Dido. Sure, include the works by, about, or taught by black lesbians if they have enough substance. But not just because they're about or by black lesbians. Because if you emphasize that quality alone, you disappoint many of the black lesbians who don't think seeing characters of that description is enough in a work of literature, and who want more substantial themes to chew on. Readers aren't as narcissistic and mirror-gazing as much graduate school propaganda about force-feeding literature from marginal groups seems to think. And the straight white boys will stay away.

My least favorite poem of all time is the much-anthologized A. E. Housman hymn to early death, "To an Athlete Dying Young" (which yes, I thought profound at age nineteen—there's the ignorance of youth again, in this case mine). "Smart lad, to slip betimes [early] away/ From fields where glory does not stay" Die young, you're better off? Die after you set a village record for a footrace? You really think there is nothing beyond that? Not marriage, say, and children, and passing it on? Housman was another repressed bitter old man—even when young. At twenty his narrator in "Loveliest of Trees" is thinking about his death at seventy as a reason to enjoy the cherry blossoms in the spring. Makes me sick. I knew I wouldn't be able to do one-armed pushups forever, my party trick to impress the midshipmen, but I did know that they loved it when I did them. Don't give up until you have to. Old age gets us all, but that doesn't mean you should run toward it,

Some things I taught, I realized, were probably beyond them at their age—Tennyson's "Idylls of the King," for example, which I taught as part of a class in poetry in order to read something other than the more accessible short lyric poems that were its staple. (At the Naval Academy, short homework is good, and long is death—for the midshipmen, class preparation is an imposition, something to be done in a hurry and not well, and with a thousand other things they have to do for their company officer.) It's all in blank verse, unrhymed iambic pentameter (duh-*dah*-duh-*dah*-duh-*dah*-duh-*dah*-duh-*dah*)—we talk about all these terms—and also other forms of poetry: What is a sonnet? A sestina? Terza rima? To be sure, I discovered that I could make some parts of it speak to their situation—Arthur's death, for example, "Le Morte [sic] d'Arthur," written first in the book of "Idylls." It's about battlefield death and survivors' guilt and loneliness. That they get, because they are at a military institution, and I read this poem aloud in many classes. (Me reading aloud is good for them, as it brings the words off the page and makes the events live. I also read *Charlotte's Web* with some skipping, and always cry. I identify with Charlotte.)

But the larger theme of the whole collection of Tennyson's Arthur poems is the fragility of order in a world of chaos. And this was simply not accessible to them. We can create the Round Table, but it's fated to dissolve from the beginning because it's made of humans who can't help being human, and sexes that can't help being sexual. Tennyson is clear that Arthur is a temporary phenomenon—brought by Merlin to bring order. But Arthur himself is perhaps (since there are several versions of his birth) the result of a rape, a violation of order brought on by lust, but that makes him the legitimate king, given his apparent biological father. Which means that for Tennyson here, legitimacy is produced by individual error. And of course, Guinevere's love for Lancelot is totally understandable, since Lancelot is a real and hence fallible man, and Arthur, while perfect, is a stick. She says so, using other terms. The knights are fallible as well, too taken with the excitement of running after the Grail rather than staying home and doing their boring day job of keeping order. So of course it all falls apart, as Tennyson knew it would. That's his point. The ideal isn't real.

The fact that, as Tennyson knew, order is possible but by definition transitory, is something I cannot convey to twenty-one-year-olds who hate their lives at the Naval Academy and who think that, when they are let out of prison at graduation, they will soar. They don't, as they come back to tell me years later. But at that point they still believe it. Camelot was what they dreamed the Naval Academy would be and now know is not. So, they have transferred their dreams to the fleet, the real Navy or Marine Corps. What Tennyson knew is that Camelot is intrinsically transitory, wherever you locate it.

This is also the message of Keats's "Ode on a Grecian Urn," which I call the "Universal Poem." (I got a text recently from a young Marine officer, a student of mine who graduated several years ago—his wife was also a student of mine whom he met in my class—saying he had managed to talk about this last poem with his enlisted men. I guess my life hasn't been in vain!) And this one is short enough that I have a decent chance of making headway with it. You'd think the best part of life is when you've achieved your goal. But it isn't. It's the moment before, because once you achieve it, it becomes reality, the everyday. You have it, so you have to strive for something else. Or crumple.

The boy on the urn, who is physically so perfect he could be a Greek god ("what men or gods or these?"—Keats starts with several males, then focuses on only one) is about to kiss the girl, but cannot because (surprise!) he's carved marble and can't move. But that means he never gets old, he never stops chasing, and the girl never gets old (and so, by extension, undesirable—yes, the poem is written from the boy's point of view). We humans get to achieve our goals, at least sometimes. However, we also grow older and lose steam, and the goal probably becomes less desirable. We, unlike the boy, can achieve our goals. But does that make us happy?

Not at all, the narrator tells us. When we humans achieve our goals, we are left with a "heart high-sorrowful and cloy'd"—cloyed meaning satiated or overfilled, as I have to discuss with students. Maybe we even get the flu: "a burning forehead and a parching tongue." What that means is that we have to find another goal to chase after—and so for the rest of our lives. I discuss this necessity to always have a goal—its attainment is secondary, perhaps (according to Keats) even a let-down. If you win a Nobel Prize one day, you still have to get up the next day and go for a run. Human beings are not frozen like the people on the urn, but caught in the flow of time, so we always have to be doing something. I'm trying to encourage teenagers to never give up. I don't know if it works.

The boy chasing the girl shouldn't be disappointed he can never get her ("do not grieve," the narrator says, addressing the excited boy), because he's at the peak of perfection, and so is his desire, just like the trees around them that will never lose their leaves. (This is a sort of joke, the narrator telling the boy not to grieve. The reader realizes that the fact the boy is frozen, and marble, means he's not grieving—nor can he be reasoned with.) In sum, the urn is so beautiful because it freezes desire at its peak, which also means the desire for the urn boy, who is made of marble, can never be achieved.

In real life, by contrast, people with "breathing human passion" (unlike the non-breathing carved people) can achieve their goals. But it's not their achievement that satisfies us, only chasing them. That's where art comes in: we imagine what it would be like to stop things at their high point. Wouldn't it be nice! We can only dream—or make urns, or poems about perfection. That's the human lot: we create things, here the urn, or the poem, that are more perfect than (Keats says "above") our endless cycle of pursuit, possible attainment, and disappointment, followed by another pursuit, and so on until death. But what they represent is unattainable for us.

Yet we can dream. And this is precisely why we make depictions of a perfection we can never actually achieve—given that, being human, we aren't frozen, but always part of a process. Our best shots at portraying this ideal may be the physically perfect marble statues of the Classical world—or many other things meant to last forever. Of course they don't actually do this. Consider Percy Bysshe Shelley's "Ozymandias," about the monument to a powerful king now destroyed by time. And centuries before Shelley, Shakespeare pointed out (in "Sonnet 55") that time gets even marble monuments—so actually, according to Shakespeare, only poetry is eternal, not even the monuments. But certainly, stone monuments are at least longer lived than people. And that makes them unreal depictions of unattainable perfection because they escape (at least for a while) the endless degradation of time or the cycles of pursuit in a human's life. Certainly we like to look at them. Maybe, I suggest, they inspire us. Maybe I also want the students to understand that their own physical perfection as worked-out late teenagers and early twenties adults is something they will have to sweat to keep going, and that it won't last forever. Maybe I want them to see my situation of "pretty darn good, if not perfection, kept going by hard work," which also will be theirs in a few decades. Unless, of course, they just give in to time, letting it work its will on them as they let the Academy do so now.

It's certainly sad how short a time youthful physical perfection lasts. I have former students knock on my door to say hello whom I barely recognize, even though it hasn't been all that many years since I saw them as fresh-faced twenty-year-olds. They are out of the Navy and don't have to work out, so they don't. One midshipman said to me one day, "I can't wait to get fat." Many of those who knock on my door have done so; many more have apparently lost their quickness, gone gray or balding, the light of striving gone from their eyes. Maybe that was because of a divorce, a cheating spouse, or the reality of military life—and then, what to do after? Once the Navy or Marine Corps no longer tells you what to do, you have to self-motivate—something most of them have never had to do.

"What happened to you?" I want to say. But I know what happened: life. And of course, I don't say that. I say "Hey, good to see you, howyadoin?" To myself, I think they could have, indeed should have, resisted the passage of time more strongly. Because that's what we have to do. That, or just give up, as it seems they may have done. Maybe they weren't paying attention when we read Keats. Or thought it didn't apply to them.

I'd say that the fact that we are all caught in the flow of time is precisely why we love these unreal depictions of perfection that never grow old. So for an essay, rather than writing a standard English class analysis of the poem's structure or word choice, I ask plebes to find a monument in the Naval Academy Yard that is as inspirational, but as unreal as the eternally desiring and eternally muscular men and beautiful women on Keats's urn, and write about it using the poem as a point of comparison. Many choose the fairly recent statue to Admiral James Stockdale behind the gym I used for decades (until I went to an even better one on the other side of campus), who came back from imprisonment in the Hanoi Hilton a broken man.

But what's this statue? It's a cocky, young buck in the prime of life striding purposefully forward with his helmet under his arm: eternally beautiful, eternally young. That's the nature of many, if not all, monuments at the Naval Academy, all of which prove Keats's point: we want to freeze eternity before the trajectory goes down. And in real life, it always does. I know this, and I can at least tell them, so that when they are no longer at the top of the arc, they aren't surprised. That's pretty sour stuff, but I can get most of them to see it by comparing their golden dreams of what the Naval Academy would be to its slogging, inchoate reality. Even after a few months, almost all get this.

I don't think this filling them full of dreams that will be shattered is fair to the young: if you're going to drop them, don't build them up so much. Be realistic with applicants—and the world at large—about what the Academy is and isn't. But, of course, the brass will never tell the truth as their self-image and standing in the world are built on the fantasy. See VADM Buck's hooya quoted above.

It's not just this poem that punctures illusions. I've also come to realize that the bitterness of most literature is itself foreign to the hope-fulness of the young—these young in particular, who are perhaps more full of dreams than the average. And we talk about that: I have to be honest with them and also explain to them why they and most people, especially young people, typically find literature so foreign. It says: You don't get what you want. We all die. Plans fall apart. That's the message of Great Literature. All of it. Yet, of course, this is so. *Oohrah* doesn't make it off the page—I can give them *oohrah* in person, with my pres-ence and voice and body, but the voice of literature is too soft, and its attempts at *oohrah* seem ridiculous. The only emotion that can survive on the page is a qualified "yes, but." Serious literature is like preserved food—it's emotion recollected in tranquility. So, it all has a common taste and a common message: it says, consider this. Not: go get laid. Or go for a run. Or cook up a nice dinner. Or hug your honey. So sure. Literature is selling a specific bill of goods. Let's admit this and discuss it.

But why read literature with the young at all? That is a question that has to be posed, and answered. They don't understand half of it. A third. A tenth? I guess I'd say: the point of talking about big topics with the young who can't possibly understand them is that doing so immunizes them, at least to a small degree, against despair. Oh, they think later on: I got what I thought I wanted but I'm not happy! That's Keats. He knew. I guess that's normal. We get old and realize we were all alone in a lonely wood—Frost. Spring is rebirth and winter death: almost all Western poetry. When it happens to us, we realize it's not just us, it's everybody. And somehow, they all kept going. So, I can keep going too.

Life's a bitch and then you die. Literature can't change that. But it can help prepare you for it. And accept it. Because you don't have a choice. But the professor who tells you this can't be old and crabby, or too young and shrill and trying to shove something down your throat: s/

he has to be enthusiastic, well dressed (if possible), athletic, and not too pushy. Otherwise, it's all too bleak and unpleasant.

So every semester it's plebes, always plebes: their same listlessness to be turned into enthusiasm and forming the same audience for the same performance; they making the same grammatical errors; and me making the same points about anticipating objections in their arguments and highlighting their best argument, called their "flex," and giving the same exhortations to "write for Bill," the audience, imagined as the Bill the Goat mascot of the Naval Academy. Me to me: You gotta wake 'em up. And carry on. Pushups, or jumping up and down when they were falling asleep (called "getting floppy"), the same five-minute life lessons—how to avoid fried food in King Hall, the dining hall; how to try on a jacket or help a boyfriend do so. Even how to tie a bow tie—we had a bow tie day where I brought in twenty bow ties, and I showed them how. They have Navy-issue bow ties to go with the mess dress, but they're fake, like for six-year-olds. Use sunblock, dental floss, and condoms. (That lecture came before spring or fall break.)

And all that carrying on made them listen to the important stuff. Sure, it was entertainment, but it was also personal, not the transmission of brute information—that they would have mind-dumped after the test—but me being with them. I needed them to be paying attention to me, so I could take them where we needed to go. It was a form of leadership, which requires personal investment in the people you lead. You have to get them to respect you by respecting them, and you have to prove yourself to them every day, over and over. You lead with strength, not weakness—which is why the current craze to claim status as the greatest victims leaves the military, and most others, cold. It's better to use smiling strength, so the strength is empowering to those you lead, not directed against them, which is ineffective—what I call snarling strength, which doesn't turn out to be strength at all.

Leadership is not for people unsure of themselves—as many tiny individuals rattling around in the armor of military uniforms with stripes and stars are—because you expose who you really are to get them to bond with you. Not with your rank, but with you as an individual.

You have to look forward to seeing them, and they have to look forward to seeing you. So, you put on a show, look sharp in your clothes, do the pushups with them or for them, crack a joke, show them how to do stuff, smile broadly, then get down to business. Leadership for the secure is fun, but it's also hard work. You have to be "on" all the time. For the insecure, it's hell—as it also is for the people they are attempting so ineptly to lead.

WAR

Here's a fact I had to be conscious of 24/7: I teach literature to people whose job it will be, if ordered, to kill other people. They have to know this. Some don't. I'll never forget the student who was so shocked at finding out what really went on in war from a cluster of works I read with them in plebe English—the German novel *All Quiet on the Western Front* and some English World War I poets, including Wilfred Owen, Siegfried Sassoon, and Rupert Brooke—that he transferred to an Ivy League university, where he was very successful. The Naval Academy is all about playing soldier or sailor and does not make clear to these idealistic eighteen- to twenty-one-year-olds that war is about killing other people and possibly being killed or wounded yourself. The Naval Academy is all about putting on a show for tourists. Which means, lying to the students.

All Quiet on the Western Front is a translation into English of Erich Maria Remarque's most famous novel, which in German has the more clearly ironic title *Im Westen Nichts Neues, Nothing New in the West (of the War)*. The German title is ironic because, as we learn on the last page, it's the newspaper headline the day Paul Bäumer, the very last of the group we have followed for several years, dies (deployments for German troops were until death, not measured in months or indeed as having a time limit). For the folks back home—by this point Germany has all but lost the war, that sputters on for only a few more months before ending—the death of one soldier is meaningless. It's certainly not news.

The novel is written about, and from, the perspective of, a group of German boys who, under the influence of their high school teacher who extolls the virtues for young men of defending the fatherland, join the German army and are stuck in the trenches of the Western Front fighting the Allies. The Eastern Front with Russia (all this from the German perspective) figures in the novel only peripherally in the last section when Paul has contact with Russian prisoners of war and realizes that they are just people too, and rather sad ones at that.

The German title makes it clear that German civilians ask every day whether something meaningful has occurred in the war—something new—and are told that this day, there was "Nothing New in the West." Everybody in Germany knew West refers to the Front, so it doesn't even have to be spelled out, as it is in English. The fundamental point of the book is clear. Namely that war isn't about individuals at all; it's about groups. Individuals are a means to an end. And the military, therefore, cannot be about becoming a man, being all you can be, or pushing your limits, as midshipmen are told and as Hollywood movies tell us (and as recruiting ads nowadays say), because the individual is treated in fundamentally unindividual terms, un-Kantian in fact because the individual is not treated as an end in him- or herself but as part of a larger scheme.

In order to make this clear to the students, usually the plebes who have been engaged in their playacting roles for only a few months (novels are taught second semester along with poetry), I tell a story I concocted about pebbles. Let's postulate that the objective is getting a single pebble through a very small, high-up hole in the wall. To make this happen, a lot of pebbles have to be thrown. How many?

Perhaps the analogy they can visualize from countless World War II movies is a bunch of guys storming a beach. Only one has to make it to the top and throw the grenade in the place where the machine gun fire is coming from to win the battle—and who knows, maybe the war! They have all seen such movies, and I am amused to see them laugh sheepishly when I note that all of them visualize themselves as the one guy who throws the grenade and saves the day.

But, as I say to them, numerically speaking, the probability that you would be the single pebble that gets through the hole is small, and whether you are or not isn't up to you. So, I ask them to visualize scooping up pebbles in both hands—each pebble is a soldier. (Even though this is the Navy, they rarely imagine themselves reading a computer screen in the bowels of a ship.) If too many pebbles are scooped, that is bad strategy because that uses up the pebbles that now cannot be thrown somewhere else. If too few, that's bad strategy too because the likelihood of the objective being reached is too small. So, strategy intrinsically means using individuals as parts of a larger movement. Somebody else scoops you up in a war, in an offensive, in a battle. And then throws you.

Some pebbles will dribble out of the hand. Some will fall too low, some arc too high, and some fall wide and never reach the wall. With luck, one out of the middle of the spray will get through—that will be the guy who wins the medal, perhaps posthumously—as they acknowledge, by visualizing the hero, the fresh-faced, all-American boy we have identified with, who throws the grenade after fighting up the beach. But at the same time as he throws, a bullet with his name on it crosses its path and, in slow motion and to a Bach organ chorale, he dies after saving the day. That is glorious death in battle.

But that death is only for one guy, if that is glory. I evoke the opening sequence of Steven Spielberg's *Saving Private Ryan*. Some of the men in this assault—all of whom have trained just as hard as the others—never make it off the amphibs, dying in the water with colorful spirals of scarlet blood caught by the underwater cameras. Some make it to the beach and are mowed down as they emerge from the water. Some make it a bit further—and so on. And it's sheer luck who lives and who dies; the old days of you being stronger than the other guy so that your sword thrust is more telling being long over—what I call, laughing with them as we are all fellow gym rats—the bench press paradigm. In the age of mechanized warfare, begun in the first World War, it's not about anything you are responsible for: a machine gun is a machine gun, and a grenade is a grenade.

And gas is gas. That's the point of a poem I read with plebes just after Remarque's book, Wilfred Owen's most graphic poem, "Dulce et Decorum Est." One soldier is too slow to get his gas mask on and dies horribly with "froth-corrupted lungs" and his eyes "writhing" in his head. And then the punch line, blaming the old people who told him the "old lie" to get him to enlist: *Dulce et decorum est pro patria mori.* (The title of the poem, in truncating the phrase, hides the death.) It is sweet and fitting to die for your country—Horace's dictum. Dying from a sword thrust to the stomach as you might have done in Roman days when a barbarian's attack went home, or from sepsis afterward, is only marginally better than dying by coughing up your bloody bits of lungs. It isn't sweet for sure, nor could anyone have thought that even Horace meant that the act of dying painfully and violently felt *dulce et decorum* to you, just to others.

For several years the *Washington Post* published every couple of months "Faces of the Fallen" with pictures of dead soldiers from Iraq and Afghanistan. I'd bring it in to class. The deaths were organized by dates, so I'd ask them to give me a date, and we read the stories of that day—or the closest day to their dates. The people in the newspaper usually died by IEDs, the roadside bombs made from fertilizer, which I called shit bombs. Or they died by so-called friendly fire when the Afghan troops they were training turned on them. Or they died in a training accident. All seemed totally random. Most were enlisted, but a few were officers. Most were male, but not all.

I cited Carl von Clausewitz and his famous "fog of war" from his classic *On War*, and summarized his point that war is subject to Murphy's Law—if something can go wrong, it will. You can make a plan of "first this happens, then this, then that," but it's almost certain that things won't follow this progression. And why not? I ask them. Because the enemy is trying to undo everything you do. So, everything can take another path at any moment. That, ladies and gentlemen, I tell them, is why you have to be able to think outside the box, to synthesize data and be able to justify new conclusions—precisely what I am teaching you to do here with English: what you thought on day one had no connection to being an officer.

Back to Remarque. The Western Front wasn't supposed to happen at all, I remind them. There is usually someone who has had some exposure to military history who can tell me about the Schlieffen Plan, the German notion that the Germans could swing through Belgium, and up from the south, and capture Paris, easy peasy. The same way I remind them that American "shock and awe" was meant to make Iraq greet our soldiers as liberators. Only, Murphy's Law kicked into effect: the French stopped the German movement. The result was the stalemate of trench warfare, pointless killing over many years. And Murphy's Law took effect in Iraq as well.

The conditions in the World War I trenches were horrible: rats, foot fungus (trench foot), the noise of the guns, gas attacks—and bullets. If they put a helmet on a rifle and lifted it over the top of the trench, it got a bullet through it. Men sent out on patrols or to get prisoners frequently didn't come back, and there was no way to recover their bodies, or bring back the wounded, without dying yourself. Dead and dying men hung on the barbed wire, and horses screamed in agony as they were dying. Worst of all, there seemed to be no point to any of it. Your side might take a few yards of no-man's-land, but after the next attack the enemy took them back. And they were worthless yards. Dirt was blasted so often there was nothing left but shell holes between you and the enemy lines.

How did things come to this? The German boys, old men before their time—as they tell us frequently—talk about this question in the lulls of battle. They note that they were snookered in by their authority figure, the professor in their school (which is called the Gymnasium in German, confusingly to us; German Gymnasia go longer than American high schools, so they would have been US junior college age) who glorified war and told them they were cowards if they didn't go. Remember, the Germans hadn't known war since the easy victory in 1870 over the French that gave them Alsace-Lorraine. And as I point out to them, the easiest way to motivate young men is to question their manhood. They laugh sheepishly and agree.

They also note that political leaders start wars that are fought by the young—the really young, as there are few officers in this book. Maybe, the enlisted oldest soldier suggests, the two leaders should fight man to man and not kill off the young? This would be a proxy war. The midshipmen object to this idea. I remind them that all wars are proxy wars—with less than 1 percent of the US population in uniform. Make everybody serve! They suggest. Bring back the draft! To do what? I ask. Soldiers are expensive, and we don't need many. If we have World War III, we will need universal conscription. Even so, the soldiers are a small fraction of the population, and young, so it's still a proxy war. Do they want World War III? They are silent.

The German boys are well aware that giving one man power over the others makes him sadistic. Their training sergeant had been a postman in civilian life and now loves throwing about his insubstantial weight. We have a discussion about whether tall men are more or less likely to be sadistic toward other men—all say, far less. The dean who kept after me is a short man with a squeaky voice. Just saying. They are aware that if they see the enemy as fellow humans like themselves, it will be difficult to kill him—the only way to do it is to dehumanize him.

Paul, for example, our hero, spends the night in a huge shell crater with a French soldier he has stabbed. It takes hours for the man to die, during which Paul feels overwhelming guilt when he looks at pictures he has taken from his victim's wallet of the man's family. He feels terrible and vows to contact them after the war. Next morning, back with his unit, his friends see his funk and bring him back to reality by using far-off Allied soldiers for target practice. "See him jump!" the marksman says when he hits one. Paul is mollified. They aren't people like him, just targets. The war goes on.

All of our group of school friends die, with Paul's death on the last page on the day when there is nothing worthwhile of report in the newspapers. They were good soldiers, too, which meant they survived far longer than many of the raw recruits, who died instantly. And also that they killed a lot of British and French boys their age. But finally, they too died, for nothing. And—get ready for the punch line, class—on the wrong side. The German emperor, most historians agree, started this war as a war of conquest and personal assertion—so the Germans should have lost. And they did. But what about the boys it killed? As Wilfred Owen asks in another poem, What church bells ("passing-bells") ring for those who die "as cattle"? It's not an individual death at all but a collective one. Paul dies with a smile on his face: finally it's over.

But it's not over when it's over. I assigned this book for several years, and one year I added a book by the journalist Chris Hedges called *What Every Person Should Know About War*. It had a powerful effect on some students. It's based on a World War I field manual of sober answers to questions about war, arranged in a roughly chronological sequence, from basic training to the aftermath of combat. Will I think about sex in a battle situation? What does it feel like to die in war? Hedges has sources for all his answers; this one comes from men who nearly died but didn't. Apparently, the shock is so great it's not that painful. And after: will I be close to my buddies? No. Will my marriage survive? Probably not.

Because Hedges's consideration of the actual shooting war is only a small part in the middle, sandwiched between preparation and aftermath, the gist of the book is that war isn't just what it means to combatants. It has ripple effects. And it's not over when it's over, not even for survivors. For the survivors who make it home, there's PTSD, divorce, and the surreal transition from a war zone to peacetime at home where nobody around you knows what you went through. For the amputees, life is different (here we read Siegfried Sassoon's poem "Disabled" about the amputee sitting in a hospital where the women no longer look at him except in pity). And the dead leave families who never get over their death, no matter how glorious, possibly young children who will resent him (or her) for going off and dying.

Americans typically invade other countries, so though our soldiers suffer casualties, civilians here don't. So, Americans tend to forget about the fact that in wars, there are many civilian casualties, both direct (bad bomb aim) and indirect—the hospitals are bombed, or the electricity or water are cut off, so people can't get medical treatment, women die in childbirth, and so on. The figures of estimated Iraqi civilian deaths are hundreds of times those of American soldiers. There are civilian effects of other sorts for returning Americans: families that fall apart, most typically.

Hedges underlines the point that wars are all alike. It's like playing in an orchestra: it's the same, with only minor variations, in Chicago, Paris, St. Petersburg, or Tokyo. And that brings us back to one of the most basic lessons of Remarque: you don't get to choose your side in war—you fight for your country, whatever that is, as the German boys did. Another is this: You don't get to choose how you will be used, or what campaign you will be used on. If the people throwing the stones are stupid, arrogant, or just inexperienced—or unlucky—you died for nothing. And the probability that you are the one guy who takes out the snipers' nest so the invasion succeeds and the war is won is close to zero. Far greater is the chance that you will be hit getting off the amphibs.

Plebes at the Naval Academy need to know these things. Why? Well, if they want to leave, they can leave. They have another year to decide. On the positive side, not all wars are as bad as in Remarque's novel. Trench warfare was probably the nadir of pointlessness in modern warfare—a pointless war, a pointless campaign, no visible officers of any effect—that your side probably started. And it was a world war—a great war, as they called it. Nowadays, I reassure them, we don't have this mass of soldiers; our wars are smaller and more focused (maybe), increasingly they are technology-based, and in the Navy, sailors are usually in a ship.

This doesn't hold for Marine infantry, of course, or SEALs. And if the Afghans you are training turn on you, there's no help in technology. Then there are those improvised explosive devices made from fertilizer, shit bombs.

But the same unclarity about whether we should be there at all still holds. I don't have an answer for them about greater purpose of the wars they might be in, I tell them; a lot of the time, history gets to decide if we should have invaded or not. But I caution them against thinking that any other country will necessarily bow down to geared-up, beef-fed

American boys trampling on their territory. We think we are in it for good, sure, but what they see are scary invaders. Giving chewing gum or Hershey bars to the kids in the off-hours won't do it. Nor will three cups of tea. You are still foreign invaders—maybe useful for a time as we fight the enemies of the locals and bring money. But at the end of the day, they will want us gone. And they won't say thanks. And then you'll come home to the Americans who don't have any idea why you were there. And who have spent the time shopping.

You have to know these things, I tell them. If I were teaching at Parris Island to Marine recruits, I wouldn't say these things, I assure them. My job would be to be oohrah. But you will be officers, I tell them. You have to know these things so when your enlisted figure it out and ask you, you can at least show the idea isn't catching you unawares. After all, the cluelessness of young officers was what led to all those fragging deaths in Vietnam, fresh-faced lieutenants from West Point arriving in the jungle and threatening the lives of their men with their naivete and self-confident ignorance who were blown up by their own troops.

I have a bad conscience here, because I'm actually teaching them how to more effectively further the aims of what may be stupid people using them as pawns for bad reasons; the enlisted will fight harder for an officer who isn't clueless, even if the goal remains unjustifiable. But that's life. We are all caught in situations: we can change some things but not all. And I work for the military, and you pay me to do it. I can't stop the military, and my job is just to treat my students in a way the military never does—as individuals. And to get them to think—possibly so that they can save the lives of their people when Murphy's Law and the fog of war kick in.

LIFE WITH MIDSHIPMEN

'*ve learned many things from over thirty years with midshipmen, one of which is certainly that thing about the importance of leaders looking good, something they don't teach you in graduate school. Another scene in Remarque's book the mids wanted to talk about is when the soldiers in Paul's group prepare for inspection from the Emperor. It's like God in the burning bush, without the bush. They will see the Emperor! They all work on looking good—uniforms inspected, boots polished. This is the man for whom they are fighting, after all. He's the one who makes it all worthwhile. It's hero worship, a big part of the military mindset, roping in midshipmen who grew up playing with GI Joe and watching movies of steroid-swollen soldiers mowing down the enemy. In fact, the German soldiers are disappointed: the Emperor is small, and far away, and had a withered arm. They clearly wanted a man-mountain. Why do they care about the body of their male leader?

Much has been made by feminist theory of what is called the "male gaze" directed only at women. But the military blows to smithereens feminist theories about the gendered nature of "the gaze." In the military, the looked-at men show off to the looking men, and then sometimes they change places. Come to the MacDonough Hall weight room on a Friday night to swim in a sea of sweating muscular midshipmen (only a few women) getting swole for the mirrors and for each other. It doesn't mean straight boys aren't so straight after all; it just means that being straight usually entails a large component of interest in other men and their bodies.

The fact that men look at themselves and at other men clarifies why women in the military are on the wrong track for busting males for checking them out—especially if they are in a command position, the one facing them in the front of the room or outside. Of course, the men are checking them out. Why not? They are far worse with other men, though to be sure the purpose is usually different. In the case of males in a command position, it's to see if they are worthy of giving orders. And yes, men are superficial. If you have bigger guns than I do, OK, I'll listen to what you say. If you don't, you'll have to have other qualities to make up for it. So that's one quality a military (or other?) leader needs to have. What are others? I discuss this with students. Is it possible to teach leadership as an end in itself, and what is being taught? The Naval Academy claims it can do this, but without saying what it is teaching. In fact, that is the basis of its claim to legitimacy, what justifies this gush of taxpayer money.

"Leaders to Serve the Nation," say banners repeating the USNA theme and placed all over the Yard and that pop up on the Web site (for example when you search for VADM Buck's inspirational words, quoted above). This implies, perhaps—I raise this essential question again— that all graduates are leaders? That leaders cannot be got elsewhere? That only Naval Academy graduates serve the nation? That all of them do? Don't ask so many questions! We're the leadership institution—though, of course, West Point claims the same. Its website says, "The Preeminent Leadership Development Institution." I guess "leadership" is what you learn at a military institution.

And everywhere else, it seems. The sign down the dirt road to the Adirondack-style summer camp where I took my sons when they were younger (run by the YMCA on a former tobacco plantation) reads: Slow Down! Future Leaders at Play! All the kids who go to this camp are going to be leaders? Perhaps this means: if you can afford to send your kids here, or care enough to do so, your kids will have the advantages that mean they'll go to good schools and drift into cushy jobs. And it's not just the military institutions nowadays that claim they produce leaders, though we certainly beat the drum louder. It's all colleges, as well as most high schools, elementary schools, after-school programs, and even summer camps. Every state university has, and most private ones have a "leadership" program, and some give degrees in it. Google "university leadership"—your eyes will blur if you look at them all. With all these leaders, who will follow?

This is part of our discussion about "leadership," a word the students hear incessantly. (To repeat: discussion is anathema to most people in the military. It shouldn't be, as that is the inbred weakness of the military, and leads to death and defeat.) Are the officers at USNA good leaders? Is anyone else? I'll toot my own horn and say that I have had students say they learned more about leadership from me than from all the officers put together. But I'd never say I was teaching it, only exhibiting or modeling it—and yes, talking about what that means.

The consensus and summary of these discussions with midshipmen over decades is this: leadership, when abstracted from a particular subject matter, is a set of facts about real people who enter a room, not a body of knowledge. It's what you'd expect would be required of a person who needs to earn the respect of the people he or she is trying to encourage what he or she needs to happen. Namely: competence, confidence, interpersonal skills, positive demeanor, boundless energy, and the ability to focus, prioritize, and keep going no matter what. It's a combination of many factors: body posture, facial gestures, use of language, ease with self and subject matter, and that most intangible of intangibles, does the person seem to like those who will be led? If the leader doesn't like the led, why should the led like the leader? Is "led" even the right word, rather than, say, inspired?

Thus, many things follow that are nowadays frowned upon as subjects for judgment, starting with body appearance, touched on in Remarque's novel (do you like looking at this person?), and also whether or not they make you nervous and irritable, or happy, to be around. A jittery or apologetic or nervous person cannot lead a fly. These are joined to what the person says and how it is said. The result is like going to a play: everything contributes to whether the experience is a success for the viewer or not. A good leader, midshipmen tell me, has to be comfortable in his or her skin, not looking for insults, and ready to praise others while showing s/he can do those things too. Leaders have skills that turn out to be identical to the skills of good social interaction, except that they're the one in front—which means you know they are looking at you and waiting for you to inspire them.

So do it. Don't be petty or mean, lead by example, praise when you can, be able to perform, and then perform. And then give a wide grin. You're doing this for them, not you. Can these ways of interacting with others be taught if they're not evident to you already? In a classroom? At any institution over any other? I don't think so, and the insistence of the service academies that they produce "leaders" shows how functionless they have become and how hungry for justification.

In fact, there are a number of factors that work against successful leadership in the military. One such factor is that many people go into the military in order to have their rank elicit the show of respect they would not otherwise get in real life, like the postman who becomes the sadistic drill sergeant in *All Quiet on the Western Front*. They aren't leaders; they are people handed power that they abuse. Abuse of power is an endemic problem in the military, because of the way the power is structured as a series of pyramids, each of which ends in the choke point of one individual, who is part of a pyramid above, and so on. The military is a series of bottlenecks. A lot of individuals try to please one individual, who is one of many individuals trying to please another individual further up the chain of command, and so on. And the very top has to deal with politicians. It has everything to do with individual personalities and prejudices and very little to do with rationality. It isn't about thinking; it's about following orders. If you are the top of your pyramid, you are an individual within that pyramid—like the one guy who survives the fire up the beach to take out the snipers' nest. All the others are just other stones that fall short or miss. But not for the next pyramid up. You have to please the man or woman in charge of you, who has to please the one in charge of him/her, and so on. Subordinates give options to a superior, who decides. There is little discussion, no attempt to forge a consensus, no putting things up for a vote, and no decision by committee.

This structure of individual whim at increasing levels is what passes for "leadership" in the military. I've got the stripes, and I say what's what. The military is the happy hunting ground of personal desire passing for rational decision making, or supplanting it entirely. It's a fundamental weakness of the military that personal whim is massaged into a smug sense of personal "leadership" on the part of so many officers, and almost to a (wo)man, the brass. Most feel offended when their desires are thwarted, or their dictates even questioned. That's why things go wrong so often in the military. And they don't seem prepared to justify what they do with rationality; at least, I've never gotten them to justify what they do or why they do it at Annapolis. And talking with graduates convinces me that things are the same in the fleet.

The military needs more rationality and less "leadership." It would be stronger with more thinking, more collective brainstorming, more encouragement of divergent views, and more justification by rationality—outside, of course, of battle situations, where you just have to act. But there is plenty of time for discussion in the military, and it shouldn't be seen as threatening to the officer in charge, but rather welcomed. We need to get people to be able to say: "I have looked at the available evidence, and this is the best course of action because X, Y, and Z." Not just: "Because I have the rank and I say so." We civilians need the military to be less about working individual will and more about justifying courses of action.

When asked on media programs what my goal is, I always say this: to help create thinking officers, people who have the strength to act decisively, but who do so only after looking at all the available data (not just some), listening to opposing viewpoints (not just the ones that agree with theirs), considering options (even scary ones), and implementing the most justifiable one, the one that seems a little less gray in a world of grays. The world is not black and white, though you'd never know it from the military, who are fond of talking about good guys and bad guys.

I can't change this system of successive bottlenecks based around personalities that defines the military. What I can do is help the future officers I teach see that they can't just come in and stomp around to express "leadership": they have to gather information, find out what the real situation is and what their people are really thinking, and be able to explain their decision, which they need to be able to justify, not merely say it's them exhibiting "leadership." Synthesize data, reach a position, be able to justify it, and respond to dissent as a way to show why you got to where you got. And be willing to change your mind if the data suggests you should.

I teach these skills through literature: What is the point of this story? What data do you have? What are divergent readings? Does any reading seem preferable? Justify. The administration of the Naval Academy usually does none of this, and is, in fact, typically among the worst "leaders" I, or the midshipmen (so they tell me), have ever seen. And this is when I typically hear, "Sir, you can learn as much from bad leadership as from good!" So that's when I draw on my decades more of experience with the world and say, "Taxpayers should not be paying half a million dollars per student to give you examples of bad leadership. That happens naturally. You'll see."

But what justification do I have for thinking that anything I do at the Naval Academy matters? Can I transmit anything meaningful to young people a third of my age, unmotivated, and sleepy to boot? I know I amuse them with my theatrics. Do they take anything else on board? Sometimes I wonder. There are built-in problems with the old teaching the young, not least of all that the things we'd most like to pass on to the young can't be passed on at all. We'd love to transmit wisdom—but isn't this just the point of view of the old? Will the young listen to it? Why should they? Will it do them any good if they do? There will be time enough for them to grow wise in their turn.

Can we prevent them from making our mistakes? Maybe not. The common mistakes are the ones we want most of all to prevent, and those are the hardest to head off, because in all people the compulsion to make them is too great. And they will find mistakes of their own I didn't even know about. The most important thing, therefore, seems to me to be to reassure them that adults are not another species but merely a more finished version of themselves, further down the road. I know what they know and more. But they don't know what I know.

Most don't know who they really are. Until that point, they have been defined by their parents and institutions. Annapolis continues this definition by institution, since the point of departure of the military is the opposite of mine. For the military, the point of departure is that they have no individuality to develop, at least none the military is interested in, or indeed even knows or cares about. For some of them, settling into the womb of control by others is welcome relief: they don't have to make any decisions, as the military does this for them.

And for these, longing for the huge hand of the drill sergeant on their necks and not getting it, the Naval Academy is the biggest letdown of their young lives. I even joke to them about this. I say, I know what you wanted. You wanted a jacked drill instructor to smash your face into the mud and then make you puke from pushups. And what you found was scolds and wimps. Right? They grin. It's true. Our hype and their own overheated adolescent imagination lead them to believe that the Naval Academy will be the ultimate challenge, the hyper alphas putting the raw recruits through hell until, by sheer force of will and muscle strength, they succeed. And then the hard-bodied, hard-faced man who has been their tormenter and their god relents and says, "Welcome to the Corps."

Oh, you who went to liberal arts colleges full of pencil-necked intellectuals, or to state universities full of frat boys who drank too much, or to community colleges with adults trying to make something of their lives once they realized how hard life actually is—do not mock these kids. It's silly, I know. And it wasn't my dream at their age either—I laugh and say I'm the drill instructor, not the recruit. And yes, I do try and make it as intellectually tough for them as I can make it. They frequently earn failing grades on early papers, then they rewrite to get a C. And maybe the next time a B. And then I crack a smile and say, "Welcome to the end of plebe English. You have passed. Congratulations!"

Some of them have other issues. I make no secret to the students of having had a gay brother, Keith, who died of AIDS. I even mention that he told the most virulently antigay jokes I have ever heard until the day he was pulled out of the closet by his first boyfriend, who now lives in Florida with his partner—we exchange Christmas cards every year. I say that in the context of explaining why I had to shut down "joke Friday" in my classes—they have joke Friday in the mess hall too. I explain that I got tired of hearing oral sex and anal sex jokes from eighteen-year-olds. I mention that Keith was clearly trying out his fascination and anxiety with his gay jokes, and mention Sigmund Freud's theory of jokes that underline this. Then I say, geesh, if you're so fascinated, why not try it? Anyway, I can't stand listening to you. They laugh uncomfortably. Don't want it? Don't do it. This spiel, by the way, was reported to the eager administration and showed up in legal documents as "talking about oral and anal sex in class." (Needless to say, I was never asked what really happened.)

Being open about my brother has encouraged a few of them to come out to me in my office, just to see if the heavens opened. This didn't happen, and they seem reassured. One woman asked me to tell her how awful she was because she was sure she was a lesbian. Good grief, I said. I'm not going to be very good at doing that, am I? She gave me a hug when she left my office. Another woman brought her wife back to meet me years later—she was in the creative writing class where we had the prom. Guys sometimes come out to me as well, though the price at the Naval Academy is far higher for a man to say he's gay than for a woman. We discuss how open they should be—they will unquestionably lose points if they are out, so discretion is not the worst option. I'm not telling them to stay in the closet: I want them to come out to the people they trust. But be aware that the world doesn't have the right to any knowledge about them, especially if they are in a position of authority over younger men whose views are unknown to them.

The students who rebel in big ways—by saying they are gay (no longer an offense for which they can be thrown out or court-martialed but still not desirable), a pacifist (I've had some), or not into the military (many)—sometimes have choices, and sometimes not. If they decide this in their first two years, and can withstand the almost inevitable strong parental pressure to stay (Free tuition! Service to country! Prestige! Best and Brightest! Regret it all your life if you leave!), they can, as noted, simply leave. But if they decide this later, they are generally stuck.

It can be argued that this is just—that indeed the ability to leave with no problem after two years is already too generous, given the taxpayer investment in half their college career, in some cases three years including the prep school. But it does set up an inherent conflict between Bancroft Hall, standing in for the pseudo-military side of things (we're not fighting anybody, just putting on parades and changing clothes a lot and saluting and saying sir/ma'am) and the academic buildings. Back in the days when there was no pretense to being a college, and when everybody clearly had to share the same values and be versions of the same person—all straight white males between eighteen and twenty-one who wanted to be in the military—I don't think education had a chance.

But nowadays, education is given the appearance of having a fighting chance, while it is sent into the ring with two broken arms and two broken legs. Nobody tells the professors they are fighting an uphill battle, and the pseudo-military thinks the goals of education are actually the same as those of training. In education, we are supposed to teach them to figure themselves out, which goes directly against what the military wants to accomplish, namely to get them to march in lockstep and follow orders. However, the best interests of the military, which means the best interests of the civilians they defend, are that officers should be able to assess situations they are unfamiliar with and "think outside the box." That's what I have committed my life to.

The paradox of educating the young is the difficulty of getting their expanding crescendo of knowledge to coincide with their decrescendo of steadily reducing possibilities as they discover the specific people they are. They may have some notion of their interests, of their strengths and weaknesses, but anything you offer them may not be a fit at all. They probably don't know themselves—they discover their tastes by trying new things. And you certainly don't know what these tastes will be, because it's difficult to tell who people are by looking at them. And what if they don't even know that there is a lot they don't know about themselves?

Education acknowledges this imprecision; training ignores it. Training is much less complex: individual variations are irrelevant in teaching people (say) how to shoot a rifle. But the thing about education is that you have to teach something specific as well, so it may look like training: everybody is reading the same book, perhaps. But the point is that you do the same thing because you can't cater to individual variations in the future that nobody knows about yet, including, usually, not even them. So with education you give it your best shot and hope you affect some of the people some of the time.

Both training and education have a point. The problem in uniting these is that it's far more usual for educators to acknowledge the point of training (for example, grammar exercises by literature professors) than it is for those who deal only in training to acknowledge the more imprecise nature, but the necessity, of education. I think I understand Bancroft Hall, but I'm pretty sure Bancroft Hall does not understand my classroom, as my experiences at USNA over three decades have shown.

I have to say I loved the fact that I shared a commitment to physicality with my students. I've also loved my life of running. It made me feel independent of the constraints of others. At an early hour of the morning when it was still dark, or before anyone was up, I'd go conquer the streets. Or so it felt, moving faster than people who, in any case, weren't around. I ran in Munich, Berlin, Barcelona, outside Venice (where I turned my ankle), and around the date palms at Furnace Creek Ranch in Death Valley before the sun rose and became unbearable. I ran up the road from the bristlecone pines on the Westgard Pass and the crabby trees of the Sierra Nevada that are the oldest living things on the planet, some, in the so-called Methuselah Grove, four thousand years old. I've run in Rwanda, outside Hyderabad, India, at the university where I was teaching (I was too chicken to run in downtown Bombay/ Mumbai, and it seemed disrespectful of the people who were begging on the streets, so I swam in the pool of the Taj Mahal Hotel instead), along the Nile in Cairo and the Sea of Marmara in Istanbul (I could see Florence Nightingale's hospital over on the Asian side), along the Seine in Paris to Notre Dame where I did pullups on a bus shelter by the police station, in Salisbury, outside of Annapolis where I live now, down FDR Drive in New York and over the Williamsburg Bridge, across the Walt Whitman Bridge from Philadelphia to Camden, along the Midway in Chicago, around Vanderbilt, and around Haverford College when I went back to lecture after my first novel came out: how small it seemed! Everywhere I was, I ran. It gave me the sense of owning the world.

In retrospect, I should have gotten signals from running beginning many months before the heart attack that things weren't going well with my heart—or, as it turned out, my coronary arteries. But it was close to impossible for me to receive the signals I was getting. I thought I was Superman. I ate right—nothing fried, take the skin off chicken, no sugary soda, olive oil, loads of steamed vegetables—and even preached it to my students. My father, despite a lifetime living off bologna (baloney) and bourbon, had made it to ninety. Then there's my mother, still going pretty strong at this writing in her late nineties. Keith's death at forty to AIDS didn't count.

I got chest pains several times that year on runs, but they went away, and I ignored them. Anyway, I had looked up the symptoms, which seemed those of exercise gastritis, and Dr. Google said basically that there was nothing I could do. So fine. Just suck it up.

In the summer of 2018, my wife had a fellowship in Berlin, where the boys and I accompanied her. I had more of the same pains while running, probably more frequently. I told myself I'd give up and go to the doctor when I went home. The day we left for the airport to fly back, I bounded up multiple flights of stairs in the Frankfurt airport, Superman again. We got on the plane. I took a nap, sitting separately from the rest of the family because I had gotten my ticket at a different time. The plane took off. My chest got tight.

That digestive thing again! I got up multiple times to walk around. I went to the bathroom and vomited, which I thought was sure to fix things. It didn't. After nine hours of discomfort but not agony, we were at Dulles airport. While I waited for the family to get the luggage, I sat down on the floor, something I never do. It didn't help. All that night I couldn't sleep, sitting up on a chair, lying on the couch, the floor, walking about. In the urgent care place, where I finally went the next morning, I gave the nurse practitioner my story of exercise gastritis. She sent an aide in with the EKG machine and a few minutes later came in with the tape in one hand and nitroglycerin in the other. You're having a heart attack, she said, and you're going to the hospital.

The techs loaded me into the ambulance. They were waiting for me in the ER. I was admitted immediately. The doc arrived, her hair still a blonde mess as they had apparently called her in from her tennis game in order to fix me up: thank you! I don't remember the stent, and the next day I went home. Before I left, the doctor explained that I needed other, but more complicated, stents, an operation that had to be done in Washington. She had sent the pictures to the doc who did this operation to see if it was even feasible. It was, but it would have to wait a month.

I wasn't totally stupid not to have thought of cardiovascular disease, which was my diagnosis. I am—I swear!—a poster boy of healthy living. So, it was revelatory when the doc came by after the second set of stents to talk to me about stress—even without knowing me or my ongoing battle with the Naval Academy. He was telling me to chill. I said, "Isn't it an old wives' tale that stress causes heart attacks?" "Not at all," he said, and launched into an explanation of how when you get agitated, it clenches your (my) arteries, which ruptures the plaque that everybody has. Then the white blood cells rush in to repair what they see as damage, and the wall builds up. And after the next time, and the next, a heart attack. My body had been clogging and unclogging for months. Those were the chest pains.

And then he told personal stories of how, as a New York Italian, he used to get irate about bad drivers on the New Jersey Turnpike, or erupt about idiots, to the surprise and consternation of his calmer, non-Italian wife. He was telling me he had to learn not to do that, which by the way frightened his wife. And so did I. Just smile.

The thing is, I thought I was totally blasé about the attacks of the Naval Academy. There's a proverb that's older than Geoffrey Chaucer, who quotes it: to eat with the devil, you need a long spoon. And I'd comment, when repeating this, well, I guess my spoon isn't long enough.

I thought I was handling it all perfectly. After all, I was right, and they were wrong. Plus, of course, I was Superman.

The heart attack now feels like a speed bump, nothing more. Of course, there's always no problem until there is: the car accident happens after countless hours, years, and decades of no accident. I was going strong before until I wasn't—and I even misread signs I should have heeded. If I had gone to the doctor after the first incident, I might not have a damaged heart now. But it hasn't stopped me. I'm not sure that I lift quite as much or can run quite as far, but what I can do feels good; I still push myself, and I feel in control of what I do. I am back on my old schedule of workouts and do it every morning in the basement with the weights.

One of the main reasons it was important for me to remain strong in my late sixties despite a heart attack was my sons, who are athletes and also weight-train to be strong and to look good. So, I get to mentor and guide them, show them proper form, make sure they remember to breathe, focus, and don't rest too long between sets. And most of all, keep their back curved and look up during squats and other leg exercises. Most people have no idea what they are doing with weights. If you go to a normal gym, you will see dozens of clueless guys grunting away, flopping their bodies, using weights too heavy for them to control or so light the weights are clearly not doing them any good.

And I'm not going to have them remember me as weak. I never say, "Take out the trash so your old dad doesn't have to." I just say, "You forgot to take out the trash." I never say, "For Pete's sake, I had a heart attack!" I don't want pity, and I don't deserve it. I am back at it, as close to 100 percent as I could possibly be. For how long, of course, I don't know. But precisely because I don't know, I can't think too much about it. I had to allow the possibility that I would have a radically new and weaker body to get used to after the heart attack—but I don't. It's the same one.

Certainly the heart attack, coupled with the Naval Academy finally throwing a Hail Mary pass and saying, "Fuck this shit, let's just fire the fucker," put a natural pause in the rhythm of my life. I had two more fights to win, and both at the same time. And I did.

Poisonous mediocrities like the Naval Academy dean will always be around. The midshipmen have learned that the only way to survive is to bow your head and shut your mouth. But I say no. You can't live in fear. You have to stride forward. And if you shut your mouth all the time, you shrivel inside. You don't have to be a constant pain in the butt. But when it counts, you have to speak up.

What's most mysterious about life is life. I am not there, or rather there's no me at all, and then slowly I come to be, entering the light but still completely dependent on others. I become who I am whether by nurture or nature, or both, and then help make others. I have a time when I see, feel warmth, and love—or as the poem "In Flanders Fields" has it, a time when I "lived, felt dawn, saw sunset glow, loved and [was] loved"—and then begin to wear out, the body at least and usually the mind, and then am no longer there at all. Or am snuffed out: "Out, out, brief candle," says Macbeth. "Life's but a walking shadow, a tale told by an idiot, full of sound and fury and signifying nothing." I'd say that's a bit harsh. I'm more positive.

We're given a gift. Our job is to maximize our potential for as long as we can. Opposition was made to be overcome. As the midshipmen are fond of quoting Admiral David Farragut, usually in full-throated chorus: Damn the torpedoes—full speed ahead!

HOW CAN WE FIX IT?

The world has changed since the service academies were founded, and the service academies have changed. Add to that the fact that now we want to use them to drive social change rather than confining them to their former mission of hardening warriors for battle. We want inclusive colleges that play sports with other colleges, and where social relations reflect the goals we want to see in society at large, rather than technical institutions for a specific career path with a specific set of skills. There's no going back to the all-male, all-white world of the academies in, say 1950, a world of no sex (because gay sex was prohibited and there were no women) and marching to class—and no one wants to, least of all me. But if we admit women and out gays in a world with far more universal access to data about the world outside through the internet, how can we keep the top on a pot that boils ever more furiously? The answer by the brass has been to pretend that we don't have problems at all and to cover up the inevitable explosions when they occur.

That is untenable in the long run. We have to take the top off the pot, starting with lifting the ban on sex within our 338 acres. It's not 1950 anymore. And we have to admit that we are running a hugely expensive taxpayer-supported government giveaway, and we want to serve as military Disneylands for tourists and proof that the military is on board with achieving liberal societal goals. If we admit that we

217

are about a racial rainbow and football and parades, and then ask tax-payers if they are willing to pay for that, I would have no objections. Frankly, I don't think enough of them would think it a good investment to continue.

What Congress wants of the service academies has changed over time. The academies can't do anything about that. Nor are the academies responsible for the post-World War II expansion of ROTC and OCS that have left the academies now producing fewer than one new officer in five and hence without clear purpose, at many multiples of the cost of ROTC or OCS, whose officers are equally effective. But the gulf between the hype, which continues to make the academies sound as if it were still 1925, and the reality the students discover, is precisely what disillusions them.

There's no way to go back to the old days, if that's what they were. Women are here to stay, for starters, as are racial considerations. One way to fix the gap between what we say we are and what we actually are is to be open about what we, in fact, are: ceremonial places to play an annual football game. That would solve the students' sense of disconnect, but it wouldn't please the brass, whose self-image is based on the hype—that they may actually believe themselves, for all I know. They certainly responded to my articles as if they did, shooting the messenger time and time again, and never once even pretending to refute what I say. My problem is that I think institutions that ask for this degree of commitment from members for a specific purpose, and that cost the taxpayers what these institutions do, ought to actually achieve their stated goals. Currently, the service academies do not do this.

So, what are we going to do?

There are answers. For a time, I looked at service academies in allied countries. I had lectured in Canada at their Royal Military College (Collège militaire royal), which amalgamates their services, and found it a more functional version of those in the USA. Students don't have to live on base, there is no wall, students can be any age so long as they can meet physical requirements, and they can marry. (US service academy students cannot do so until they graduate, with the result that many do so the week after graduation day, seeing it as forbidden fruit that there-fore has to be good; divorces are numerous.) In Australia, the service academy is run by the University of New South Wales. In Germany, the students wear civilian clothes. I liked the Belgian military academy's sep-aration of academics and military training into separate blocks, not the stirred-up mess of the US, which results in the watering down of both.

But the academy I paid most attention to was Britain's Royal Military Academy Sandhurst, which is now out of the undergraduate education business and acts as a center for military training for people who already have been educated (and sown their wild oats) elsewhere. They're not eighteen; they've committed to the military as adults and not for the "free education." The training courses are measured in months not years, which allows greater intensity and largely seems to prevent eye-rolling or burnout. All Naval and USMC officers could come through a graduate program at Annapolis, rather than the 18 percent undergraduate rate for Navy as it is now, fewer for USMC. This intensive prespecialty training would not compete with the Naval Postgraduate School or with the fact that USNA graduates complete a specialty school afterward, whether BUD/S for SEALs, flight training for pilots, SWO training for ship officers, or others. It would be a generalized military course for students who had graduated from civilian universities, with or without having done ROTC.

Or would it also incorporate some of the specialty training? We have classrooms and labs. Creative thinking is necessary. What's clear is that the Navy doesn't need to, and indeed shouldn't, be running an undergraduate college. Of course, I think it ought to have a writing and literature component, because with so many different schools produc-ing officers, we just don't know what they may have learned about jus-tifying their conclusions, or not. To be determined, TBD. Colleges can do the general education. If we think there's more they have to learn, they can do it at Annapolis and the other service academies, once out of the undergraduate education business.

Our problem with trying to keep this institution going as an under-graduate one is that we're still trying to keep the control going that may have worked in 1925. There's no need for undergraduate education by the military, as it's exactly what all colleges offer—unlike in 1845. Plus it's clearly training that we offer (or force) at the academies, not education. Students nowadays have access to more information than their grandparents did and take behaviors for granted that their grandparents didn't. We want the service academies to "look like" what we envision for our society, which means a far wider variety of types of people—but we aren't willing to admit that that means we have to loosen the control, and be clearer with these divergent groups about what we want to achieve. And we've refused to face the question: are they meant to train warriors or be Disneylands for tourists? One way to solve our problems is to be like Sandhurst and get out of the undergraduate education business. That way we may get our purpose and our self-respect back—and the respect of our students, which the service academies currently do not have.

How likely is this to happen? If Congress says it will happen, it will. That's how we got women, after all, and the abolition of the hunting down of gays. But how much political appetite is there for this? People who haven't spent decades in these institutions, as I have, believe the hype and have no idea what they really are. The military brass would scream bloody murder as well, carry on about tradition, and try to kill such a move. Some of them went to these places decades before, and their memories have hazed over in nostalgia for their youth. Nobody wants to see his (or her) college close.

Besides, the likelihood of the military admitting that it has been faking it all these years at its showpiece academies is close to zero. Faking it means not producing "leaders" in any higher proportion than any other institution from which young men and women in their early twenties can emerge and, in fact, producing demoralized graduates that are no more effective than the competition at being Naval and Marine officers—it all depends on the individual, as midshipmen say. That would be admitting failure, and the military does not like to admit failure. We kick ass—that's who we are (that's what midshipmen tell me). Except, of course, when we don't—say every conflict past World War II, which may be why there is so much nostalgia for a time when the bad guys were so clearly bad (which made us clearly good) and which produced our last big win. Just as the South built its memorials to the "Lost Cause" fifty years after the Civil War, the US largely built its World War II memorials a half century after the War, one in Washington DC by the Lincoln Memorial, and another overlooking the Naval Academy on the highway that crosses the Severn River. Of course, we won and the South lost, but a half century allows the nostalgia to build in any case.

Why should they change? What of the fact that the academies cost hundreds of millions of taxpayer dollars with no purpose but symbolic, or theater for tourists? Probably that won't cut much mustard either. Nobody is concerned with the national debt these days except as a political club to beat the other party with. And the military continues to be allocated more and more money. Besides, the cost of the academies to the taxpayers is small potatoes compared to what we wasted on useless exercises in, say, Afghanistan—all of our fruitless "nation building" and the hardware left behind.

How about the psychic pain to midshipmen as they see their dreams destroyed and count the days until they can get out (as almost all do)? Well, it's not fun for them, and it's painful for me to foresee the process in the newbies and then see it all play out, class after class, decade after decade. But they're young, and most of them shed the influence of their four years of what is largely frustration like water off the proverbial duck's back, beginning the day of their graduation. I joke with them that the moment they are declared officers on graduation day (there is a huge cheer at this moment at graduation), the golden cloud of nostalgia begins to descend. It was something they survived. Probably no more service academy graduates are psychically maimed for life than others their age.

Of course, they are immature and unsocialized, having been controlled and lectured at for four years and denied normal social interactions on campus. And what we do to them with the relentless lecturing not to be rapists (the men) and that they are never responsible for their own actions (the women) is almost guaranteed to produce more of the problems the advocates of such programs think they are addressing. Any therapist or counselor will tell you that constant harping on something by one partner in a relationship is almost certain to produce resistance or indifference on the part of the person being constantly attacked. And so it is at the service academies.

Many former students corroborate that the academies are worse than the fleet in this regard because they are only play-acting, whereas the fleet or the Army are the real thing—or realer, anyway. So the academies' lies and their pettiness, their arbitrary punishments and their currying of favor, frustrate more because they are just part of a vast Disneyland staffed with unwilling cast members who thought they were signing up for something completely different. Is the utility of these institutions found in the deflowering process itself, the disappointment they suffer at an early age so the world doesn't surprise them after? Maybe the students are right in saying, "Sir, if you can put up with the bullshit here, you can put up with the bullshit anywhere." Maybe it's harsh but useful in the long run, this disillusioning of the young.

I am not so cynical as to believe this. It's better if people are shown how to do things the right way rather than the wrong way. Especially if it's based on lies, and you're paying for it. I believe that all the temptations that ranks and uniforms and sirs/ma'ams offer people to use with others are to merely feel important, and that these can be refused if we alert people to their dangers—if not by all, then by most. Most people are decent human beings, I believe, and can be educated to resist the things that they will be presented with as perks of office or being officers. The military careens between the two extremes of kissing the ass of its members and treating them like shit. More discussion, more rationality, less preening, less self-aggrandizement is what we need—and it can be achieved. This I believe.

More of all this at the service academies, if they are to continue as four-year institutions for undergraduates rather than abandoning this as unrealistic (which is what I propose), is also what we need. That would be Plan B if we can't get the Plan A of following Sandhurst. Officers should be shown that they can get people to follow them without browbeating them. This is always more effective in situations of stress than cowed troops kept in line by punishments. And people subjected to arbitrary punishments become like whipped dogs, cringing and distrustful. So, changing the academies to eliminate this—to have them function because the people want to do what is asked of them rather than out of lassitude or fear of punishment—would make them exponentially more effective as training tools of officers.

However, this is impossible in their current form as vanity projects of transient brass in a world that has changed so radically around them. The pettiness and arbitrary punishments are the direct result of the fact that they produce such a small proportion of officers, that students could have gone to ROTC or OCS, that the lure of these places for many people is financial, that they recruit so many people committed to playing their sport rather than a career in the military, and perhaps most of all, that there is so much more information floating around on the internet. The students know that what they hear about this being necessary to produce "leaders" is all lies. But the harder the pot boils, the more firmly the lid is clamped down. They could just take the pot off the fire and open it up.

Some immediate personnel changes would bring down the pressure in the short run. Immediate relief will be produced if the current, even-more-than-usually toxic and vindictive administrators are stripped of power or shown the door. Of course, there is every indication that this degree of vitriolic nastiness is what the military brass who run the place want, to keep everyone under their thumb. Still, it would help.

And then there is the problem of our being "commanded" by a superintendent, a Navy admiral with no understanding of education and out to protect his retirement. Almost every one of the many I've seen come through the revolving door and out again in over three decades has been more clueless than the last and projected more self-assurance. They exhibit the killer combination of ignorance and arrogance, what an old-timer professor in our department who called the place "Sing Sing on the Severn" said was characteristic of our students. (He had been born on base, when his father was an officer here, in the hospital that is now gone from what we still call Hospital Point.)

Two decades ago, I wrote a column for the website Military.com that suggested that instead of an admiral with no higher education experience as a chief (superintendent/president), we have a civilian PhD like a real college—preferably a woman. At that point, I even had a specific person in mind: Nan Keohane, who had been the president of my wife's alma mater, Wellesley, and then of Duke. Since then, of course, female presidents in top-level schools have become commonplace, which is a good thing for all because it tends to eliminate some of the testosterone jockeying that gums up the works of institutions that are supposed to be based on collegiality. But it's especially necessary for a military institution, which is so prey to the tussles of men showing their power over men. As I imagine it, she would have a military XO (executive officer) who would try to explain anything she found odd. If she wasn't convinced, she could simply eliminate it. Maybe that way we'd clean out the ghostly shadows of things done in 1925.

But this still wouldn't be enough to solve the central paradox of the places: you can't get people enthusiastic about learning if you are micro-controlling their lives. As Ezra Pound, then incarcerated at St. Elizabeth's mental hospital in Washington as punishment for what may have been profascist statements during World War II, put it to explain why he had ceased writing poetry, "caged bird doesn't sing." Midshipmen are caged, and they don't sing. Instead, they sit listlessly in the corner of the cage and wait to be released. Remove the prohibition on sex; give them more freedom; treat them like adults.

One day in a class, I let the midshipmen talk about what they wanted to talk about for a while, which was how bitterly the place had disappointed their expectations. One of them demanded that I put my money where my mouth was: how would I fix the Academy? I reeled off ten things, which he wrote down on his laptop as I talked. This is what he typed up and sent to me:

10 ways to change USNA overnight-a discussion with Bruce Fleming, my English Prof.
*These are his words and ideas, I thought the world would benefit.

1. Change the attitudes toward students
A. Don't micro manage them-don't give them 20+ rules and expect them to be able to follow them or want to follow them all the time.

2. Acknowledge that this is a land institution (not a fucking ship)
A. Treat students as if they live in a dorm.
B. "Sex is not our affair" - treat them like young adults.
C. Sex on a ship is different than sex in a dorm.

3. What students do on their free time is up to them
A. "What they do and who they fuck is their business, not yours! As long as they show up to whatever evolution on time and able to work."

4. Talk to them about goals instead of regulations
A. Do not embitter them
B. We take people with a lot of potential and determination and make it all go away by October of their plebe year. (If not sooner)

5. Have an administration that is here more than 3 years and realize this is a military COLLEGE
A. This is college, not the pacific fleet.
-mandatory meals\formations?
-this is college, people!
B. Have a non-military supe with a military XO
-XO can explain tradition and things that generally work.
-civilian supe can be fired right away instead of promoted to get them out.

6. Cut out the hype
A. The naval academy could be more down played.
B. Cut out the bullshit-best of the best-
C. Hollywood is terrible with this stuff.

7. Don't act as if every time there is an issue its only "one bad apple"
A. Don't act like every problem has only occurred once and like other mids aren't doing it.
-if one mid has done it: its more than likely other have, or at least thought about it.

8. Get rid of the plebe system-doesn't produce better officer.
A. Was traditional back in the 19th century
B. Distracts from studies
C. Typical plebes are worn out by class-forget the varsity athletes who had practice that morning on top of the crap they are forced to partake in.
D. Need a USNA that doesn't kill your idealism.

9. Stop the mother hen
A. Get rid of interm grades.
B. Have the academic standards set in stone and then set them free like any other college.
C. USNA does anything to prop you up.
-how will that help in the fleet.

10. Let for your interpretation or for a shitty day.
A.

So open up. Give the students some real responsibility. Dial back the hype. And stop lying about what you are. The service academies are kept afloat on lies—about their selectivity, the quality of the students, their necessity. And lying is never good, though we see a lot of it in politics. It kills the spirit. And the academies in their current form are based on lies. Yet truth is the antidote to lies. If students enter knowing what they face, they won't be disillusioned. And they can make a better decision about whether to go at all. As a colleague of mine with whom I discussed these matters observed: "So, the Naval Academy sells itself to outsiders as a highly selective institution with tenured professors, and neither is true." "Yup," I said. "Weren't we gullible to believe it."

West Point professor Tim Bakken makes other ingenious suggestions for how to fix the academies in *The Cost of Loyalty*, a book whose pattern of exposition is similar to mine, starting with an introduction called "Breaking the Myth" (of the academies as they were through World War II). He favors turning the academies into national universities (I would say "colleges") with civilian students, albeit with some on a military track. They would be staffed by civilians able to exercise academic freedom; after graduating, students would be obligated to five years of government service. Those who chose to join the military would receive additional military training for a year. The prep schools would close. (Bakken, p. 285)

My reaction to this proposal is that we already have programs that do these sorts of things, and that it's unclear what such institutions would add to the already crowded educational landscape if they really are as open as Bakken envisions. ROTC already gives scholarships to students committed to military service to matriculate at civilian colleges, and trains them in specialties after, just as Academy graduates go to specialty schools. The obligation to government service is already a fundamental principle (though not a requirement) of Princeton University's School of Public and International Affairs (named, until student outcry, the Woodrow Wilson School), as it is of Harvard Kennedy School (and other institutions as well), though these are graduate programs. Indeed, it is unclear how an entering freshman at such a school as Bakken envisions can make the decision to commit to government service (hardly a solid concept people can picture in their mind's eye), or how this would affect the teaching of, say, freshman English, or any other subject, to justify these separate (and taxpayer-supported?) colleges. (Bakken implies it would not.)

Would such places be free to students? That leaves the problem of the vast cost gulf between a handful of European-style, state-supported civilian colleges and all other US colleges that offer the same things to students: a secular undergraduate education. If costing what other colleges cost, it's hard to see how they would be anything but new colleges, which we arguably don't need. How about sports recruiting or racial admissions at such places? If a student left or failed to enter government service, would s/he be liable for fees if the education is otherwise free? (And what would count for this—only federal government? The local school board?) And this: would they be run with the student freedom of other colleges and universities? In other words, no policing for, say, sex or physical location of students? If you make the former academies somewhat like civilian schools, it's hard to see how they could avoid being completely like these. Any tighter rein would be seen as constricting.

Make the academies ROTC central? Let students from ROTC programs at civilian schools trade place with midshipmen and cadets for a year? The fact that midshipmen and cadets are in the military and are subject to military discipline and ROTC students are not makes this problematic if not impossible. So, we'd have to reclassify midshipmen and cadets as being of the same legal status as ROTC students, like students at the Merchant Marine Academy. Doable? Sure. And this would mean a massive loosening of regulations at places like Annapolis. Yet when you do that, it's clear that they serve no purpose. They once did, but they no longer do—as undergraduate colleges, that is.

As graduate centers for committed adults in training programs for future warriors, however: aah. Yes. They're beautiful places and, under these circumstances, duty, honor, and country could once again be primary. Sadly, in places like Annapolis as they currently exist, they no longer are. I want them back.

APPENDIX:
REPORTS FROM
THE TRENCHES

James Barry

James F Barry, "Adrift in Annapolis," *Washington Post*, March 31, 1996, https://www.washingtonpost.com/archive/opinions/1996/03/31/adrift-in-annapolis/42d59e44-b910-4326-8cd5-6d140a25a224/.

Selected Articles and Videos Relating to USNA by Bruce Fleming

Bruce Fleming, "Nobody Asked Me, But...The Academy Can Do Better," February 2005, U.S. Naval Institute Proceedings, https://www.usni.org/magazines/proceedings/2005/february/nobody-asked-me-but the-academy-can-do-better.

Bruce Fleming on CNN, October 13, 2009, YouTube, https://www.youtube.com/watch?v=eQ2PvSamP0s.

Bruce Fleming, "Not Affirmative, Sir," February 16, 2003, *Washington Post*, https://www.washingtonpost.com/archive/opinions/2003/02/16/not-affirmative-sir/ca79a51d-2e31-4221-a80e-2342d5bde8e8/.

Bruce Fleming, "The Academies' Drift to Mediocrity," May 21, 2010, *New York Times*, https://www.nytimes.com/2010/05/21/opinion/21fleming.html.

Bruce Fleming, "How to Stop Sexual Assault at the Service Academies: First, Legalize Sex," January 16, 2013, *The Atlantic*, https://www.theatlantic.com/sexes/archive/2013/01/how-to-stop-sexual-assault-at-military-service-academies-first-legalize-sex/267208/.

Bruce Fleming, "Does the US Military Have a Clear Purpose?" July 1, 2011, *Christian Science Monitor*, https://www.csmonitor.com/Commentary/Opinion/2011/0701/Does-the-US-military-have-a-clear-purpose.

Bruce Fleming, "On Gay Issue, Military's History Will Repeat Itself," April 19, 2010, *Baltimore Sun*, https://www.baltimoresun.com/opinion/bs-xpm-2010-04-19-bs-ed-ending-dont-ask-dont-tell-20100419-story.html.

Bruce Fleming, "Alienating Men on the Topic of Sexual Assault," December 6, 2013, *Capital Gazette*, https://www.capitalgazette.com/cg2-arc-a9256a63-b7c5-50cb-a7da-dcec864f506c-20131206-story.html.

Bruce Fleming, "The Few, the Proud, the Infantilized," October 8, 2012, *The Chronicle of Higher Education*, https://www.chronicle.com/article/the-few-the-proud-the-infantilized/.

Bruce Fleming, "Bruce Fleming Said It: 8 Naval Academy Criticisms from a Newly Fired Professor," August 24, 2018, *Capital Gazette*, https://www.capitalgazette.com/education/naval-academy/ac-cn-naval-academy-bruce-fleming-quotes-0825-story.html

CDRSalamander, Navy, "Separate Water Fountains," U.S. Naval Institute Blog, https://blog.usni.org/posts/2009/07/02/separate-water-fountains.

Bruce Fleming, "Loyal Opposition Isn't Disloyal," September 2001, U.S. Naval Institute Proceedings, https://www.usni.org/magazines/proceedings/2001/september/loyal-opposition-isnt-disloyal.

Bruce Fleming, "The Service Academies: Eminent Victorians," *Society*, 49.1 (January 2012), 3-12, https://link.springer.com/article/10.1007/s12115-011-9497-5

C-Span Interviews

"Bruce Fleming on Military Issues," C-Span, May 27, 2013, *Washington Journal*, https://www.c-span.org/video/?312930-3/bruce-fleming-military-issues&event=312930&playEvent.

"Military Purpose and Mission," C-Span, July 4, 2011, *Washington Journal*, https://www.c-span.org/video/?300332-4/military-purpose-mission.

"Military Academies," C-Span, May 31, 2010, *Washington Journal*, https://www.c-span.org/video/?293806-6/military-academies.

"Bridging the Military-Civilian Divide," C-Span, November 28, 2010, https://www.c-span.org/video/?296766-5/bridging-military-civilian-divide&event=296766&playEvent

Books by Bruce Fleming Related to USNA

Bruce Fleming, *Annapolis Autumn: Life, Death, and Literature at the U.S. Naval Academy* (New York: New York Press, 2005), https://www.amazon.com/Annapolis-Autumn-Death-Literature-Academy/dp/1595580026.

Bruce Fleming, *Why Liberals and Conservatives Clash: A View from Annapolis* (Routledge, 2006), https://www.amazon.com/Why-Liberals-Conservatives-Clash-2006-04-16/dp/B01A64PHLG.

Bruce Fleming, *Masculinity from the Inside* (Routledge, 2022), https://www.routledge.com/Masculinity-from-the-Inside-Gender-Theorys-Missing-Piece/Fleming/p/book/9781032191478.

Earl Kelly, *Capital Gazette*

Earl Kelly and Tina Reed, "Capital Investigation: Drug Use, Party Culture, and the Naval Academy," December 16, 2012, *Capital Gazette*, https://www.capitalgazette.com/cg-capital-investigation-drug-use-party-culture-at-naval-academy-20140730-story.html.

Earl Kelly and Staff Writer, "Academy Justice Was Tilted Toward Women, May 17, 2009, *Capital Gazette*, https://www.capitalgazette.com/news/cg-academy-justice-was-tilted-toward-women--20150115-story.html.

MSPB Hearing May 20, 2019, and Judgment Reinstating July 24, 2019

Tim Prudente, "Naval Academy, Ousted Professor Bruce Fleming Present Cases on Whether He's Fit for the Classroom," May 22,

2019, *Baltimore Sun*, https://www.baltimoresun.com/bs-md-bruce-fleming-closing-arguments-20190522-story.html.

Bruce Fleming v. Department of the Navy, July 24, 2019, United States of America Merit Systems Protection Board, https://acrobat.adobe.com/link/review?uri=urn:aaid:scds:US:e5f227b5-5829-415e-b7f3-6386646e29de.

Bruce Fleming v. Department of the Navy, May 22, 2019, United States of America Merit Systems Protection Board, https://acrobat.adobe.com/link/review?uri=urn:aaid:scds:US:8d028e58-c8bb-43d8-9d32-45bf493b656e.

Susan Svrluga, "Judge Orders Reinstatement of Fired Naval Academy Professor," July 24, 2019, *Washington Post*, https://www.washingtonpost.com/education/2019/07/25/judge-orders-fired-naval-academy-professor-be-reinstated/.

Documentation/Further Reading
General/ Comparison of Commissioning Programs/Retention

William J. Astore, "How America's Broken Service Academies Create a Broken Military," August 18, 2015, *The Nation*, https://www.thenation.com/article/archive/how-americas-broken-service-academies-create-a-broken-military/.

Tim Bakken, "Corruption in U.S. Military Academies Is Harming Our National Security," March 9, 2020, *The American Conservative*, https://www.theamericanconservative.com/corruption-in-u-s-military-academies-is-harming-our-national-security/.

M-VETS Student Advisor, "The Most Bang for Your Buck," May 22, 2018, M-VETS, https://mvets.law.gmu.edu/2018/05/22/the-most-bang-for-your-buck-are-the-united-states-military-academies-the-most-cost-effective-way-of-producing-officers/.

Bruce Fleming, "Let's Abolish West Point," January 5, 2015, *Salon*, https://www.salon.com/2015/01/05/lets_abolish_west_point_military_academies_serve_no_one_squander_millions_of_tax_dollars/.

Stephen Kershnar, "Statistical Discrimination at the Military Academies," International Society for Military Ethics, https://www.inter-
nationalsocietyformilitaryethics.org/uploads/5/3/8/9/53896955/
kershnar_statistical_discrimination_military_academy_admissions.
pdf.

Scott Beauchamp, "Abolish West Point," January 23, 2015, *Washington Post*,
https://www.washingtonpost.com/opinions/why-we-dontneed-
west-point/2015/01/23/fa1e1488-a1ef-11e4-9f89-561284a573f8_
story.html.

Thomas E. Ricks, "USNA Prof to USMA Flack," April 27, 2019,
Foreign Policy, https://foreignpolicy.com/2009/04/27/usna-prof-
to-usma-flack-ricks-is-basically-right/.

Active Component Officers Source of Commission, CAN.org, https://
www.cna.org/pop-rep/1999/html/chapter4/c4-commission.htm.

History of USNA, United States Naval Academy, https://www.usna.
edu/USNAHistory/index.php.

"U.S. Army Cadet Command, The 10-Year History," Cadet Command
Historical Study Series, https://apps.dtic.mil/sti/pdfs/ADA317940.
pdf: Arthur T. Coumbe and Lee S. Harford, U.S. Army Cadet
Command—The 10 Year History (Fort Monroe, VA: Office of the
Command Historian, U.S. Army Cadet Command, 1996).

"Labels Are Not Required, but if Used Must be Proven, " U.S. Merit
Systems Protection Board, https://www.mspb.gov/studies/adverse_
action_report/9_Labelsnotrequired.htm.

James Webb, "Women Can't Fight," November 1, 1979, *Washingtonian*,
https://www.washingtonian.com/1979/11/01/jim-webb-women-
cant-fight/.

"Comparative Analysis of ROTC, OCS and Service Academies as
Commissioning Sources," Advanced Management Program,
November 19, 2004, https://cdn.shopify.com/s/files/1/0059/6242/
files/tenchfrancisprose.pdf : *Comparative Analysis of ROTC, OCS
and Service Academies as Commissioning Sources*, Tench Francis
School of Business (Nov. 19, 2004).

U.S. Coast Guard Officer Training Programs, Cal Maritime, https://www.csum.edu/academics/military-options/coast-guard-officer-programs.html.

William D. Lehner, "An Analysis of Naval Officer Accession Programs, https://www.thenavycwo.com/the-archives/send/6-the-archives/289-an-analysis-of-naval-officer-accession-programs or: https://apps.dtic.mil/sti/pdfs/ADA479949.pdf.

Meghann Myers, "Is the Military Too 'Woke' to Recruit?" October 13, 2022, *Military Times*, https://www.militarytimes.com/news/your-military/2022/10/13/is-the-military-too-woke-to-recruit/#:~:text=The%20Army%20missed%20its%20recruiting,struggling%20to%20meet%20their%20benchmarks.

John Stuart Mill, "On Liberty," 1859, https://socialsciences.mcmaster.ca/econ/ugcm/3ll3/mill/liberty.pdf.

Tim Bakken, "A Tale as Old as West Point," March 2, 2020, *Lit Hub*, https://lithub.com/author/timbakken/.

"Direct War Deaths of U.S. and Allied Forces in Afghanistan and Pakistan," October 2001–October 2019, Watson Institute, https://watson.brown.edu/costsofwar/costs/human/military.

Casualty Status, May 22, 2023, U.S. Department of Defense, https://www.defense.gov/casualty.pdf.

Faces of the Fallen, *Washington Post*, https://apps.washingtonpost.com/national/fallen/branches/navy/.

Shelby Simon, "How Many People Die from Car Accidents Each Year?" Updated October 10, 2022, *Forbes*, https://www.forbes.com/advisor/legal/auto-accident/car-accident-deaths/.

"Welcome from the Superintendent," United States Naval Academy, https://www.usna.edu/About/Welcome-from-the-Superintendent.php.

George Ziezulewicz, "Why Can't the Navy Keep Its Surface Warfare Officers?" July 7, 2021, *NavyTimes*, https://www.navytimes.com/news/your-navy/2021/07/07/why-cant-the-navy-keep-its-surface-warfare-officers/.

Navy Readiness, June 17, 2021, U.S. Government Accountability Office, https://www.gao.gov/products/gao-21-168.

Ryan Guina, "A Military Retirement is Worth Millions of Dollars," February 16, 2023, *The Military Wallet*, https://themilitarywallet. com/military-retirement-worth-millions/.

Jim Absher, "Here's the 2023 Pay Raise for Vets and Military Retirees," October 13, 2022, Military.com, https://www.military.com/benefits/military-pay/allowances/cola-for-retired-pay.html.

College Rankings and USNA Selectivity

Robert Morse and Eric Brooks, "How U.S. News Calculated the 2022–2023 Best Colleges Rankings," September 11, 2022, *U.S. News & World Report*, https://www.usnews.com/education/best-colleges/articles/how-us-news-calculated-the-rankings.

Christina Kreznar, "America's Top Colleges 2021: For the First Time a Public School Is Number One," September 8, 2021, *Forbes*, https://www.forbes.com/sites/christiankreznar/2021/09/08/americas-top-colleges-2021-for-the-first-time-apublic-school-is-number-berone/?sh=2205903241ad.

"Google Search: What Is the Naval Academy Acceptance Rate?" 2021, Google.com, https://www.google.com/search?rlz=1C1RXQR_enUS1004US1004&q=What+is+the+Naval+Academy+acceptance+rate%3F&sa=X&ved=2ahUKEwjhwe7ShtH7AhVZFlkFH-TEuA-IQsZYEegQIPhAC&biw=1536&bih=656&dpr=1.25.

Theodosia Stavroulaki, "Antitrust and Law Schools' Exit from U.S. News Rankings," November 22, 2022, *The Regulatory Review*, https://www.theregreview.org/2022/11/22/stavroulaki-antitrust-and-law-schools-exit-from-u-s-news-rankings/#:~:text=Expressing%20some%20of%20these%20concerns,Stanford%2C%20and%20Michigan%20followed%20suit.

Sam Fellman, "Record Academy Applications," June 15, 2012, Adobe Acrobat pdf, https://acrobat.adobe.com/link/review?uri=urn:aaid:scds:US:c66f47a9-d2d1-48cb-bc81-8e5ac1237799.

U.S. Department of Education College Scorecard, 2021 Cohort, https://collegescorecard.ed.gov/data/glossary/.

Colin Diver, "The Rankings Farce," April 6, 2022, *The Chronical of Higher Education*, https://www.chronicle.com/article/the-rankings-farce.

Brianna Hatch, "College Rankings Are 'a Joke,' Education Secretary Says," August 11, 2022, *The Chronicle of Higher Education*, https://www.chronicle.com/article/college-rankings-are-a-joke-education-secretary-says.

SAT Understanding Scores, 2022, College Board.org, https://satsuite.collegeboard.org/media/pdf/understanding-sat-scores.pdf

Abigail Johnson Hess, "University of Wisconsin Produced Most Current Fortune 500 CEOs," November 29, 2018, CNBC, https://www.cnbc.com/amp/2018/11/28/these-30-colleges-produced-the-most-current-fortune-500-ceos.html

USNA Class of 2026 profile
https://www.usna.edu/Admissions/_files/2026_Class_Profile.pdf

Daniel de Vise, "Naval Academy professor: A veneer of selectivity," December 30, 2011, Washington Post, https://www.washington-post.com/blogs/college-inc/post/naval-academy-professor-a-veneer-of-selectivity/2011/12/29/gIQA9droQP_blog.html

USNA graduation rate
https://www.collegefactual.com/colleges/united-states-naval-academy/academic-life/graduation-and-retention/#:~:text=Annapolis%20Graduation%20Rates&text=The%20official%20graduation%20rate%20of%20Annapolis%20is%2091%25.

Cost of Academies/Colleges

Academic Year 2019–2020 Reimbursable Rate for Service Academies Foreign Cadet and Midshipman, July 30, 2019, Comptroller, Defense.gov, https://comptroller.defense.gov/Portals/45/documents/rates/fy2020/2020_a.pdf.Student

Student Budgets, Berkeley Financial Aid & Scholarships, Berkeley.edu, https://financialaid.berkeley.edu/how-aid-works/student-budgets-cost-of-attendance/.

2022–2023 Nontuition Charges & Fees, Stanford University, https://studentservices.stanford.edu/my-finances/tuition-fees/non-tuition-charges-fees/2022-2023-non-tuition-charges-fees.

Tuition and Aid, Haverford College, https://www.haverford.edu/admission/tuition-and-aid.

Gregory Korte, "Congress and the Academies: A History of Patronage," September 15, 2014, *USA Today*, https://www.usatoday.com/story/news/politics/2014/09/15/service-academies-congressional-nominations-history/15660721/.

"DOD Needs to Enhance Performance," September 2003, Military Education, https://www.gao.gov/assets/gao-03-1000.pdf.

Letter Regarding Military Education and Additional DOD Guidance, February 27, 2012, https://www.gao.gov/assets/gao-12-327r.pdf.

Cost of NAPS to taxpayers
https://www.nytimes.com/2016/12/09/sports/ncaafootball/navy-midshipmen-army-football.html

Diversity

Lester L. Lyles, Final Report "From Representation to Inclusion," Final Report, Military Leadership Diversity Commission, https://diversity.defense.gov/Portals/51/Documents/Special%20Feature/MLDC_Final_Report.pdf.

"Navy's Top Admiral Wants More Diversity at Top," July 26, 2008, *Daily Press*, https://www.dailypress.com/news/dp-xpm-20080726-2008-07-26-0807250127-story.html.

Rebekah Blowers, "Diversity Remains a Top for CNO," July 1, 2009, *The Flagship*, https://www.militarynews.com/norfolk-navy-flagship/news/top_stories/diversity-remains-a-top-priority-for-cno/article_4e1127d6-5fad-511c-b530-e5900a333874.html.

"U.S. Naval Academy Settles Complaint with Professor Critical of Affirmative Action Policies," January 27, 2011, *The Fire*, https://www.thefire.org/news/us-naval-academy-settles-complaint-professor-critical-its-affirmative-action-policies.

U.S. Naval Academy Diversity and Inclusion Strategic Plan, USNA, https://www.usna.edu/Diversity/_files/documents/D_I_PLAN.

J.A. Cauthen, "The U.S. Naval Academy Is Adrift," November 11, 2022, James G. Martin Center, https://www.jamesgmartin.center/2022/11/the-u-s-naval-academy-is-adrift/.

J.A. Cauthen, "Merit and Preferences Never the Twain Shall Meet," January 9, 2013, James G Martin Center, https://www.jamesgmartin.center/2013/01/merit-and-preferences-never-the-twain-shall-meet/.

Students for Fair Admissions, Inc v President and Fellows of Harvard College, June 29, 2023. https://www.supremecourt.gov/opinions/22pdf/20-1199_hgdj.pdf

Sherrilyn Ifill, "When Diversity Matters," January 19, 2023, *New York Review of Books*, 24-26, https://www.nybooks.com/articles/2023/01/19/when-oral-arguments-matter-sherrilyn-ifill/

Racial composition of the Navy, officers and enlisted, 2016, https://diversity.defense.gov/Portals/51/Documents/Presidential%20Memorandum/20161018%20Abbreviated%20US%20Navy%20by%20Gender,%20Race,%20and%20Ethnicity%20v1.0.pdf?ver=2017-01-04-135118-310

Background of black Harvard students https://www.thecrimson.com/article/2023/2/17/michaela-harvard-generational-african-american/

Sexual Assault

Appendix 2, Uniform Code of Military Justice, December 20, 2019, JSC Defense, https://jsc.defense.gov/Portals/99/Documents/UCMJ%20-%2020December2019.pdf.

Executive Summary, Department of Defense Annual Report on Sexual Assault in the Military, Fiscal Year 2012, *New York Times*, archive, https://archive.nytimes.com/www.nytimes.com/interactive/2013/05/08/us/politics/08military-doc.html

SAPR/SAVI Reports starting in 2012 www.sapr.mil/reports

Annys Shin, "Three Former Naval Academy Football Players Face Accuser at Hearing on Rape Charges," August 28, 2013, *Washington Post*, https://www.westhawaiitoday.com/2013/08/28/nation-world-news/three-former-naval-academy-football-players-face-accuser-at-hearing-on-rape-charges/.

Annys Shin, "Academy Leader Denies Political Facet to Rape Trial," January 25, 2014, *(Sarasota FL) Herald-Tribune*, https://www.heraldtribune.com/story/news/2014/01/25/academy-leader-denies-political-facet-to-rape-trial/29225123007/

Annys Shin, "Two Ex-Navy Football Players to Go to Trial for Rape Case Despite Judge's Recommendation," October 10, 2013, *Washington Post*, https://www.washingtonpost.com/local/two-of-three-ex-navy-football-players-charged-in-alleged-rape-will-face-court-martial/2013/10/10/0544abaa-31ae-11e3-8627-c5d7de0a046b_story.html?hpid=z3.

Melinda Henneberger and Annys Shin, "Aggressive Tactics Highlight the Rigors of Military Rape Cases," September 1, 2013, *Baltimore Sun*, https://www.baltimoresun.com/maryland/anne-arundel/annapolis/bs-md-navy-rape-trial-20130901-story.html.

Annys Shin, "Accuser in Naval Academy Rape Case Granted a Day Off from Testifying," August 31, 2013, *Washington Post*, https://www.washingtonpost.com/local/defense-cross-examines-accuser-in-naval-academy-rape-case-for-a-third-day/2013/08/30/b45db992-1165-11e3-bdf6-e4fc677d94a1_story.html.

Lisa M. Schenk, "Informing the Debate About Sexual Assault in the Military Services," 2014, George Washington Law School, https://scholarship.law.gwu.edu/cgi/viewcontent.cgi?article=2343&context=faculty_publications

Annys Shin, "Naval Academy Rape Case Investigator Testifies that One Midshipman Changed His Story," September 3, 2013, *Washington Post*, https://www.washingtonpost.com/local/naval-academy-rape-case-investigator-testifies-about-her-interviews-with-alleged-victim/2013/09/03/9f604298-14ae-11e3-a100-66fa8fd9a50c_story.html.

Annys Shin, "Judge Finds Midshipman Not Guilty in Naval Academy Sex Assault Case," March 20, 2014, *Washington Post*, https://www.washingtonpost.com/local/judge-to-rule-in-naval-academy-sexual-assault-case-after-hearing-closing-arguments/2014/03/20/d9211394-b040-11e3-b8b3-44b1d1cd4c1f_story.html.

Dan Belson, "Navy Midshipman Acquitted in Anne Arundel Sexual Assault Jury Trial," September 21, 2022, *Capital Gazette*, https://www.capitalgazette.com/news/crime/ac-cn-usna-midshipman-rape-verdict-20220921-kfs35q2qp5ebjg3g4efbm24uiy-story.html.

"Not Guilty: Jury Clears Midshipman in Rape Trial," September 21, 2022, *Report Annapolis News*, https://www.reportannapolis.com/2022/09/not-guilty-jury-clears-midshipman-in.html.

Danielle Ohl, "Naval Academy Midshipman Acquitted of Sexual Assault Charges," April 15, 2019, *Capital Gazette*, https://www.capitalgazette.com/education/naval-academy/ac-cn-midshipman-acquitted-20190415-story.html.

Michael Muskal, "Former Midshipman Is Acquitted in Naval Academy Sexual Assault charges," *Capital Gazette*, https://www.latimes.com/nation/nationnow/la-na-nn-naval-academy-acquittal-20140320-story.html.

Standage v. Braithwaite, December 22, 2020, Casetext, https://casetext.com/case/standage-v-braithwaite.

Heather Mongilio, "After Lawsuit Settlement with Head of Naval Academy," May 29, 2021, *Stripes*, https://www.stripes.com/branches/navy/2021-05-29/After-lawsuit-settlement-with-head-of-Naval-Academy-midshipman-who-had-faced-expulsion-over-tweets-graduates-1602390.html.

USNA and USN Malfeasance

How to report government fraud, waste, and abuse:
https://www.gao.gov/blog/2017/08/24/we-want-you-to-report-fraud-waste-and-abuse#:~:text=If%20you%20suspect%20that%20these,saving%20millions%20of%20taxpayer%20dollars

Mark F. Light, "The Navy's Moral Compass," 2012, *Naval College War Review*, https://digital-commons.usnwc.edu/cgi/viewcontent. cgi?article=1472&context=nwc-review.

Sam Fellman, "LCS Freedom CO Fired after Engine Damages," October 14, 2016, *NavyTimes*, https://www.navytimes.com/news/ your-navy/2016/10/14/lcs-freedom-co-fired-after-engine-damages/.

Sam LaGrone, "Updated: Naval Academy Graduate Faces Bribery," June 26, 2017, USNI News, https://news.usni.org/2017/06/ 26/naval-academy-graduate-faces-bribery-corruption-charges-first-military-prosecution-fat-leonard-case.

Geoff Ziezulewicz, "How Did Fat Leonard Attend This Former CNO's Former Chain of Command?" July 23, 2021, *NavyTimes*, https:// www.navytimes.com/news/your-navy/2021/07/23/why-did-fat-leonard-show-up-this-former-cnos-change-of-command-he-was-on-the-vip-list/.

United States District Court January 2016 Grand Jury document, Justice.gov, https://www.justice.gov/opa/press-release/file/948061/ download.

Greg Moran, "Jury Convicts Four Former Navy Officers in 'Fat Leonard' Bribery Trial, June 29, 2022, *Los Angeles Times*, https:// www.latimes.com/california/story/2022-06-29/jury-convicts-four-former-navy-officers-in-fat-leonard-bribery-trial.

"The United States Merchant Marine Academy," July 1, 2021, Congressional Research Service, https://crsreports.congress.gov/ product/pdf/IF/IF11868/2#:~:text=Sealift%20Midshipmen%20 are%20not%20subject,UCMJ%20and%20military%20 criminal%20investigations.

John Woodrow Cox, "A Marine's Convictions," March 10, 2016, *Washington Post*, https://www.washingtonpost.com/graphics/local/ marine/.

"Naval Academy Superintendent Quits After Probe," June 5, 2003, *The Washington Times*, https://www.washingtontimes.com/news/2003/ jun/5/20030605-025222-7995r/.

Scott Calvert, "Slush Fund Was Factor in Naval Academy Super-intendent's Retirement," June 29, 2010, *The Baltimore Sun*, https://www.baltimoresun.com/maryland/bs-xpm-2010-06-29-bs-md-naval-academy-report-20100629-story.html.

Tim Prudente, "Former Naval Academy Superintendent Reprimanded Amid Investigation into Bribery Scandal," February 11, 2015, *Capital Gazette*, https://www.capitalgazette.com/ph-ac-cn-miller-0212-20150211-story.html.

Craig Whitlock, "Three U.S. Naval Officers Censured in 'Far Leonard' Corruption Probe," July 17, 2015, *Washington Post*, https://www.washingtonpost.com/world/national-security/three-us-admirals-censured-in-fat-leonard-corruption-probe/2015/07/17/7f29ca1a-2b1f-11e5-a5ea-cf74396e59ec_story.html.

Steve Walsh, "Trials Are Finally Wrapping up in the 'Fat Leonard' Bribery Case," June 16, 2022, NPR, https://www.npr.org/2022/06/16/1105633340/trials-are-finally-wrapping-up-in-the-fat-leonard-bribery-case.

Tim Prudente, "Navy: Former USNA Superintendent Censured over Gifts," July 17, 2015, *Capital Gazette*, https://www.capitalgazette.com/ph-ac-cn-miller-retires-0718-20150717-story.html.

Milton J. Sands III, "The Delta of Command: The Increasing Gap Between Character and Competence in the Navy's Commanding Officer Screening and Selection," April 21, 2014, Sanford School of Public Poicy, https://cttp.sanford.duke.edu/wp-content/uploads/sites/16/2015/09/TheDeltaofCommand_21April14_Final-1.pdf.

"18 Are Expelled or Resign from Naval Academy Amid Cheating Inquiry," August 23, 2021, *New York Times*, https://www.nytimes.com/2021/08/23/us/us-naval-academy-cheating.html#:~:text=Eighteen%20midshipmen%20resigned%20or%20were,general%20physics%20course%20on%20Dec.

Eric Schmitt, "An Inquiry Finds 125 Cheated on Naval Academy Exam," January 13, 1994, *New York Times*, https://www.nytimes.com/1994/01/13/us/an-inquiry-finds-125-cheated-on-a-naval-academy-exam.html.

"Legacy of a Scandal," June 22, 2003, *Baltimore Sun*, https://www.baltimoresun.com/news/bs-xpm-2003-06-22-0306210061-story.html.

Bill Brubaker, "Six Navy Football Players Face Expulsion for '92 Scandal," April 23, 1994, *Washington Post*, https://www.washingtonpost.com/archive/sports/1994/04/23/six-navy-football-players-face-expulsion-for-92-scandal/e1d506a5-9839-4da7-b0c8-741cb07aa08a/.

May-Jayne McKay, "Truth and Consequences: A Navy Scandal," May 30, 2002, CBS, https://www.cbsnews.com/news/truth-and-consequencesbra-navy-scandal/.

Earl Kelly and Tina Reed, "Capital Investigation: Drug Use, Party Culture at Naval Academy, December 16, 2012, *Capital Gazette*, https://www.capitalgazette.com/cg-capital-investigation-drug-use-party-culture-at-naval-academy-20140730-story.html.

Drug Use at the Naval Academy: http://www.stripes.com/news/navy/investigation-finds-significant-drug-use-party-culture-at-naval-academy-1.200984.

"DOD Service Academies: Comparison of Honor and Conduct Adjudicatory Processes," April 25, 1995, GovInfo., https://www.govinfo.gov/content/pkg/GAOREPORTS-NSIAD-95-49/html/GAOREPORTS-NSIAD-95-49.htm.

Damien Fisher, "Former Athol Man Convicted," October 10, 2014, https://www.thegardnernews.com/story/news/2014/10/10/former-athol-man-convicted-in/11348145007/.

Heather Mongilio, "Naval Academy Midshipman Dismissed," April 8, 2021, https://www.capitalgazette.com/education/naval-academy/ac-cn-naval-academy-matthew-mosley-20210408-3penxgayq5g-prelip353v2vjcy-story.html.

Michael Graczyk, "A Former Naval Academy Midshipman Loses Appeal," July 24, 2018, *NavyTimes*, https://www.navytimes.com/news/your-navy/2018/07/24/a-former-naval-academy-midshipman-lost-her-appeal-in-a-1995-love-triangle-murder/.

Dan Belson, "Navy Veteran from Odenton Sentenced to Six Years," June 20, 2022, *Capital Gazette*, https://www.capitalgazette.com/news/

crime/ac-cn-navy-pornography-sentence-20220620-lkno4i2pvfc-jvh2f7lxepwpoqm-story.html.

Sam LaGrone, "Updated: Naval Academy Graduate Faces Bribery, Corruption Charges," June 26, 2017, https://news.usni.org/2017/06/26/naval-academy-graduate-faces-bribery-corruption-charges-first-military-prosecution-fat-leonard-case.

"Earl Kelly: Memorable Stories," January 15, 2015, *Chicago Tribune*, https://www.chicagotribune.com/cg-earl-kelly-memorable-stories-20150115-storygallery.html.

"Capital Investigation: Drug use, party culture at Naval Academy," December 16, 2012, *Chicago Tribune*, https://www.chicagotribune.com/cg-capital-investigation-drug-use-party-culture-at-naval-academy-20140730-story.html.

Earl Kelly, "Academy Justice Was Tilted Toward Women," May 17, 2009, *Chicago Tribune*, https://www.chicagotribune.com/cg-academy-justice-was-tilted-toward-women--20150115-story.html.

Promotion and Commissioning, Numbers

David A. Schwind and Janice H. Laurence, "Raising the Flag: Promotion to Admiral in the United States Navy," December 15, 2009, https://www.tandfonline.com/doi/abs/10.1207/s15327876mp1803s_7?journalCode=hmlp20.

Matthew D. Sharra, "U.S. Naval Officer Accession Sources," Theses and Dissertations, 2015–16, Calhoun Institutional Archive of the Naval Postgraduate School, https://upload.wikimedia.org/wikipedia/commons/9/95/U.S._Naval_Officer_accession_sources-_promotion_probability_and_evaluation_of_cost_%28IA_usnavalofficercc1094545939%29.pdf.

Hasan Celik and A. Faruk Karakaya, "An Analysis of the Effect of Commissioning Sources on the Retention and Promotion of Surface Warfare Officers in the U.S. Navy," March 2011, Theses and Dissertations, Calhoun Institutional Archive of the Naval Postgraduate School, https://core.ac.uk/download/pdf/36699513.pdf.

"A Qualitative Analysis of Selection to Flag Rank in the United States Navy," Dudley Knox Library, Calhoun Naval Postgraduate School, https://calhoun.nps.edu/handle/10945/1515?show=full.

Kimberly Jackson, et.al, "Raising the Flag," 2020, RAND Corporation, https://www.rand.org/content/dam/rand/pubs/research_reports/RR4300/RR4347/RAND_RR4347.pdf.

"Nonacademy Graduates Get to Navy Jobs," February 3, 1985, *New York Times*, https://www.nytimes.com/1985/02/03/us/non-academy-graduates-get-to-navy-jobs.html.

Mark Cancian, "U.S. Military Forces in FY2022: Navy," November 2, 2021, Center for Strategic & International Studies, https://www.csis.org/analysis/us-military-forces-fy-2022-navy.

"Active and Reserve United States Military Force Personnel in 2021, by Service Branch and Reserve Component," 2023, *Statista*, https://www.statista.com/statistics/232330/us-military-force-numbers-by-service-branch-and-reserve-component.

"Defense Primer: Department of Defense Civilian Employees," *In Focus*, Congressional Research Service, February 6, 2023, https://sgp.fas.org/crs/natsec/IF11510.pdf.

"Total Military Personnel of the United States Navy from the Fiscal Year 2024, by Rank," *Statista*, https://www.statista.com/statistics/239345/total-military-personnel-of-the-us-navy-by-grade/.

Guy M. Snodgrass, "Keep a Weather Eye on the Horizon: A Navy Officer Retention Study," 2014, https://digitalcommons.usnwc.edu/cgi/viewcontent.cgi?referer=&httpsredir=1&article=1352&context=nwc-review.

Zafer Kizilkaya, "An Analysis of the Effect of Commissioning Sources on Retention and Promotion of U.S. Army Officers," June 2004, ResearchGate, https://www.researchgate.net/publication/235101131_An_Analysis_of_the_Effect_of_Commissioning_Sources_on_Retention_and_Promotion_of_US_Army_Officers.

Diana Stancy Correll, "Retention of surface Warfare Officers Is Improving," January 10, 2021, *Navy Times*, https://www.navytimes.com/news/your-navy/2023/01/10/retention-of-surface-warfare-

officers-is-improving-swo-boss-says/#:~:text=Even%20so%2C%20
retention%20among%20SWOs,%2C%E2%80%9D%20
Kitchener%20told%20reporters%20Jan.

Geoff Ziezulewicz, "Why Can't the Navy Keep Its Surface Warfare
Officers?" July 7, 2021, *NavyTimes*, https://www.navytimes.com/
news/your-navy/2021/07/07/why-cant-the-navy-keep-its-surface-
warfare-officers/.

"Navy Readiness: Actions Needed to Evaluate and Improve Surface
Warfare Officer Career Path," June 17, 2021, U.S. Government
Accountability Office, https://www.gao.gov/products/gao-21-168.

Oversight

"The Five Service Academies: A Followup Report," November 25,
1977, U.S. Government Accountability Office, https://www.gao.
gov/products/fpcd-77-78.

"DOD Service Academies: Improved Cost and Performance Monitoring
Needed," July 16, 1991, U.S. Government Accountability Office,
https://www.gao.gov/products/nsiad-91-79.

"Officer Commissioning Programs: More Oversight and Coordination
Needed," November 6, 1992, U.S. Government Accountability
Office, https://www.gao.gov/products/nsiad-93-37.

"DOD Needs to Enhance Performance Goals and Measures," September
2003, U.S. Government Accountability Office, https://www.gao.
gov/assets/gao-03-1000.pdf.

"Military Service Academies: Actions Needed to Better Assess Organi-
zational Climate," July 29, 2022, U.S. Government Accountability
Office, https://www.gao.gov/products/gao-22-105130.

Teaching Officers

Dickey, James L., "Cherrylog Road," Poetry Foundation, https://www.
poetryfoundation.org/poems/42712/cherrylog-road.

Frost, Robert, "The Road Not Taken, Poetry Foundation, https://www.
poetryfoundation.org/poems/44272/the-road-not-taken.

SAVING OUR SERVICE ACADEMIES

Housman, A. E., "To an Athlete Dying," Poetry Foundation, https://www.poetryfoundation.org/poems/46452/to-an-athlete-dying-young.

Keats, John, "Ode on a Grecian Urn," Poetry Foundation, https://www.poetryfoundation.org/poems/44477/ode-on-a-grecian-urn.

McCrae, John, "In Flanders Fields," Poetry Foundation, https://www.poetryfoundation.org/poems/47380/in-flanders-fields.

Owen, Wilfred, "Dulce et Decorum Est," Poetry Foundation, https://www.poetryfoundation.org/poems/46560/dulce-et-decorum-est.

Shakespeare, William. Sonnet 55, https://www.poetryfoundation.org/poems/46455/sonnet-55-not-marble-nor-the-gilded-monuments

Tennyson, Alfred, "Morte d'Arthur," Poetry Foundation, https://www.poetryfoundation.org/poems/45370/morte-darthur.

Trowbridge, William, "Kong Looks Back on His Tryout with the Bears," Poetry Foundation, https://www.poetryfoundation.org/poems/89546/kong-looks-back-on-his-tryout-with-the-bears.

Books Mentioned

Achebe, Chinua. *Things Fall Apart*. London: Heinemann, 1958.

Bakken, Tim. *The Cost of Loyalty: Dishonesty, Hubris, and Failure in the U.S. Military*. New York: Bloomsbury, 2020.

Clausewitz, Carl von. *On War*. Edited and translated by Michael Howard and Peter Paret. Princeton: Princeton University Press, 1989.

Dworkin, Andrea. *Intercourse (20th Anniversary Edition)*. New York: Basic, 20066.

Fleming, Bruce. *Annapolis Autumn: Life, Death, and Literature at the U.S. Naval Academy*. New York: New Press, 2005.

Hedges, Chris. *What Every Person Should Know About War*. New York: Free Press, 2003.

Lovejoy, Paul E. *Transformations in Slavery: A History of Slavery in Africa (3rd edition)*. Cambridge: Cambridge University Press, 2011.

Orwell, George. *Burmese Days*. New York: Mariner, 1974.

Remarque, Eric Marie. *All Quiet on the Western Front*. New York: Ballantine, 1987.

Rever, Judi. *In Praise of Blood: The Crimes of the Rwandan Patriotic Front*. New York: Random House Canada, 2018.

Ricks, Thomas. *The Generals: American Military Command from World War II to Today*. New York: Penguin, 2012.

Sartre, Jean-Paul. *Being and Nothingness*. Translated by Hazel E. Barnes. New York: Washington Square, 1966.

Webb, James. *A Sense of Honor*. New York: Bantam, 1983.

ABOUT THE AUTHOR

A native of Maryland's Eastern Shore, Bruce Fleming graduated from Haverford College at nineteen with a degree in philosophy (BA '74), and holds graduate degrees in comparative literature from the University of Chicago (MA '78) and Vanderbilt University (PhD '82). He was a Fulbright Scholar in West Berlin and taught for two years each at the University of Freiburg in Germany and the National University of Rwanda, the latter as a Fulbright professor. He has taught at the US Naval Academy since 1987 and is the author of over twenty books. His nonfiction titles concern a variety of subjects ranging from military-civilian relations to the liberal-conservative clash in politics, and from literary modernism to dance criticism, and his fiction work includes a novel and short fiction. His personal essays have been published in many leading US literary magazines, including *The Yale*

Review, *The Antioch Review*, *The Gettysburg Review*, *Michigan Quarterly Review*, and *Southwest Review*. He has won an O. Henry Award and the *Antioch Review*'s Award for Distinguished Prose, as well as the US Naval Academy's Award for Excellence in Research and a US Navy Meritorious Civilian Service Award. Fleming has published op-eds in national media outlets including the *New York Times*, the *Washington Post*, *Christian Science Monitor*, *The Chronicle of Higher Education*, *The Atlantic*, and *The Federalist*, and been interviewed on CNN, C-SPAN, NPR, and the BBC. He lives with his family outside Annapolis, Maryland.